EATING
THEIR
WORDS

EATING THEIR WORDS

Cannibalism and the Boundaries of Cultural Identity

Edited by
Kristen Guest

Foreword by
Maggie Kilgour

STATE UNIVERSITY OF NEW YORK PRESS

Published by
State University of New York Press, Albany

For information, address State University of New York Press,
90 State Street, Suite 700, Albany, NY 12207

Production by Marilyn P. Semerad
Marketing by Fran Keneston

Library of Congress Cataloging-in-Publication Data

Eating their words : cannibalism and the boundaries of cultural identity / edited by
Kristen Guest ; foreword by Maggie Kilgour.
     p. cm.
Includes bibliographical references and index.
ISBN–7914–5089–9 (alk. paper) — ISBN 0–7914–5090–2 (pbk. : alk. paper)
1. Cannibalism in literature.   I. Guest, Kristen, 1967–

PN56.C34 E19 2001
809'.93355—dc21   00–053152
                    10 9 8 7 6 5 4 3 2 1

Contents

Foreword

Maggie Kilgour

> Go to the meatmarket of a Saturday night and see the crowds
> of live bipeds staring up at the long rows of dead quadrapeds.
> Does not that sight take a tooth out of the cannibal's jaw?
> Cannibals? Who is not a cannibal?
>
> —Hermann Melville, *Moby Dick*

At the beginning of the twenty-first century, Ishmael's rant seems uncannily prophetic. Eating people is *in*, or at least "interesting," as cannibalism has emerged as one of the most important topics in criticism today, one which pierces to the very heart of current discussions of difference and identity. At the same time, however, the question might need to be inverted, to read: Who "is" a cannibal? Since the publication of William Arens's controversial 1979 study, *The Man-Eating Myth: Anthropology and Anthropophagy*, we have become aware that too often the myth of the cannibal has been precisely that: a myth constructed about others that cultures have used to justify hatred and aggression. Cannibalism is the ultimate charge: call a group "cannibals," and you not only *prove* that they are savages but authorize their extermination. It is easy to conclude then that cannibalism is "only" a fiction. Since Arens, many critics have assumed just this and deny the reality of cannibalism as a practice. Postcolonial studies especially have suggested that the figure of the cannibal was created to support the cultural cannibalism of colonialism, through the projection of western imperialist appetites onto the cultures they then subsumed.

Arens himself, however, never denied absolutely that cannibalism occurred; what concerned him more was understanding why his discipline (anthropology), had so much invested in proving that cannibalism had occurred, despite often inadequate evidence. As his subtitle suggested, anthropology seemed to need the idea of anthropophagy in order to create itself as a discipline. Following Arens's lead, other critics have shown how the figure of the cannibal plays a central role in defining western ideals. If in the past the cannibal was used to construct differences, today it is invoked in order to deconstruct them. The chapters in this volume subsume a wide range of sources, from Homer, the great oral poet of what Fielding called "the eating poem," *The Odyssey*, to here. Close analyses of the individual works enables the contributors to follow some of the different and ambiguous desires that cannibalism has been used to embody, of which imperialism is just one manifestation. The most extreme image of the subhuman is intensely revealing of a culture's vision of what it means to be human and of its appetites both spiritual and material. The focus on cannibalism today seems to reflect our current desire to renegotiate differences and relations with others in a multicultural world in which the idea of the "savage" and, indeed, even "nature" is questioned. The cannibal presents a disturbing fiction of otherness because it both constructs and consumes the very possibility of radical difference. As these chapters note, the boundary between the "cannibal" and "civilized man" traditionally has been the marker of absolute opposition. But since Montaigne, we have known that that difference is illusory: the cannibal is us. For a post-holocaust culture especially, the question of whether one can distinguish civilization from barbarism seems especially urgent, yet difficult. The figure of the cannibal dramatizes the danger of drawing boundaries too absolutely. But perhaps it equally reveals the peril of not drawing them at all, as the act of cannibalism is the place where self and other, love and aggression meet, where the body becomes symbolic, and at the same time, the human is reduced to mere matter. If it is not adequate to cry with Ishmael that we are *all* cannibals, it seems important still to look carefully at what our current fascination with this unsavory subject is able to tell us about our needs and desires.

Acknowledgments

It is a pleasure to be able to acknowledge the personal debts accrued while completing this project. Linda Hutcheon and Raymond L. Williams both provided crucial advice in the early stages. Through several stages of review, Maggie Kilgour's thorough and conscientious input was enormously helpful as was that of the unnamed readers for SUNY Press. Rebecca Leaver, John Leaver, Bonnie Harrison, and Kevin Alcock provided tremendous personal support at a crucial stage in the editing process, and Grace Kehler has—as always—been a great sounding board as well as a most wonderful friend. Throughout it all, Dale Guest has been my best friend and biggest supporter.

Finally, putting together an edited volume is a lengthy and sometimes frustrating process. I would like to thank the contributors to this volume for their unfaltering patience, diligence, and remarkable professionalism.

Two of the chapters that appear in this volume have been revised from previous publications. Minaz Jooma's "Robinson Crusoe Inc(orporates): Domestic Economy, Incest, and the Trope of Cannibalism" originally appeared in *Literature, Interpretation, Theory*. Marlene Goldman's essay on *Wilderness Tips* appeared in *Etudes canadiennes/Canadian Studies* 46(1999):93–100.

1

Introduction: Cannibalism and the Boundaries of Identity

KRISTEN GUEST

U ntil fairly recently, literary scholarship often relegated the theme of cannibalism to the margins of critical discussion, dismissing anthropophagic representations as the concern of particular authors or periods. With the publication of Maggie Kilgour's seminal study of cannibalism in literature, however, scholars have begun to reconsider the complex history of representations of the cannibal. Now, rather than relating cannibalism to contemporary events or a particular period's interest in sensationalizing its others, critics have begun to rethink how representations of cannibalism help us to produce, contest, and negotiate our identity as subjects. The wide variety of critical work now being done on cannibals and literature indeed owes much to Kilgour's argument in *From Communion to Cannibalism*, which takes as its starting point the binary definition of self and other that underpins most representations of cannibalism. As Kilgour points out, the notion of incorporation central to the idea of cannibalism "depends upon and enforces an absolute division between inside and outside," yet at the same time, the act "dissolv[es] the structure it appears to produce."[1] Insofar as it examines the relationship between cannibalism and our dominant western mode of producing meaning through strategies of exclusion, Kilgour's work has paved the way for such important reevaluative readings

1

of cannibalism as the cross-disciplinary collection *Cannibalism and the Colonial World,* edited by Francis Barker, Peter Hulme, and Margaret Iverson (1998), as well as for the translation of Frank Lestringant's *Cannibals: The Discovery and Representation of the Cannibal from Columbus to Jules Verne* (1997), previously unavailable in English. This volume represents another step in this reevaluative process, bringing together literary scholarship on a variety of texts and contexts—from classical epic to the contemporary novel—both to advance our understanding of how cannibalism has historically "enforced" and "dissolved" the boundaries of identity through forms of representation and to suggest how cannibalism emerges as a useful focal point for ideological critique.

It is the intention of this book to show that the cannibal, long a figure associated with absolute alterity and used to enforce boundaries between a civilized "us" and savage "them," may in fact be more productively read as a symbol of the permeability, or instability, of such boundaries. As Kilgour suggests—noting that the pair sets up a circle of cannibalistic consumption that shifts from literal to metaphoric modes—"the definition of the other as cannibal justifies its oppression, extermination, and cultural cannibalism (otherwise known as imperialism) by the rule 'eat or be eaten.' "[2] In some circles, the metaphorical notion of "cultural" cannibalism represented by imperialism has even come to be identified with the act itself. For both William Arens and Peter Hulme, the term *cannibalism* is so inextricably bound up with discourses of colonial oppression that its meaning must be separated from the act itself.[3] While the term *cannibal* is certainly inseparable from its roots in colonial enterprise, it has a lengthy history within western culture as well. In fact, vague, often unsubstantiated charges of cannibalism have historically been evoked to undermine the political, social, or economic power of marginal groups, to explore the psychopathology of criminal "others," or simply to generate the sensationalistic frisson associated with the growth of mass culture. Traditionally used in colonial enterprises to justify acts of genocide or assimilation, then, the opposition between civilization and savagery also performs significant ideological work within western culture both by containing marginal groups and by helping to articulate the anxieties of their dominant social counterparts.

In this volume, the historically uneasy relationships that have evolved between the discourse of cannibalism and the diverse ideological positions it has been evoked to support are explored in a variety of literary texts from across a range of periods and cultures. Alternately wielded to express the contradictions that exist within mainstream culture or to critique mainstream practices and construct oppositional identities outside the dominant culture, cannibalism has seemed to function either as a monolithic (and oppressive) expression of power or as a radically utopian gesture of defiance. In their own ways, each of the chapters included here questions the extremes represented by these two positions. From readings of Elizabethan "self-fashioning" to postmodern critiques of consumer culture, the contributors collectively argue in this book that the discourse of cannibalism persistently gives voices to the diverse marginal groups it is supposed to silence and questions the dominant ideologies it is evoked to support. Thus, while readings of Oswald de Andrade's Anthropophagist *Manifesto* and Ian Wedde's *Symmes Hole* recognize the value of cannibalism as a metaphor of reverse appropriation, other chapters—on Maturin's *Melmoth the Wanderer* and Atwood's *Wilderness Tips*, for example—use cannibalism to help us understand the anxieties that haunt the apparently stable center of western culture.

If cannibalism generally fails to produce the intended domesticating result—either in the colonies or at home—it is probably because considerations of anthropophagy historically have as much to say about the convergence and exchange between apparently opposing terms as they do about their differences. The paradox, as Montaigne points out in his essay "Of Cannibals," turns on the relativity of terms like *civilization* and *savagery*. "Indeed," he suggests, "we seem to have no other level of truth and reason than the example and pattern of the opinions and practices of the country wherein we live."[4] When comparing "noble" savages to their dissolute European "others," Montaigne does not query the oppositional logic that underwrites the distinction; instead, he simply condemns his own culture for combining savagery and hypocrisy.[5] Yet, if we look beyond the oppositional logic of cannibalism as a discourse, we see that as a taboo its efficacy relies not on its participation in differential systems of meaning but rather on its recognition of corporeal similarity. Even when it seems to reinforce dominant ideologies or mainstream discourses, then, cannibalism also reveals the catch twenty-two of oppositional logic by drawing our attention to the relatedness of bodies that lie beneath the ideas they express. Indeed, the idea of cannibalism prompts a visceral reaction among people precisely *because* it activates our horror of consuming others like ourselves. Ultimately, then, it is the shared humanness of cannibals and their victims that draws our attention to the problems raised by the notion of absolute difference.

By calling our attention to the idea of a "common humanity" that unites "civilized" self and "savage" other, cannibalism would seem to represent a movement back to an older humanistic mode of understanding founded on the notion of shared essence. In the context of this volume, however, cannibalistic discourse is treated as a critical vehicle that allows us to move away from the either/or logic that has characterized both traditional humanism and much contemporary theoretical discourse. Unlike the more visually coded relationships between ideology and biology that govern distinctions based on race and gender, "savagery" is a problematic point of reference that draws our attention to the difficulties of dividing self from other by calling traditional boundaries of identity into question. This view of cannibalism is founded on the notion that the designations "civilization" and "savagery" (traditionally associated with cannibalism) are entrenched in a wider—often seemingly unrelated—network of relationships particular to distinct cultures and historical periods. Among anthropologists cannibalism is now widely viewed as a complex, diverse cultural practice whose meaning is determined by the sociohistorical context in which it is practiced rather than through a preset "universal" pattern.[6] Insofar as they see the act of cannibalism enabling the production of meanings and values within a particular social system, anthropological descriptions of the social function of cannibalism bear a striking resemblance to contemporary theoretical notions of ideology as a structure that is, in Slavoj Žižek's words, "a kind of reality whose very ontological consistency implies a certain non-knowledge of its participants."[7] While ideology is almost always theorized as an imaginary structure that is functional only insofar as it remains imperceptible, cannibalism draws our attention to the problematic relationship between real acts and the imaginary structures available to make them meaningful. One result of this convergence is that the discourse of cannibalism invites us to reflect on how the construction of difference is always limited by the sociohistorical context in which it is produced. Thus, as a critical figure the cannibal does not just call into question the universality of binary structures that generate meaning, it also, as Geoffrey Sanborn argues in this volume, challenges us to "stop thinking of the co-existence of what we call 'humanity' and 'savagery'." Sanborn encourages contemporary critics to resist the binary assumptions that undergird much recent theoretical discourse, arguing instead for a model of reading which, he argues, "first became available within the discourse on cannibalism over two hundred and fifty years ago." In his or her own way, each contributor in this volume reflects on both the possibilities and limitations that the discourse of cannibalism offers textual critics. Together, we tell the story of how the anxieties surrounding difference were (and are) addressed through literal, symbolic, and figurative representations of cannibalism.

Because it offers an imaginative context for framing and addressing ideological issues related to identity and difference, literature is an ideal vehicle through which to focus questions related to cannibalism. Not only does it allow us to address real issues on an imaginative level, it also provides a context in which broad social anxieties can be addressed on a symbolic level. The earliest literary representations of cannibalism occur in mythology, where familial cannibalism explains shifts in the balance of divine power as the gods consume each other in the struggle for authority. Among mythic human figures, too, myths of cannibalism often reflect the struggle to enforce the boundaries of social identity. Such myths depict cannibalism as the most extreme act of vengeance imaginable, an act so monstrous that it cannot be resolved within the boundaries of human society. While this taboo demarcates the boundaries of "civilization," however, it also calls attention to the tenuous nature of such distinctions. As Mark Buchan points out in his contribution to this volume, even to *imagine* cannibalizing another person calls attention to the realm outside existing social boundaries that structure our identities. For Buchan, cannibalism evokes both the "socially prescribed limits of wrath" and the fantasy of transgressing or exceeding these limits in ancient Greek warrior culture. Insofar as he argues that myth, ideology and community converge in representations of cannibalism, Buchan establishes a context for the chapters that follow, charting the mechanism through which differential systems of meaning help to produce and mirror identity.

In various ways, this volume expounds on questions about the formation and dissolution of personal and cultural identity central to literary studies today. Thus, for instance, Robert O'Brien's piece on book 6 of the *Faerie Queene* extends Buchan's argument about heroism in warrior culture to the Renaissance ideal of the gentleman and its implications for colonial enterprise, while Marlene Goldman examines the relationship between consumer culture and cultural identity in a series of modern short stories by Margaret Atwood. While such questions are raised in a variety of contexts, they address remarkably similar issues. Most significantly, they suggest the relationship between a social identity founded on a "civilized" ideal and the various types of consumption that take place within "civilized" communities that challenge these boundaries of identity. Throughout this volume, problems posed by identity are explored in relation to a variety of historically specific texts. While the chapters are arranged chronologically, then, they also introduce and complicate a series of questions related to the specific texts and contexts in which cannibalism emerges as a theme.

The chapters that follow Buchan's examine the various roles cannibalism plays in responding to "colonizing" projects depicted in literature and criticism from the Elizabethan period to the present. Most of these essays evoke the relationship between civilization and savagery as a defining structure in western culture, where real and metaphorical forms of cannibalism are used to justify acts of domination. While the texts examined all appeal to civilization and savagery as an opposing pair, the chapters also discuss the instability of the opposition and the meanings it supports in different contexts. In "Cannibalism in Edmund Spenser's *Faerie Queene*, Ireland, and America," for example, Robert Viking O'Brien discusses cannibalism as a metaphor and model for the discursive violence necessary to accommodate the "civilizing" ideal of self-fashioning articulated by Spenser. O'Brien reflects on how the colonial encounters with New World savages depicted in the *Faerie Queene* are complicated by Spenser's use of cannibalistic metaphors in his writing about the Irish, a connection that is further developed by Julia Wright in her essay on the gothic novel *Melmoth the Wanderer*. For Wright, Maturin's novel enacts the breakdown of imperial stability during the Romantic period. In this context, she considers how the metaphors of familial cannibalism evoked in late eighteenth and early nineteenth-century debates about inheritance law parallel the imperial disinheritance of the Irish by the British, a group whose identity was uncomfortably positioned as "other."

Taking up this question from the perspective of a different marginalized population, Kristen Guest considers both how the colonial discourse of cannibalism was evoked to contain the perceived threat to "civilization" by the lower classes and how the poor turned this discourse against the dominant middle class. Guest's suggestion that the Victorian melodrama *Sweeney Todd* engages in a pointed critique of dominant values by treating cannibalism as a model of "reverse assimilation" is further amplified in the essay by Santiago Colás that follows it. Colás takes up the issue of postcolonial resistance in a different period and context, considering how the figure of the antropófago has been appropriated by Latin American writers who attempt to reconceive this traditionally negative term in a revolutionary framework. Finally, Colás reflects on the history of this movement and its ultimate failure to bring about a true culture of the masses, a problem he suggests is implicit in the notion of cannibalism itself—which functions so well as a metaphor because of "its internal ambivalences and contradictions."

Another aspect of cannibalism that is central to many of the treatments of colonial or postcolonial enterprise here is the uneasy relationship between cannibalistic consumption and emerging consumer culture. In Minaz Jooma's reconsideration of *Robinson Crusoe*, for example, cannibalism is linked to the mercantilism that underpins the colonial enterprise. Jooma argues that in this context cannibalism focuses the relationship between consumption and power, expressing "the anxiety generated by the expansion of the domestic economy to the worldly economy." Jooma's conclusion that cannibalism represents the fear of being consumed is a theme that is also addressed by other contributors, including Wright and Guest—both of whom suggest that attempts to characterize other groups as cannibals are implicated in the discourses of emerging consumer culture.

For twentieth-century writers, the idea of the cannibal as consumer has assumed even more powerful associations, particularly for postcolonized nations that have adapted cannibal metaphors to address the imperialist threat of multinational consumer culture. Following Colás's consideration of attempts by colonized nations to appropriate the discourse of their colonizers, Brian Greenspan and Marlene Goldman both address questions about the convergence of postcolonial and postmodern concerns in texts that self-consciously pair consumerism and cannibalism. In his reading of New Zealand author Ian Wedde's metafictional novel *Symmes Hole*, Greenspan suggests that cannibalism represents "the fear of the colonizer when confronted with the emptiness of his own identity." Greenspan argues that the hollow identity associated with colonization has been carried forward in multinational consumer culture. Ultimately, Greenspan claims, Wedde uses the figure of the cannibal to challenge a passive, "easily devoured," consumer culture by placing it alongside the complex intertextual connections explored in *Symmes Hole*.

Unlike Greenspan, who examines connections between figures of past imperial power and present postcolonial resistance, Goldman draws on an indigenous cannibal figure—the Wendigo—to explore the dark side of consumer culture in Canada. For Goldman the cannibal monster central to Cree and Ojibway mythology provides an interpretive key to Margaret Atwood's *Wilderness Tips*, a collection of short stories that explore the relationship between colonial past and consumerized present by emphasizing the debilitating effects of different forms of consumption on personal identity. Through her readings of individual stories in *Wilderness Tips*, Goldman identifies the Wendigo as a "symptom of cultures in crisis," a figure of "excess" rather than monstrosity.

The final essay in this volume addresses the epistemological implications of the cannibal encounter in order to critique the political underpinnings of recent literary theory. The idea of criticism as a form of cannibalistic consumption gained currency with J. Hillis Miller's seminal poststructuralist essay, "The Critic as Host."[8] Here, however, Geoffrey Sanborn brings a more historicized approach to bear on the enterprise of criticism. Taking eighteenth and nineteenth-century European accounts of cannibalism among native groups as his starting point, Sanborn suggests that the colonial discourse of cannibalism is haunted by anxieties about evidence that belie the excessive desire among westerners for proof of a savagery that remains unauthenticated. Drawing on the work of such Lacanian social theorists as Ernesto Laclau, Slavoj Žižek, and Homi Bhabba, Sanborn argues that critics who treat the cannibal as a secure symbol of savagery cover over the complex interests at stake when we use the term *savage*. If we restore questions about evidence to the visibility they enjoyed in the eighteenth and nineteenth centuries, Sanborn suggests, we may reconceptualize the cannibal encounter as an example of the way colonial enterprises are already haunted by the possibility of postcolonial subversion. Insofar as it applies the critical methods employed throughout the volume to the enterprise of criticism itself, Sanborn's essay seems an appropriate place to conclude: reminding us not only that historical and literary representations of cannibalism may illuminate our attempts to define ourselves, but also that the function of criticism is best served when we reflect on the ways that the absorption and digestion of texts and theories shape our own identities as interpreters.

NOTES

1. Maggie Kilgour, *From Communion to Cannibalism: An Anatomy of Metaphors of Incorporation* (Princeton, N.J.: Princeton UP, 1990), 4.

2. Kilgour, 148.

3. See William Arens, *The Man-Eating Myth: Anthropology and Anthropophagy* (New York: Oxford UP, 1979), and Peter Hulme, *Colonial Encounters: Europe and the Native Caribbean, 1492–1797* (London and New York: Methuen, 1986), 83–87. The "discursive" reading of cannibalism in both *The Man-Eating Myth* and *Colonial Encounters* has been highly controversial. In *Divine Hunger: Cannibalism as a Cultural System* (Cambridge: Cambridge UP, 1986), Peggy Reeves Sanday responds to Arens's work from an anthropological perspective. Hulme's argument is addressed by Myra Jehlen in "History Before the Fact; or, Captain John Smith's Unfinished Symphony," *Critical Inquiry* 19

(Summer 1993), 679–685. Jehlen's article subsequently sparked further debate with Hulme; see Hulme's "Making No Bones: A Response to Myra Jehlen" and Jehlen's "Response to Peter Hulme," both in *Critical Inquiry* 20 (autumn 1993). More recently, Arens has revisited the controversy in an essay included in *Cannibalism and the Colonial World*, edited by Francis Barker, Peter Hulme, and Margaret Iverson (New York: Cambridge UP, 1998).

    4. Michel de Montaigne, "Of Cannibals," in *The Essays of Michel de Montaigne*, vol. 1, trans. Jacob Zeitlin (New York: Knopf, 1934), 181.

    5. Montaigne, 185. Frank Lestringant offers a useful and interesting discussion of the context for Montaigne's essay in *Cannibals: The Discovery and Representation of the Cannibal from Columbus to Jules Verne*, trans. Rosemary Morris (Berkeley: University of California P, 1997).

    6. See, for example, William Arens's *The Man-Eating Myth*, Peggy Reeves Sanday's *Divine Hunger*.

    7. Slavoj Žižek, *The Sublime Object of Ideology* (London: Verso, 1989), 21.

    8. J. Hillis Miller, "The Critic as Host" in Harold Bloom et al eds. *Deconstruction and Criticism* (New York: Seabury, 1979), 217–53.

2

Food for Thought:
Achilles and the Cyclops

MARK BUCHAN

If we were to indulge in cannibalism, would we enjoy our meal? If we did enjoy the meal, would we be satisfied afterward? These questions are perhaps the crucial *ideological* questions of Homer's *Iliad*; for they go to the heart of the problem of the socially prescribed limits of wrath. In this poem of boundless anger, where all sorts of social prohibitions are transgressed, it is notable that no act of cannibalism ever occurs; cannibalism is imagined as a way of satisfying a limitless fury, but the act itself is never performed. This refusal is exemplified in the actions of the central hero, Achilles; after the death of his friend Patroclus, he attempts to satiate his anger in a variety of ways and indulges in a series of transgressive acts (rejection of suppliants, human sacrifice, mutilation of Hector's corpse) which he seems to enjoy as he performs them. Ultimately, however, they provide him with no lasting satisfaction. Yet although he considers the possibility of cannibalism, he cannot actually bring himself to carry it out. It is this rejection which signifies that he has not wholly divorced himself from society; for it leaves in place a fundamental taboo which is shared by the other Greeks and which preserves a fixed point of social solidarity. Achilles, in anger against Agamemnon, first rejects his Greek comrades, refusing to fight; later, on his return to battle, he rejects the norms of heroic warfare. But we discover that for all his isolation, he remains tied to them because of this shared taboo. The fantasy of cannibalism functions as a kind of test case; if the best of the Achaeans, Achilles, were to indulge in cannibalism, then his

11

rejection of society and the shared ideology that sustains society would be complete. But it is a strange test case, since its efficacy, in *The Iliad*, depends on its not being tested.

It is because of this refusal to test the test case that *The Iliad* leaves us at an ideological impasse. Achilles, on the point of defeating Hector in battle and caught up in the fury which has raged since the death of his friend Patroclus, raises the possibility that eating Hector could provide the ultimate satisfaction for his anger:

> I wish only that my spirit and fury would drive me
> to hack your meat away and eat it raw for the things
> that you have done to me. (*Il.*22.346–48)[1]

Yet he swiftly pulls back from the brink. It is significant that he cannot even imagine directly desiring cannibalism; he only desires that his fury would drive him to desire it, as if such a desire is abstractly conceivable, but not conceivable *for him*. The mention of the possibility of cannibalism, together with the marked change from transgressions which are acted out to a transgression which is only imagined, suggests that Achilles' wrath has reached its apex. For once he has rejected the possibility of eating Hector, he is well on the way to returning (somewhat meekly) to the society of Greek warriors which he had so powerfully rejected at the start of the poem.[2] It is therefore tempting to suggest that the true tragedy of the poem resides in Achilles' *failure* to cannibalize Hector. For Achilles' obedience to the supreme social taboo of cannibalism seems to render irrelevant his former critique of heroic society. This sequence of events suggests that the poem provides a fundamentally conservative moral message. Achilles' challenge to authority leads nowhere; the social cost is the thousands of corpses predicted in the poem's proem.[3] But an even more disquieting problem destabilizes such a reading. Because Achilles bows to the social prohibition on cannibalism (the implicit *thou shalt not cannibalize*), he leaves behind the danger of an ongoing fascination with what is prohibited—a fascination which is amply attested by Achilles' fantasy. The logic of prohibition makes the act that it formally prohibits all the more intriguing by means of the prohibition itself. The poem thus leaves us with a nagging question: what would have happened if Achilles *had* eaten Hector? Our initial question regarding the possibility of cannibalistic satisfaction seems to be left unanswered, and quite purposively so.[4]

Is this ideological impasse of *The Iliad* a Homeric impasse, a "structured silence" that reveals the social limitations of archaic Greek society? Are we forced to accept, along with Achilles, that cannibalism is simply too horrific to be indulged in, and that therefore the only solution is to join in a moralizing denunciation of cannibalism?[5] There is a good Homeric reason for not doing this: *The Odyssey*. For if real cannibalism is taboo in *The Iliad*, it plays a significant role in *The Odyssey*, most notably in the poem's best-known episode, the blinding of the man-eating Cyclops in book 9.

In this chapter, I want to argue that the different depictions of cannibalism in the epics (only imagined by human characters in *The Iliad* but actually performed by the seemingly monstrous, quasi-human cyclops in *The Odyssey*) are closely related, and that *The Odyssey*'s most famous man-eater helps us disentangle the logic lurking behind Achilles' refusal to cannibalize. Odysseus's tale of his interaction with the man-eating cyclops is, at least in part, intended to demonstrate what would have happened if Achilles had gone "all the way," if he had indulged his cannibalistic wish. The imaginary universe of the Cyclopes can thus tell us a great deal about the underlying logic of Achilles' fury, and thus about the functioning of ideology as such.[6] In psychoanalytic terms, if Achilles clings to the fantasy which allows him to sustain a relationship with the social world by refusing to indulge openly in cannibalistic enjoyment, the Cyclops episode *traverses* this fantasy—for us, the readers—by providing a picture of the consequences of the illicit desire that Achilles deliberately keeps at a distance. I begin with a closer look at the ideological impasse of *The Iliad*—a fundamentally Achillean impasse—and end by suggesting the manner in which *The Odyssey* can be read as a commentary on this impasse.

ILIADIC CANNIBALISM AND THE "ETHICS OF ANGER"

In response to the death of Patroclus, Achilles returns to battle and embarks on a furious killing spree. Yet although Achilles' actions are clearly transgressive, violating a series of the heroic norms which regulate Iliadic warfare, they are not transgressive enough to undermine the overall workings of heroic society. The poem seems to assume a distinction (never explicitly articulated) between "permissible" and "impermissible" transgressions of the social order. Consider the following taxonomy of "the ethics of anger" by Van Wees, who has carefully established the range of options available to an angry Iliadic warrior:

> The range of expressions of anger runs from the ubiquitous "scowling" at one's opponent, via insulting, threatening, robbing, beating and wounding him, to killing him and mutilating his corpse. In

extreme fury, one may wish to eat one's enemy, but cannibalism remains in the realm of angry fantasy.[7]

I think we should take Van Wees's remarks that cannibalism *remains* in the realm of fantasy quite seriously: cannibalism is not simply rejected *tout court*; it is stubbornly held onto in fantasy. An immediate consequence is that the warrior society is defined not so much by what it includes (the endless variations of what can and cannot be performed within heroic culture) but by what it excludes as the price to be paid for the ongoing cohesion of the social world. The functioning of Homeric society can withstand every attack upon its validity, every challenge to the legitimacy of its everyday functioning, but not *that*, not cannibalism. One can mutilate a corpse, rob, beat, insult, and all this can be done *within* society. Even if these activities go beyond officially prescribed limits, they are still the sorts of trangsressions which can be accounted for (any such symbolic debt to society incurred by individual anger can be repaid by making use of a given calculus of right and wrong).[8] But to eat human flesh seems to menace the existence of any meaningful society at all. It threatens to set in motion a process similar to the one described by Richard Rorty in his discussion of Winston's breakdown during torture in Orwell's *1984*. People go through

> the ultimate humiliation of saying to themselves, in retrospect, "Now that I have believed or desired this, I can never be what I hoped to be, what I thought I was. The story I have been telling myself about myself . . . no longer makes sense. I no longer have a self to make sense of. There is no world in which I can picture myself as living, because there is no vocabulary in which I can tell a coherent story about myself." For Winston, the sentence he could not utter sincerely and still be able to put himself back together was "Do it to Julia!" and the worst thing in the world happened to be rats. But presumably each of us stands in the same relations to some sentence, and to some thing.[9]

For Achilles, the thing which he cannot imagine consciously desiring (and yet which is raised as something which could satisfy his fury) is cannibalism.[10] Were the best of the Achaeans to engage in cannibalism, the social story he had been telling himself about his status as a Greek warrior (the social story which he shares with the other Greeks) would no longer seem to make sense. What we are dealing with is a particular sort of act: if it is carried out, the worry is that the social narrative itself, the story the community tells itself about itself, will no longer be possible.

This fundamental situation has been theorized by Lacanian psycho-analysis through the logic of the working of the "Name of the Father." Language, the regime of sense, only functions when access to a certain "enjoyment" is forbidden—classically, the incestuous enjoyment of the mother prohibited by the symbolic agency of an ideal father.[11] The Name of the Father functions when there is an acceptance of a certain renuncia-tion of enjoyment; in Achilles' case, it is the enjoyment of cannibalism which is socially prohibited. To indulge in this would be not merely to transgress a social law, but to undermine the gap (between language and senseless enjoyment) which allows the realm of meaning to exist at all. A community is not simply held together by a set of shared positive beliefs but, more fundamentally, by a shared prohibition. Insofar as this prohibi-tion is fundamentally of something *impossible*—the shared illusion is that what is prohibited might satisfy desire, render complete the failure endemic to language itself—the taboo functions as the *proton pseudos*, the original "lie" around which the community is structured. Were the falsity of this lie to be made public, the community would fall apart. We can now appreciate the importance of Achilles' attitude to cannibalism in *The Iliad* 22. He comes close to articulating openly the unconscious *proton pseudos* which holds the community of heroes together.

Of course, Achilles' nerve fails. And yet it is worth pausing over the radical nature of his challenge to the social, his suggestion of the possibility of a cannibalistic enjoyment which would destroy it. Indeed, within ancient Greek culture, it is ultimately *ideology itself*, the illusion of a per-fectly sublated father supervising the workings of the Symbolic order, which is challenged by cannibalism. This logic is elucidated in a later philosophical argument between the sceptics and dogmatists, as reported by Diogenes Laertius:

> And when the dogmatists say that the skeptic's position is such that he will live a life in which, were he commanded, he would not shrink from cannibalizing his father, the skeptics reply that he will be able to live so that he can suspend judgement about dogmatic questions, but not about matters of everyday life and of observance.[12]

The skeptics, heirs to the tradition of Socratic doubt, are ultimately also the descendants of the radical doubt cast on the functioning of the social by Achilles. For to the extent that they doubt everything, they seem to be veritable revolutionaries with regard to ethical behavior. This is certainly what the dogmatists seem to be afraid of. The skeptics to them are not reasonable people who indulge in debate within a given social framework. Rather, they challenge the coherence of the framework itself. They seem to threaten paternal authority *tout court*, and the cannibalization of their fathers illustrates the destruction of the workings of paternal authority implicit in their skepticism. Insofar as they doubt this, the skeptics seem to flirt with an utter rejection of the founding assumptions governing public discourse.[13] Of course, Diogenes Laertius suggests the skeptical position is much tamer and that the dogmatists' anxiety (revealing though it is) is unwarranted. The skeptics continue to exist by *prohibiting* any doubt with regard to everyday, ideological questions. Their challenge to society thus falls short of the challenge provided by Achilles. For at least Achilles confronts the possibility that behind the taboo on cannibalism lurks the possibility of an obscene enjoyment: he *wants* to be able to want it and articulates that desire. The skeptics shy away from this and become instead typical "beautiful souls," thoroughly dependent on the normative workings of the society they cast doubt upon.

CYCLOPEAN PSYCHOSIS

It is this link between the functioning of the Name of the Father and cannibalism which recurs in the Cyclops episode in *The Odyssey* 9. For the Cyclopes are a species which thoroughly rejects any kind of socially structured symbolic world; in psychoanalytic terms, they seem to be a species of psychotics. The key elements of Odysseus's encounter with the Cyclops are well-known. He journeys with a few of his men to the island of the Cyclopes; they enter the cave of one Cyclops and help themselves to food. The Cyclops returns, traps them in the cave, and begins to eat the men, two by two. Odysseus gets him drunk with wine and the Cyclops then asks Odysseus to tell him his name. Odysseus replies that his name is "No one." The Cyclops replies that, as a reward for this disclosure, he will eat "No one" last. Odysseus goes on to blind the Cyclops, and when he cries out that 'No one' has tricked him, the other Cyclopes ignore his plight.

A conventional, structuralist-inspired reading of Odysseus's blinding of the Cyclops sees it as a victory of civilization over barbarism, of cunning over might. Odysseus's guile (and in particular, his use of the "No one" trick) overpowers the brute strength of the uncivilized, man-eating boor. The problem with this reading is that it can proceed with its enumeration of what is "civilized" and "uncivilized" only by tacitly identifying with the position of Odysseus, with the position of "civilization" itself. It chooses civilization, the Name of the Father, and then uses the symbolic system it has chosen retroactively to justify the choice itself. *If* this critical choice of identification with Odysseus is made, then it is easy to list the Cyclops's symbolic deficiencies. Walter Burkert, for example, provides four contrasts between civilization and barbarism: man with weapon against unarmed savage, the sober man against the drunkard, the seeing against the blind, the master of language against the stupid. Vidal-Naquet has drawn attention to the perversion of sacrifice on the Cyclopes' island as evidence of impiety and, in particular, the Cyclopes' cannibalism.[14] But what is missed is that the Cyclopes utterly reject these terms of reference, this implied accounting system of what is good and bad. What is overlooked in the tracing of this series of individual broken laws is that the Cyclopes are quite simply outside the law. Their lack of concern for the supreme figure of authority, Zeus, is represented in the words of the Cyclops himself:

> The Cyclopes do not concern themselves over Zeus of the aegis, nor any of the rest of the blessed gods, since we are far better. (*Od*.9.275–276)

The rejection of this law cancels out any significance the others might have insofar as it means that the Cyclopes are a law unto themselves. The rejection of the law of Zeus signposts the interchange between Odysseus and the Cyclops as a failed interchange; they have no common terms of reference by which their respective behavior can be judged.[15] By "taking sides" with Odysseus, critics miss that something more basic is at stake—the possibility of finding any meaning in *choosing* the Symbolic in the first place. The paradox is that any choice for sense can only be explained in terms of sense retroactively, after the identification with the position of sense. The Cyclopes, in contrast, seem to refuse this choice of sense, to never have made it.

Because of this, it is worth looking more closely at their peculiar society, which the poem carefully describes. First, we should note that it is completely asocial. Their collective lack of concern for Zeus (an authority that would provide a set of systems to guide their interactions with each other) means that they also have no concern for one another:

> These people have no institutions, no meetings for counsels; rather they make their habitations in caverns hollowed among the peaks of

the high mountains, and each one is the law for his own wives and children, and cares nothing about the others. (Od.9.112–15)

The Cyclopes are perfectly monadic, a species of ones bereft of any social institutions and utterly self-sufficient. This self-sufficiency makes communication unnecessary. They are one-dimensional beings, which is reflected in their most significant physical feature, the single big eye in the middle of their forehead. The static nature of their universe can help explain their peculiar family life. Ancient commentators at least as early as the time of Aristotle were extremely anxious about the parentage of the Cyclopes, and particularly of Polyphemus: "[S]ince neither his father nor his mother is a Cyclops, in what sense can he be said to be one?"[16] But this worry that the Cyclopes do not conform to human classifications concerning the workings of species is precisely the point: the lack of generational normality is a fundamental, if paradoxical, feature of their society. The Cyclopes are a species frozen in time, and it is this which allows them to circumvent the crucial problem which the functioning of the paternal name seeks to resolve: the passing on of the father's name from generation to generation, beyond death. For though there are certainly real fathers on the island—it is emphasized that their civilization is an amalgam of nuclear families—these fathers themselves have no Cyclopean fathers and reject Zeus as a symbolic father. They are fathers who have never had to act out the role of son. They simply do not confront the problem of generational continuity, and thus have no need of a Name of the Father—an ideal, symbolic figure of authority against which the Cyclopes could judge themselves.

Cyclopean society is not only temporally static; it is also spatially static. The Cyclopes, without ships, remain confined to their own island. Odysseus's narrative calls attention to this by emphasizing that opposite the Cyclopean island there lies another island which is perfectly cultivable, yet which the Cyclopes feel no need to visit.[17] There is a simple reason: insofar as they are perfectly self-sufficient, nothing outside of their own island can tempt them. The elaborate description of a cultivable island next door emphasizes their immunity to any human curiosity. The static nature of their society (an asocial world which is shielded from communication from both without and within) provides the context for their "cannibalism." Odysseus meets a Cyclops and attempts to engage him in a language of exchange, a social relationship. The Cyclopean reaction to the threat of the intrusion of sense is simply to consume the threat: Outsiders want to tell me of the laws of the world outside. Fine. I'll eat them. In short, we have a literal "cannibalism," an eating of human flesh but without the taboo of cannibalism – the very thing that made it so fascinating for Achilles.

In the Cyclops's reaction to his adversaries we can see the imaginary relations which, according to Lacan, are so central to the universe of the psychotic; these terms can let us revisit the story of *Odyssey* 9 and give us a vocabulary to describe the way Homer showcases a species which lacks the linguistic structures that characterize speaking-beings. Because of the psychotic's failure to assimilate language—and hence a symbolic structure that would allow him to objectify his own self and thus allow himself to relate peacefully to other objective selves through the mediating effects of a symbolic system—any symbolic incursion into his space from another presence is perceived as a threat to his very existence. Because he has suffered no loss, and there is no gap in his universe, he has nowhere else to go. The psychotic can mimic the language of others, and thus minimally relate to them—but only as long as they keep their distance. The psychotic's failure to recognize loss (castration) is to rule out the possibility of the space (and freedom) to work within the general constraints of language. In Freudian terms, the genital phase has failed to impose its order on the more primitive "oral," cannibalistic phase. In Lacanian terms, the Symbolic order has failed to overwrite the Imaginary. For the Cyclops, can we not see his cannibalistic aggression as a consequence of this? When Odysseus enters his cave, and tries to engage him in discourse, it immediately becomes an invasion of his personal space.[18]

If the Cyclops famously fails to get Odysseus's joke, we can also try to pinpoint the theoretical stakes in the Cyclops's failure to understand Odysseus's "pun" on No one. To say that the Cyclops is stupid or barbarous is certainly a common critical move, but it succeeds only insofar as it ignores this important question. What the Cyclops seems to lack is an understanding of the relationship of words to meaning—an understanding available only to those who inhabit the polysemic realm of language. Let me return once more to the terms of psychoanalysis: for the psychotic substitutional metaphors are not possible (one word cannot be replaced by another word in order to create new meaning) because the paternal metaphor itself (the fundamental replacement of the mother's desire with the father's name which is the *sine qua non* for entrance to language and subjectivity) is not operative. When Odysseus tells the Cyclops his name, we are too easily lured into seeing the joke on the name itself, which depends on *our* understanding of the gap between name and referent: in order to get the pun, *we* substitute No one for Odysseus and then embark upon the long scholarly process of trying to interpret the *meaning* of the use of the negative term No one as a way of understanding the episode.[19] But to the Cyclops, No one does not function as a proper name at all: instead, it possesses an immediate relationship to the identity of the person who confronts him. No one, and the man before him, form a single thing—a thing he can simply consume after he has consumed the other men—because the gap between words and things is missing. The Cyclops lacks a lack.[20] The Cyclops response to this disclosure is not to ask further questions of Odysseus (such as, Who is your father? Where did your name come from?—basically neurotic questions which would require a fuller integration into language), but to fall back on the certainty of what he knows will happen, a certainty which itself is a symptom of the lack of a gap between words and deeds: No one will be eaten last.

ACHILLES AND THE CYCLOPS

What is the relevance of Cyclopean society to Achilles? In the asocial behavior of the Cyclops, it is easy to detect much of the kernel of the plot of *The Iliad*. The profoundly asocial character of the Cyclopes recalls Achilles' rejection of the society of his Greek companions at the start of *The Iliad* and his prayer for their destruction. Indeed Ajax, part of the embassy in book 9, accuses him of savagery in words which come close to Odysseus's description of the Cyclops:

> Achilleus has made savage the proud-hearted spirit within his body. He is hard, and does not remember that friends' affection wherein we honoured him by the ships, far beyond others. Pitiless. (*Il*.9.628–32)

Achilles has a savage spirit, just as the Cyclops is savage. But Ajax views Achilles as savage because he engages in the sort of self-affirmation that pays no heed to his companions. Achilles begins the *Iliad* by rejecting the authority of Agamemnon—he refuses to concede that Agamemnon is "better."[21] The Cyclopes take this Achillean move a crucial step further by affirming their own omnipotence, by declaring themselves to be "far better" than the gods (*Od*.9.275–76). We have already drawn attention to another crucial similarity—and difference. Achilles flirts with cannibalism, the Cyclopes are actual cannibals. But what needs to be emphasized is the underlying logic of Achilles' desire. For to the extent that he joins his challenge to the social order with a fundamental self-affirmation (as he always does), he cannot avoid paying a social penalty for this affirmation. Cedric Whitman has elegantly summed up the substance of Achilles' impossible desire:

> Personal integrity in Achilles achieves the form and authority of immanent divinity, with its inviolable, lonely singleness, half repellent because of its almost inhuman austerity, but irresistible in its passion and perfected selfhood. Yet the scale is not weighted in favor of this gleaming vision.[22]

"Integrity," "perfected selfhood" mixed with "almost inhuman austerity": this is the dream of a self without loss, an impossible longing for a world where entrance to the Symbolic does not involve loss. In short, Achilles seeks to be a Cyclops—a perfect, whole, one-dimensional being. His is the paradoxical desire to be a being without desire, an asocial, monadic one. It is for this reason that the *The Odyssey* provides an answer to perhaps the most puzzling question of *The Iliad*: What does Achilles want?[23] What he wants, but he is unable to acknowledge fully, is *not* to want, to be free of desire itself and its metonymic logic: in short, *to be a Cyclops*.

THE NAMING OF A CYCLOPS

There is one final, crucial connection between Achilles' rejection of society and the world of the Cyclopes. But in order to see this, we need to return to the narrative of the Cyclops's blinding. The cleverness of the trick by which Odysseus blinds the Cyclops has been well explicated by scholars. But what has not been noticed is the *effect* of the trick. Odysseus pokes out the Cyclopean eye, and causes the Cyclops to scream. In response to this scream, the asocial Cyclopes come down from their mountain tops to see what has happened. Critical attention (because of the unacknowledged identification with the civilized cunning of Odysseus) has focused on the failure of the Cyclopes to provide assistance to their blinded comrade—a failure engineered by Odysseus's adoption of the persona No one. But what has been missed is the climactic nature of this event for Cyclopean society. First, the blinding of one Cyclops undermines the self-sufficiency which is crucial to the stability of his identity; the blinding forces him to look for social help. Secondly, the Cyclopean gathering in response to the scream is the first social gathering of a hitherto asocial species. In short, we are far too eager to focus on the failure of the Cyclopes to help their comrade, writing it off as a simple trick. What me miss is the significance of a

Cyclops asking for help at all and the offer of aid in return by his asocial comrades.

Because the response to the blinding stages the first act of communication between Cyclopes, it is worth paying close attention to the words used:

> Why Polyphemos, what do you want with all this outcry through the immortal night and have made us all thus sleepless? (*Od*.9.403–4)

It is noteworthy that this is the first time that the word *poly phemus* is associated with this Cyclops. It is only after the fellow Cyclopes call out Polyphemus that a name is applied to the Cyclops who has been blinded by Odysseus. In contrast, within his narrative Odysseus never calls the Cyclops he blinds Polyphemus; in the run up to the blinding he always addresses him as Cyclops, "Circle Eye," suggesting that he reacts to the single eye in the middle of his adversary's forehead. The fellow Cyclopes thus articulate the name for the first time, a name which can be roughly translated from the Greek as "man of much speech." The narrative depicts the moment when an adjectival cluster (*poly-phemus*, "much speech") is first associated with the blinded Cyclops: "Why on earth, Polyphemus, ("chatterbox" "man of much speech") are you shouting?"

The Cyclopean surprise is a reaction to the first attempt at communication by one of their number, the breaking of a perennial Cyclopean silence. Their rude awakening by the blinded Cyclops is not merely evidence of a disturbed night's sleep but of an awakening from a much longer sleep. Odysseus's tale stages the baptism of the first Cyclops, and the Cyclopes' entrance as a species into the realm of linguistic exchange. And what better name for the first breaker of silence than Polyphemus, "chatterbox"?[24] The blinding of the Cyclops also destroys his oneness, his previous self-sufficiency. Here we can see perhaps the most important consequence of Odysseus's assumption of the negative identity of No one. An external negativity—in the shape of Odysseus as No one—is transferred, in the act of blinding, into the center of the Cyclops. But because he has lost his eye, his identifying feature, *he is no longer a Cyclops*, "Circle Eye."

The blinding also retroactively adds symbolic significance to the joke that the Cyclops tried to play on Odysseus. In return for receiving the supposed knowledge of Odysseus's name, the Cyclops promised he would eat him last:

Then I will eat Nobody last, and the others I will eat first, and that shall be my guest present to you. (*Od.*9.369–70)

The Cyclops' words here are far truer than he could have realized. For after he consumes Odysseus's men, the last thing he will "consume," receive inside himself, is the stake with which Odysseus blinds him. While the consumption of the men in no way affects his identity as a Cyclops, the consumption of the stake—the hollowing out of his eye—irrevocably destroys his identity. He loses his identity as a Cyclops and becomes a *No one*, a subject who has lost his identity and who screams because of this loss; he then makes use of language to try to regain that lost identity, and hence obtains the contingent identity-in-language of "chatterbox." Eating the stake of Odysseus/No one is thus the final act of pure consumption, presymbolic enjoyment of the cannibalistic Cyclops.[25] The "negativity" consumed is an internalization of the gap which, in Lacanian terms, separates the Symbolic from the Real, a gap internal to the Symbolic itself. There is also an ironic reversal of the Cyclops's mocking of the rites of gift-exchange. Before his blinding, the Cyclops' self-sufficiency meant he had no reason to exchange gifts; in his world, gift-exchange is answered with pure consumption. But after he has lost his eye, he will embark on a frantic quest to regain this lost kernel of his being. This search inevitably leads *outside* of himself, and thus into the realm of human exchange. Accordingly, the final "gift" of Odysseus—the stake pushed into his eye— is the paradoxical act which initiates the Cyclops into exchange as such, and away from cannibalistic enjoyment. Exchange takes place against this absolute loss of identity, in an on going attempt to refind it.

NEED, DEMAND, DESIRE

The well-known Lacanian triad of need-demand-desire which is used to help describe the consequences of the entrance of the child into language, can help us clarify the consequences of the blinding and forge the final link between the Cyclops and Achilles. For Lacan, need functions at the level of the biological, as a child depends on others for its most elementary biological need. Need, then, always relates to something specific, a particular item (for example, food) which can of course be satisfied. However, an important change occurs when this need is mediated by language, when the child enters the Symbolic order. At this point, the request for the fulfillment of need is accompanied by a *demand* of the subject, a demand for recognition. Beyond any biological need articulated by the child, there is the demand for the love of the mother. This demand, in Lacan's words, "cancels out the particularity of anything which might be granted by transmuting it into a proof of love."²⁶ The child asks for food but wants the mother's love. But demand is destined to fail, because whether specific demands are met or not, the child can never be certain that the mother's love is absolute. Desire thus appears, heralding an (unfulfillable) wish on the part of the subject for a (mythical) previous totality, wholeness. Desire is a certain leftover of demand after all the specific, satisfied needs have been subtracted from it. With this terminology in mind, let us return to our blinded Cyclops. After the removal of his eye, Polyphemus produces a loud wail—a wail which is worth examining:

> He gave a horrible cry and the rocks rattled to the sound, and we scuttled away in fear. He pulled the timber out of his eye, and it blubbered with plenty of blood, then when he had frantically taken it in his hands and thrown it away, he cried aloud to the other Cyclopes, who live around him in their own caves along the windy pinnacles. (*Od*.9.395–400)

What is crucial here is the move from the initial scream of pain to the cry to the other Cyclopes. The first is a shuddering reaction to the loss of his eye. For the Cyclops, something is now missing and needs to be replaced; like a child, he recognizes his dependence on others. However, in his second cry to his fellow Cyclopes, the cry of pain immediately moves to an intersubjective level; he cries out to the other Cyclopes. Any prior self-sufficiency has been destroyed, and the Cyclops looks to others in an attempt to heal his wound. It is at this point that the Cyclopean cry for help functions as a demand.²⁷ This is the import of the Cyclopean reply:

> If alone as you are No one uses violence on you, why, there is no avoiding the sickness sent by great Zeus; so you had better pray to [your] father, the lord Poseidon. (*Od*.9.410–12)

Several things need to be emphasized here; first, the thing that had always been avoided (Zeus) can no longer be avoided. Polyphemus is now subject to the law, the law of the father (represented by the sickness sent by Zeus). Furthermore there is a nuanced use of the adjective 'οτος' "alone." In a profound way, the Cyclops is alone for the first time. Since he is no longer self-sufficient, his loneliness—the possibility of needing help, and having it rejected—is real. Though before the blinding the Cyclops was always on his own, in the perfection of his self-sufficiency, it is only now that he is truly *alone*, in that he recognizes that he is apart from others upon whom he is dependent, in that he feels lonely. Finally, and most importantly, his new subjection to this "sickness of Zeus" means that he must pray to his father. Let us consider this in detail.

Polyphemus's cry for help is, in the terms outlined above, a demand. But because his fellow Cyclopes seem unable to help, he looks elsewhere— to a father. It is worth noting again that though the other Cyclopes appear to fall victim to the No one trick of Odysseus, their words nevertheless contain an important truth. Insofar as the blinded Cyclops is alone, and victim of a sickness without apparent cause, he is in an utterly helpless situation; his self-sufficiency is destroyed and all that the other Cyclopes can suggest is that he appeal to an external father figure to heal his internal wound. This is exactly what Polyphemus does:

> So come here, Odysseus, let me give you a guest gift and urge the glorious Shaker of the Earth to grant you conveyance home. For I am his son, he claims to be my father. He himself will heal me, if he will, but not any other one of the blessed gods, nor any man who is mortal. (*Od*.9.517–21)

His appeal to Poseidon begins with an identification with his position as son, followed by a reference to Poseidon's claim to be his father. This is another Cyclopean first; it is the first time that a Cyclopean father has identified himself with the position of a son. Polyphemus is introduced to doubt because he has lost his eye; he therefore appeals to his father to heal him and return him to a doubt-free, languageless universe. But this is precisely what Odysseus declares is impossible:

> I only wish it were certain I could make you reft of spirit and life and send you to the house of Hades, as it is certain that not even the Shaker of the Earth will ever heal your eye for you. (*Od*.9.523–29)

Polyphemus appeals to a figure of authority to heal his wound. In brief, his appeal to his father, his recognition of his father, is a recognition of his entrance into the Symbolic, a recognition of the law of the father. However, the father is only called upon after the destruction of the Cyclops's self-sufficiency; Polyphemus's appeal therefore *creates, ex nihilo,* a father who had previously simply not existed for him. The appeal to the father is an appeal to an outside source to cover up an internal doubt. But the genie of doubt has now irrevocably left its bottle. This is the point of Odysseus's reply, which gives Polyphemus an elementary lesson concerning the consequences of his entry into the Symbolic, for we should emphasize that Odysseus is quite right. Poseidon will certainly not heal his son since his status as father is dependent on Polyphemus's entrance into the Symbolic, which in turn, comes from a recognition of his dependence on others. Odysseus demonstrates that the lack at the heart of the Cyclops is now constitutive, that his ongoing demands will remain unfulfilled. He introduces Polyphemus to his desire which lies beyond his demands. Polyphemus thus emerges as a mortal subject, and it is this passage from immortality to mortality which lies behind Odysseus's wry reference to Hades; the certainty that Polyphemus's eye will not be healed is already a certainty that sooner or later he will make the trip to Hades, and that he needs to be aware of this. The Cyclops is pulled back from his refusal of (the language of) society, and now must face his mortality. But more, the acceptance of his mortal status goes hand in hand with the emergence of the realm which makes him part of a system which extends beyond his mortal existence: language. It is ultimately the realm of language that is fundamentally incompatible with the sort of control the Cyclops believes he had over his universe: as Alain Grosrichard puts it, Polyphemus is a good name for the unconscious.[28]

But what is particularly striking is that Odysseus's warning to Polyphemus after the loss of his eye (the taunt which affirms that his lost eye cannot be recovered, and thus heralds his entrance to the social) recalls a warning made by Odysseus to Achilles in the ninth book of *The Iliad*:

> Up, then! if you are minded, late though it be, to rescue the afflicted sons of the Achaeans from the Trojan onslaught. It will be a pain to you hereafter, there will be no cure found to heal the evil thing when it has been done. No, beforehand take thought to beat the evil day aside from the Danaans. (*Il.*9.247–51)

Odysseus's words are typically prescient. Indeed, they seem to highlight the ideological impasse reached by Achilles in *The Iliad*, even as they anticipate Odysseus's later words to the Cyclops. Achilles' fevered attempts to gain sufficient recompense for loss will lead only to further loss: the incurable loss of Patroclus. The indeterminacy of the language of Achilles in *The Iliad* 9, his desire for something more than anything that Agamemnon can provide is a confrontation with this "lack" which structures language: Achilles does not know what he wants, but merely that he wants.[29] From a humdrum heroic existence played out on the playing field of glory, Achilles confronts the problems of his desire. But perhaps because he is not privy to the more explicit elaboration of this problem suggested in Odysseus's encounter with the Cyclops, he is far from learning the Odyssean lesson. For it is only by working through the fundamental fantasy of cannibalism, the ultimate social prohibition around which Greek social life is constructed, that such an austere message can be faced. The lesson is epitomized in a significant Odyssean pun: there is no cure, ἄκος, for grief, ἄχος.[30] For a certain pain, a primordial wound, is endemic to civilization as such.

It is, ultimately, knowledge of this primordial wound which Achilles chooses to flee; rather than return home to his father, he chooses instead to keep desiring, to keep the possibility of an end of desire at bay. He chooses not to cannibalize in order to preserve the illusion that enjoyment and language are compatible. For it allows him to preserve the (unconscious) fantasy of the possible fulfillment of desire in an obscene, cannibalistic enjoyment, while hanging on to his self-conception as a social subject. Further, we can say that it is at this point that the orgy of violence on show in Achilles' killing spree of transgression after the death of Patroclus (a killing spree which itself functions as the hidden truth of the regulated violence of Homeric warfare) is shown to be all for nothing; for it has, at least in no obvious way, altered the ideologies motivating the warriors. *The Odyssey* merely illustrates a truth lurking in Achilles' desire: you want an asocial universe, where you have no ties to other people, no dependence on anything? Fine! Then here is such a universe: that of the cannibalistic Cyclopes!

But here, we need to emphasize that Achilles' problem was *not* that he challenged the social order in the first place: rather, it was his refusal to push this challenge far enough: he "gave up on his desire," replacing it with the return to the social that can leave him with little but a scarcely veiled contempt for the Greeks and himself (as a Greek). It is accordingly only fitting that the minor matter of his later biological death can be little other than an anticlimax, a minor footnote to his epic story. It is not simply that he is as good as dead the moment he kills Hector, as he well knows; for this distracts our attention away from the prior question of his confrontation with cannibalism. He is *socially* dead the moment he decides not to eat Hector, and in consequence returns meekly to the rules and regulations of the Greeks.

It is perhaps worth ending with a few concluding remarks on what is at stake in the meeting between Odysseus and the Cyclops. The story stages the encounter between a representative of the Symbolic (Odysseus) and the representative of a limiting case to the Symbolic—a psychotic. But these questions already seem to entangle us—as readers—in the question of what is involved for us in understanding the tale. I began by the Freudian insight that any identification with any position of sense is dependent on a shared taboo (in *The Iliad*, thou shalt not cannibalize!). To violate this taboo threatens narrative as such. But significantly, this taboo structure also seems to underpin our critical reading of the episode. For in order to understand the Polyphemus story at all—for narrative to have meaning—we are lured into identifying with Odysseus, not the Cyclops. We identify with Odysseus as representative of the Symbolic ("civilization") in order to allow his narrative of the encounter with the Cyclops to work. But in so doing, the danger is that we are complicit in the violence inflicted on the Cyclops performed in the name of forcing him to enter the world of language. It is this second danger which critics seem to have missed, and this seems to be because they are caught up in the *fantasy* of Achilles – and, in the case of much humanist criticism, the consequence has been ongoing efforts to either ignore, or apologize for, Achilles' brutality. But it is this very fantasy that the narrative of the blinding of the Cyclops, if we let it, can help us to shake up.

What is this violence? The Cyclops is psychotic—in Lacanian terms—because his world is characterized by unregulated libidinism; he lacks a key signifier (the phallic signifer, the signifier of loss, of castration) which allows him to order his universe. His cannibalism—a limitless oral enjoyment—is bound up in this psychosis. Yet in his blinding we are forced to witness the price to be paid for entrance to language. If Odysseus faces "oral" incorporation from the cannibalistic Cyclops, the tale ends with just as brutal an incorporation of the Cyclops into the world of speaking-beings through the imposition of an act of symbolic violence. In this episode of *The Odyssey*, this occurs in an unusually pure form; civilization *as* such is shown to be violent, inflicting a loss upon the subjects it claims to civilize. But surely the sophistication of the text lies in its ability to draw attention to this process. Odysseus's remark on the inability of the Cyclops to heal his wound is a commentary on the dangers of the process of identification at work in our reading of the narrative. Odysseus's words to the Cyclops are also an implicit invitation to us to question our identification with him as story teller. Are we—as readers of Odysseus's travels—in search of something, in need of a certain identification, a certain tale of sense? That is, the narrative leaves us with the troubling possibility that our investment in the tale, on the side of Odysseus, is motivated by exactly the same incoherent strivings that characterize the blinded Cyclops, even as we disavow them. What has made us want to take Odysseus's side? The rebuke to the Cyclops—his wound is incurable—is also a rebuke to us. What cure are we seeking by identifying with the position of Odysseus? If *The Odyssey* is a poem about civilization, we might do well to remember that it is also a poem about the "discontents" at the heart of civilization and that our reading of it cannot but be implicated in these concerns.

This "test case" of cannibalism also provides us with some insight into the literary relationship between *The Iliad* and *The Odyssey*. For what is repressed in *The Iliad* (cannibalism) seems to return in *The Odyssey*. We should accordingly be careful before we rush to make judgments about the "separateness" of the themes of these fundamental texts at the origins of the epic tradition.[31] Instead, the monster fantasies of *The Odyssey* are the truth of the all too human fantasies of *The Iliad*. But we can take this further: the structural integrity of each text depends on the disavowal of the opposite. I have tried to argue that the fantasy of the civilization of the Cyclopes provides Achilles with the truth of his desire. Perhaps humans, then, invent monsters not so much to provide narratives that allow them some sort of identity in difference (we are not *that*, not *cannibals*) but as symptoms of their own disavowed, monstrous desires. For from the perspective of the blinded Cyclops, cannibalism itself, as transgressive desire, is "invented" retroactively, in the same gesture that rejects it as inhuman: a one-eyed monster did it, not a human. The moment the Cyclops desires, the moment he becomes human, is also the moment that a traumatic past emerges, a past that is disavowed as the past of a different species, the Cyclopean monster. The enjoyment of cannibalism is always figured as the enjoyment of a monster, never that of the desiring subject. This enjoyment itself is something that is, within the logic of the tale, both irrecoverable (the Cyclops will never recover his eye, nor will he ever *enjoy* in the same way) and something he immediately runs away from: as he looks to the world outside for a new eye, every research, every effort at looking confirms to us all that he is no longer *that*—a nondesiring, man-eating Cyclops. Yet for all that, this lost enjoyment is irrecoverable: it has effects. Indeed, the war narratives of the Homeric poems themselves can be seen as symptoms of these extended attempts at recovery of a missing object.

So perhaps we can see the story of Achilles, *The Iliad* itself, as an extended interpretation of what will happen to the Cyclops after he is blinded by Odysseus. It is as if Odysseus's "fatherly" act of blinding/castrating the Cyclops is an explanatory preface to the story of Achilles in *The Iliad*. The Cyclops would not only figure as an answer to the question of what Achilles wants; he also helps us understand why the Achilles of *The Iliad* is so "childlike" in his wants.[32] For in the depiction of the beginnings of the traumatic "childhood" of the Cyclops, we find an attempt to explain the origins of the (obsessive, neurotic) questions that Achilles is constantly asking in an attempt to find his place in the epic universe. His ongoing *failure* to find the answers leaves us with one explanation for why he is so angry: the theme of *The Iliad* is *menis*, "wrath."

NOTES

1. The *Iliad of Homer: Translated with an Introduction by Richard Lattimore*, Chicago 1951. Adaptations are my own.

2. The suggestion that Achilles has learned the lesson *not* to question social power is reinforced by the final competition of the funeral games in book 23. There, Agamemnon is about to compete with Meriones in the javelin contest. However, Achilles intervenes to halt the contest, saying that there is no need for the contest, as everyone knows that Agamemnon surpasses all others in throwing (*Il.*23.884ff.). The thematic link to the opening book seems clear; earlier, Achilles had questioned the unquestionable right to rule of Agamemnon, and therefore tested his power. Here, as arbitrator of the funeral games, Achilles orchestrates events to ensure that Agamemnon's power is *not* tested.

3. See *Il.*1.1–4:

> Sing, goddess, the anger of Peleus' son Achilleus and its devastation, which put pains thousandfold upon the Achaians, hurled in their multitudes to the house of Hades strong souls . . .

4. The fantasy of cannibalism is mentioned at two other points in the poem, which seems to confirm this hypothesis: Zeus imagines that Hera's hatred of the Trojans might be satisfied if she were to eat them raw (*Il.*4.34ff.), and Hecuba imagines eating Achilles' liver as suitable recompense for the death of her son Hector (24.212ff.). In both cases, cannibalism is only imagined, while the latter incident suggests that the possibility of cannibalism as satisfaction for human fury remains in place after (and indeed because of) Achilles' refusal to eat Hector.

5. The solution of the vast majority of Homer critics who choose to identify with the horror at cannibalism.

6. In my readings of the Homeric poems, I follow the work of Gregory Nagy, who has argued that the assorted Homeric traditions (of which *The Iliad* and *The Odyssey* are the most significant) constantly allude to each other, showing an implicit awareness of their ongoing compositions and re-compositions in an oral context. See *The Best of the Achaeans* (Baltimore: Johns Hopkins UP, 1979), and his more recent elaboration of his position in *Poetry as Performance: Homer and Beyond* (Cambridge: Cambridge UP, 1996). Nagy's insights have been put to

use by Pietro Pucci: *Odysseus Polutropos: Intertextual Readings in the Iliad and the Odyssey* (Ithaca: Cornell UP, 1987). Pucci suggests, as a reading strategy, we leave ourselves open to the possibility that the major Homeric epics, each composed with the knowledge of the ongoing development of the other, read each other. The significance of such an approach for the problem of cannibalism is elaborated further below.

7. Hans Van Wees, *Status Warriors* (Amsterdam: Gieber, 1992), 128.

8. It is precisely such a principle which Ajax stands up for in his argument against Achilles in *The Iliad* 9.624ff.

9. Richard Rorty: *Contingency, Irony, and Solidarity* (Cambridge: Cambridge UP 1989), p. 195.

10. This is the second time Achilles has come to the point of rejecting the society of warriors; when approached by the embassy sent by Agamemnon in *The Iliad* 9, and asked to return to battle, he refuses Agamemnon's gifts and claims at first that he will head home. Yet he fails to do this, and the threat of going home quickly becomes a lever used to extract more recognition, pure prestige, from the other warriors in general, and Agamemnon in particular. See the fine discussion of Michael Lynn-George in *Expos: Word, Narrative and The Iliad.* (Atlantic, NJ. Humanities Press International, 1998), chp. 2.

11. Herein lies the importance of the pun made by Lacan on *non* and *nom* in the "*Nom du Père.*" The functioning of the symbolic under the auspices of an ideal father only occurs when this father utters a no to enjoyment. An immediate consequence is that the enjoyment that seems to be *external* to the father (in the figure of the mother) is already present in the senseless no of the father himself, in its idiocy as a signifier. On this in general, see Slavoj Žižek, *Enjoy your Symptom, Jacques Lacan in Hollywood and Out* (New York: Routledge, 1992), chap. 4.

12. Diogenes Laertius 9.108, translated by Brad Inwood and L. P. Gerson, in *Hellenistic Philosophy: Introductory Readings* (Indianapolis: Appleton, 1988).

13. This threat of cannibalizing *the father* also suggests a split in the functioning of the father itself. The ideal father, supervisor of the social, is threatened with his absorption by an obscene, enjoying, cannibalizing father.

14. Walter Burkert, *Structure and History in Greek Mythology and Ritual.* (Berkeley: U of California P, 1979), 33; Pierre Vidal-Naquet, *The Black Hunter* (Baltimore: Johns Hopkins UP, 1986), 18ff.

15. This is noted by Crotty, *The Poetics of Supplication.* (Ithaca: Cornell UP, 1994), 146: "To eat human flesh is so horrific as to be utterly beyond such codes [of hospitality]. To accuse Polyphemus of "not scrupling" . . . to eat "his guests" . . . is an unwarranted importing of one culture's ethics into another realm, where ethics can have no meaning." Yet this insight (which suggests a bracketing of all that is "civilized") is not explored by Crotty.

16. S. West, in A. Heubeck, S. West, and J. B. Hainsworth, *A Commentary on Homer's Odyssey,* vol. 1. (Oxford: Clarendon P, 1988), 84. The relevant fragment of Aristotle referred to by West is fr.172, Rose, which comes from the H. Q.

Scholiast *ad Od.* 9.106: ζητεῖ Ἀριστοτέλης πῶς ὁ Κύκλωψ ὁ Πολύφημος μήτε πατρός ὢν Κύκλωπος Ποσειδῶνος γάρ ἦυ μήτε μητρός Κύκλωψ ἐγέετο αὐτός. "Aristotle questioned how the Cyclops Polyphemus himself became a Cyclops, since he was neither born from a Cyclopean father (Poseidon was his father), nor from a mother."

17. *Od.*9.116ff. Odysseus and his uoops approach the island of the Cyclopes from this island.

18. Here, and below, I follow the lucid analysis of psychosis by Bruce Fink in *A Clinical Introduction to Lacanian Psychoanalysis* (Cambridge, Mass.: Harvard UP, 1997). Fink abstracts from the arguments made by Lacan in his third seminar on the psychoses.

19. For an interesting attempt at just this, see John Peradotto, *Man in the Middle Voice* (Princeton, N.J.: Princeton UP, 1990).

20. For more on the way the psychotic treats words for things, see Fink, 86ff.

21. See Nestor's exhortation to Achilles to recognize that Agamemnon is "better" at *Il.*1.281ff.

22. Cedric Whitman *Homer and the Homeric Tradition* (Cambridge, Mass.: Harvard UP, 1958), 182. Whitman's treatment of Achilles remains deeply insightful, and is especially sensitive to the hero's savagery.

23. For a superb discussion of the difficulties, see Lynn-George 123ff.

24. The reaction of the Cyclopes to Polyphemus's blinding can be contrasted with the reaction to adversity exhibited by the Kikonians earlier in Odysseus's narrative. When attacked by Odysseus's men, the Kikonians *immediately* come to each others help, calling out to each other (*Od.*9.47). The immediacy of this response highlights their status as a community linked by (a common) language. This is in marked contrast to the lack of such group solidarity exhibited by the Cyclopes.

25. The link is strengthened by an astute observation of John Peradotto, who has noted the punning on the word for "stabbing," οὐτάω, and the word for "No one," οὔτιω. To stab is simultaneously to "render someone a nobody." See Peradotto, 143ff.

26. Jacqueline Rose, and Juliet Mitchell, eds., *Feminine Sexuality: Jacques Lacan and the Ecole freudienne* (New York 1982), 81. For a general elaboration of these concepts, see Rose's introduction,32ff.

27. We can ask a further important question: Who is the subject of this scream? It cannot yet be Polyphemus because the act of naming has not yet occurred. Is it a Cyclops? Not if we define the Cyclopes in terms of their defining quality, their one eye. For this is a Cyclops who has just lost his eye and is thus no longer properly a Cyclops. The subject of the scream is *no one*, which announces the entrance of the subject *as such* to Cyclopean civilization.

28. See Alain Grosrichard, "The Case of Polyphemus," 146, in *Cogito and the Unconscious*, ed. Slavoj Žižek (Durham, NC: Duke UP, 1998). For the work-

ings of the unconscious, structured like a language, constantly subvert any discourse of conscious self-mastery which is characteristically that of the *ego*.

29. Lynn-George, 123ff.

30.   αὐτῷ τοι μετόπισθ' ἄχος ἔσσεται, οὐδέ τι μῆχος
ῥωχθέτῃς κακοῦ ἔστ' ἄκος εὑρεῖν: (*Il.*9.249–50)

31. There have been many such efforts. Some of the more influential include the following set of distinctions: *The Odyssey* as an "imaginary" poem of fantasy and self-construction, *The Iliad* as the "realistic" poem of war and violence. *The Odyssey* as the poem of "life" and "sexuality," *The Iliad* as the poem of "death" and "politics." I hope, at least, to have gone some way in demonstrating the inadequacy of such separations.

32. See the analysis of Thomas MacCary, *Achilles: Childlike Achilles: Ontogeny and Phylogeny in the* Iliad. (Baltimore: Johns Hopkins UP, 1982)

3

Cannibalism in Edmund Spenser's *Faerie Queene*, Ireland, and the Americas

ROBERT VIKING O'BRIEN

In Book 6 of *The Faerie Queene*, Edmund Spenser describes a nation of cannibals:

a saluage nation, which did liue
Of stealth and spoile, and making nightly rode
Into their neighbours borders; ne did giue
Them selues to any trade, as for to driue
The painefull plough, or cattell for to breed,
Or by aduentrous marchandize to thriue;
But on the labours of poore men to feed,
And serue their owne necessities with others need.

Thereto they vsde one most accursed order,
To eate the flesh of men, whom they mote fynde,
And straungers to devoure, which on their border
Were brought by errour or by wreckfull wynde.
(6.8.35-36)[1]

The maiden Serena falls asleep in the "wylde deserts" where these cannibals dwell. When she wakes, she gets a nasty surprise, as the cannibals "round about her flocke, like many flies" (6.8.40), tear off her clothes, and

35

prepare to eat her. The knight Calepine arrives just in time and single-
handedly defeats the savages despite their large numbers:

> . . . swarmes of damned soules to hell he sends;
> The rest that scape his sword and death eschew,
> Fly like a flocke of doues before a Faulcons vew.
>
> (6.8.49])

Scholars have long speculated about the sources of this episode. One
lists the following possibilities: "Greek romance, Italian romance, Italian
pastorals, . . . rites of human sacrifice and anthropophagy in ancient
Greece and Celtic Gaul, the views of Elizabethan historians on the primitive Celts and contemporary Irish, and Spenser's conception of Irish ethnic
origins and social customs in his *View of the Present State of Ireland*."[2] This
long, heterogeneous list includes many historic examples of cannibalism,
yet it omits what is arguably the most popular Elizabethan example: the
cannibalism of Native Americans as described in European narratives of
the Americas. Spenser's use of cannibalism in the Savage Nation episode
plainly admits multiple influences.

In this chapter, I shall explore Spenser's Irish and American sources,
which are closely related to the process of national self-fashioning that
accompanied Elizabethan colonialism. Through this exploration, I hope
to show how Spenser's representation of cannibalism was part of the larger
process of European self-definition, a process in which cannibalism was
often used as a conclusive signifier of otherness.

Spenser's descriptions of Irish cannibalism show his difficulties in
having to see the Irish as at once other and yet also European. He devotes
much of *A View of the Present State of Ireland* to describing the barbarity of
the Irish—their criminality, their cruelty, the filth of their dwellings, and
their superstitions[3]—but he does not suggest that they are radically other,
for this would make their incorporation into the British polity impossible.
For that, they must be European. This condition makes cannibalism problematic as a signifier of Irish barbarity. We see this in both of the descriptions of Irish cannibalism in *A View*. The second of these results from a
famine during the war in Munster: "Out of every corner of the woods and
glens they came creeping forth upon their hands for their legs could not
bear them, they looked like anatomies of death, they spake like ghosts crying out of their graves, they did eat the dead carrions, happy where they
could find them; yea and one another soon after, in so much as the very
carcasses they spared not to scrape out of their graves."[4]

This ghastly portrayal of famine-induced cannibalism differs significantly from the portrayal of cannibalism in *The Faerie Queene*. While the Savage Nation practices cannibalism as a regular custom, the Irish are reduced to cannibalism because of starvation; under similar circumstances, even the English eat their dead.[5] Unlike customary anthropophagism, cannibalism *in extremis* does not, for Spenser, denote the evil nature of its practitioners. In *The Faerie Queene*, the Savage Nation's "most accursed order" signifies their innate depravity; in the passage cited above, the Irish rebels' cannibalism reveals a debasement produced by external circumstances. Although Spenser blames this "wonderful wretchedness" on the Irish themselves, who have stubbornly refused to submit to English rule, Irish cannibalism, in this instance, is the fault of "the extremity of famine which they themselves had wrought."[6]

By describing the Munster famine, Spenser hopes to show that the Irish can be quickly defeated.[7] His description of Irish cannibalism thus supports his argument that Ireland can be subjugated without much effort. Earlier in the *View*, Spenser tries to show that the Irish need this subjugation: their barbarous customs demand English correction. Spenser's first reference to Irish cannibalism is part of this rhetorical effort:

> . . . the Gauls used to drink their enemies' blood and to paint themselves therewith. So also they write that the old Irish were wont. And so have I seen some of the Irish do but not their enemies' but friends' blood as namely at the execution of a notable traitor at Limerick called Murrogh O'Brien. I saw an old woman which was his foster mother take up his head whilst he was quartered and sucked up all the blood running thereout, saying that the earth was not worthy to drink it, and therewith also steeped her face, and breast, . . . crying and shrieking out most terrible.[8]

Unlike his description of the Munster famine (1581–82), Spenser's description of this blood-drinking implies that a kind of cannibalism is customary among the Irish. A close look reveals, however, that Irish cannibalism differs from the Savage Nation's "accursed order."

In the passage cited above, Spenser refers to two distinct kinds of cannibalism. The first is connected to warfare. After a battle, "the old Irish" drank the blood of their vanquished foes, a custom they inherited from the ancient Gauls. Spenser believed that the Irish descended from both Gauls and Scythians, and he attributes many barbarous Irish customs to that descent.[9] In this instance, Spenser seems to have confused these ancestors: no classical source describes the Gauls as drinking blood. Herodotus does, however, describe how "the Scythian custom is for every man to drink the blood of the first man he kills."[10] This custom, which represents a rite of passage, is found in many cannibal cultures—among various Melanesian peoples.[11] Whether or not "old Irish" cannibalism represented a similar rite of passage, it was connected with warfare and thus a species of what Peggy Reeves Sanday calls "exocannibalism," the cannibalism of outsiders.[12] In *Cannibalism: Human Aggression and Cultural Form*, Eli Sagan writes that

> For the cannibal who eats people outside his tribe, warfare and cannibalism are inexorably connected. . . . [E]ating the vanquished is as important to warfare as victory is. For the cannibal, many metaphors are reduced to literalness: the fruits of victory are literally eaten.[13]

Spenser's Gallic and "old Irish" custom fits this description: when the ancient Gauls and Irish "drink their enemies' blood and . . . paint themselves therewith," they reify their victories.

This kind of cannibalism differs significantly from what Spenser claims to have witnessed at Murrogh O'Brien's execution.[14] When O'Brien's foster mother drinks his blood, she expresses, not victory, but grief, "crying and shrieking out most terrible." Although less common than exocannibalism, the kind of cannibalism described here (Sanday calls it "endocannibalism"; Sagan calls it "affectionate cannibalism") has occurred in a number of cultures throughout the world.[15] According to Sagan, there is "a crucial distinction" between this and the cannibalism of war: "Eating the dead is certainly cannibalism, but eating dead kinsmen is a profoundly different form of cannibalism from the aggressive eating of victims outside the clan."[16] The motives behind the two forms are different: when a cannibal eats his enemies, he symbolically expresses a victory in war; when he eats his relatives, he honors them. In the scene described by Spenser the Irishwoman who drinks her foster son's blood says that she does this because "the earth was not worthy to drink it."

Although he does not refer to it, Spenser has classical support for claiming that the Irish honored the dead in this manner. In the *Geography*, Strabo writes that the Irish "count it an honorable thing, when their fathers die, to devour them."[17] Strabo was a popular author for the Elizabethans, and many of their historians referred to this passage when they described the origins of the Irish people. Edmund Campion cites it in his *Historie of Ireland*, and William Camden does the same in *Britannia*.[18]

The passage had a certain appeal for the Elizabethans: it showed that, even in ancient times, Britons were more civilized than the Irish. Strabo explains the import of the Irish custom: "Concerning this island [Ireland] I have nothing certain to tell, except that its inhabitants are more savage than the Britons, since they are man-eaters."[19] For Spenser, the behavior of Murrogh O'Brien's foster mother provided contemporary proof of this thesis, for like Campion and Camden, Spenser believed that Irish "savagery" had a long history, as his description of "old Irish" cannibalism shows.

But are the Irish the source for *The Faerie Queene*'s Savage Nation of cannibals? Although a number of scholars have seen a connection,[20] the Irish cannibalism described in *A View* differs from the Savage Nation's cannibalism in several ways. This is certainly true of what Spenser witnessed during the Munster famine: unlike customary cannibalism, famine-induced cannibalism does not show that the Irish are savages. But even when Spenser describes cannibalism to show Irish savagery—as with "old Irish" blood-drinking and the cannibalism of Murrogh O'Brien's foster mother—that cannibalism is unlike the Savage Nation's. "Old Irish" blood-drinking, like most instances of exocannibalism, is connected to warfare, and the behavior of O'Brien's foster mother is a way of honoring the dead. Serena is neither an enemy soldier captured in war nor a dead relative being honored by her own, anthropophagic, people: she is an innocent who has wandered into a country inhabited by cannibals.

We can find better analogies for Serena's situation, and the Savage Nation's cannibalism, in European narratives of the New World. The earliest of these narratives—the *Quatuor navigationes*, the *Mundus Novus*, and the various accounts based on Columbus's voyages—contain gruesome descriptions of cannibalism. These descriptions obviously appealed to the European readers, for when a genuine account lacked such descriptions, publishers added their own.[21] The interest in Native American cannibalism did not diminish over the next century. Editions of the early accounts multiplied and were joined by newer, more explicit, narratives. The most explicit resulted from European encounters with the natives of Brazil. In his *Veritable history and description of a country belonging to the wild, naked, and terrible people, eaters of men's flesh situated in the New World, America* (1557), Hans Staden repeatedly describes, in gory detail, the preparation and consumption of cannibal feasts.[22] Similar stories appear in other works describing native Brazilians: André Thevet describes Tupinamba cannibalism in his *Singularities of Antarctic France* (1557), as does Jean de Léry in his *History of a Voyage to the Land of Brazil* (1578).[23]

Both the early and later accounts of Native American cannibalism were accompanied by gruesome illustrations. The earliest editions of the *Mundus Novus* and *Quatuor navigationes* contain crude woodcuts of Indians cooking severed heads and limbs.[24] A similar illustration, inspired by the Vespucci accounts, appears on one of the earliest maps of America.[25] Indeed, the first known European representation of Native Americans is a cannibal scene based on descriptions in the Vespucci accounts: this German woodcut depicts cannibals eating parts of human bodies and smoking limbs and a head for future use.[26] Similar woodcuts accompanied both Thevet's *Singularities* and Staden's *Veritable History*. In Theodore de Bry's edition, the *Veritable History* is accompanied by numerous, detailed engravings of the murder, dismemberment, cooking, and eating of cannibal victims.[27] Such illustrations continued to appear on maps, such as those accompanying Sebastian Münster's influential *Cosmographia Universalis* (1544).[28]

This last example shows how closely Europeans associated Native Americans with cannibalism. European mapmakers usually chose a cannibal scene to represent the inhabitants of the New World. The association was so close that mapmakers did not even need to represent the natives themselves: depicting evidence of cannibalism was enough to imply their presence. No people are portrayed on the first separate map of America, which was printed in 1544 by Sebastian Münster. Instead, Münster represents the natives with a hut of branches, but from one of these branches hangs a severed leg.

Münster expected his readers to understand the significance of that leg. The idea of Native American cannibalism was firmly established in the European consciousness even before the newer accounts of Brazilian natives appeared in the middle of the century. By the time Spenser was writing *The Faerie Queene*, descriptions and images of cannibals were everywhere in the voluminous literature on the Americas. Few educated Europeans in the period could think of man-eaters without thinking of Native Americans.

A number of references in *The Faerie Queene* show Spenser's interest in the Americas. One cited by a number of scholars occurs in the proem to book 2, when Spenser challenges anyone who would judge his "antique history" to be a forgery:

> But let that man with better sence auize,
> That of the world least part to vs is red:
> And dayly how through hardy enterprize,

> Many great Regions are discovered,
> Which to the late age were neuer mentioned.
> Who euer heard of th'Indian Peru?
> Or who in venturous vessell measured
> The Amazons huge riuer now found trew?
> Or fruitfullest Virginia who did euer vew?
>
> (2.Pro.2)

Spenser's references to Peru, the Amazon, and Virginia prove that he had an interest in, and knowledge of, the Americas. Spenser's knowledge undoubtedly included the familiar fact of American cannibalism. This fact was certainly more familiar than the "fruitful" nature of Virginia or the immense size of "Amazons huge riuer." Cannibals had entered the European popular imagination, and Spenser had only to draw on that imagination to create his Savage Nation of cannibals.[29]

We find popular ideas about Native Americans in a number of places in *The Faerie Queene*. For example, in the Masque of Cupid, Fancy's garment is made of

> painted plumes, in goodly order dight,
> Like as the sunburnt *Indians* do aray
> Their tawney bodies, in their proudest plight.
>
> (3.12.8)

Spenser probably learned about Native American skin color and feather decorations from Richard Eden's English translation of Pietro Martire's *Decades*, as well as from the *Quatuor navigationes* and the *Mundus Novus*.[30] When he describes Maleger in book 2, Spenser exhibits an even greater familiarity with European descriptions of Native Americans. Maleger contains elements of both American and East Indians, a common conflation in this period. He appears on a tiger, that most East Indian of beasts, but his arms are Native American:

> And in his hand a bended bow was seene,
> And many arrowes vnder his right side,
> All deadly daungerous, all cruell keene,
> Headed with flint, and feathers bloudie dide,
> Such as the *Indians* in their quiuers hide;
> Those could he well direct and streight as line,
> And bid them strike the marke, which he had eyde,
> Ne was their salue, ne was their medicine,
> That mote recure their wounds: so inly they did tine.
>
> (2.11.21)

European accounts of the Americas contain numerous references to bows and arrows as Indian weapons. The accounts also refer to the Indians' proficiency in using those weapons. In the *Quatuor navigationes*, for instance, the narrator says that the Indians "are sure shots, and where they aim they hit."[31] Many accounts describe how, like Maleger's arrows, Indian arrows caused wounds that could not be healed with "salue" or "medicine." Sebastian Münster notes that the Indians "are accustomed to infect their arrows with venom."[32] Fernandez de Oveido says that "the Indians are accustomed to poison their arrows wherewith they kill all that they wound."[33] And in a description that could be Spenser's source, Pietro Martire describes the arrows' venom: "that poison is of such force, that albeit the wounds were not great, yet they died thereof immediately. . . . [T]hey yet knew no remedy against this kind of poison."[34]

The Maleger episode contains details drawn from accounts of the New World but also elements from elsewhere: much of the episode comes from the legend of Antaeus, for instance.[35] The Savage Nation episode, however, could have been drawn entirely from accounts of the New World. Unlike Maleger, or Fancy in the Masque of Cupid, the Savage Nation is, in every detail, closely related to the Native Americans described in those accounts. Even the name, "Savage Nation," is one often used in the accounts to describe Native Americans: Theodore de Bry called the Algonquians a "Savage Nation."[36]

Spenser's Savage Nation is not related to all the "savage nations" of the New World, but to one in particular. The Caribs, called "cannibales" in sixteenth-century accounts, were supposed to plunder their neighbors for goods and human flesh. Pietro Martire's description of these people is especially applicable to Spenser's representation of the Savage Nation. Martire writes that "these wily hunters of men, give themselves to none other kind of exercise but only to manhunting and tillage after their manner" (149). His description implies that the cannibals are slothful, but he makes it clear elsewhere that they are energetic in their manhunting: cannibals "are wont at some time to go from their own coasts above a thousand mile to hunt for men" (69). The cannibals do not go on these raids for human flesh alone. Martire says that "the cannibals, being a wild and wandering people, and overrunning all the countries about them to hunt for man's flesh, were accustomed to bring home with them whatsoever they found . . . profitable in any place" (177). Cannibal raids result in the desolation of islands that would otherwise be "very fruitful." When the cannibals' neighbors, who tend gardens and look after the land, flee to the mountains in fear, their islands are "left desolate and wasted by reason of the cruelty of the cannibals" (98).

Essentially, Martire describes a slothful cannibal nation that lives by raiding their more industrious neighbors. This description could just as easily apply to Spenser's Savage Nation. Admittedly, Spenser's savages seem to do no farming at all, while Martire's at least have "tillage after their manner." Nevertheless, the thrust of the two descriptions is the same: both Martire's cannibals and Spenser's savages live in a desolate place and are indolent, except when they are raiding their neighbors.

The raids differ in their emphases, however, and to understand the Savage Nation's relation to American cannibals, we need to consider this difference. When Martire's cannibals go raiding, they go "to hunt for man's flesh." If, at the same time, they find something valuable, they take it (177). Human flesh is the primary goal; spoil is secondary. The reverse is true of the Savage Nation. Spenser says that these savages "liue / Of stealth and spoile"; he never says that they hunt for flesh. When they discover Serena, they are "wandring euery way / To seeke for booty," and their capture of her results from "fortune blynde" (6.8.36). Martire's cannibals discover booty when they are looking for human flesh; Spenser's Savage Nation discovers human flesh when they are looking for booty.

In this, Spenser's description of the Savage Nation curiously resembles the accounts' descriptions of Europeans who commit atrocities—though not cannibalism—as they search for booty in the Americas. Despite this curious resemblance, the Savage Nation, as we would expect, more closely resembles the natives in the European–Native American encounter. The Savage Nation usually stays in its own country, where it practices a peculiarly passive kind of cannibalism. They do not "go from their own coasts above a thousand mile to hunt for men" (69); instead, they wait for prey to come to them. The Savage Nation, it seems, are "natives" who are as slothful about cannibalism as they are about trade, farming, and husbandry. They prefer mantrapping to manhunting.

The cannibals appearing in accounts of the New World are also both manhunters and mantrappers. Martire, for example, describes how "[a]t the coming . . . of our men into their regions, they look as surely to have them fall into their snares as if they were harts or wild boars, and with no less confidence lick their lips secretly in hope of their prey" (149). Such descriptions may be sublimated expressions of European anxieties over their own "consumption" of the Americas: Europe is not devouring the Americas, the descriptions imply, the Americas are devouring Europe.

The accounts are replete with these descriptions. In them, Europeans are always the victims of mantrapping, never of manhunting. There the victims are other natives. Similarly, the accounts rarely describe other Native Americans as the victims of mantrapping. The Savage Nation episode thus most closely resembles incidents of cannibalism in which Europeans are the victims. Serena wanders into the Savage Nation's territory, is captured and almost eaten. The same sequence of events, with a more unfortunate ending, occurs repeatedly in exploration narratives. Martire, for example, describes how Juan de Solis

> chanced to fall into the hands of the filthy cannibals. For these crafty foxes seemed to make signs of peace, when in their minds they conceived a hope of a dainty banquet, and . . . began to swallow their spittle as their mouths watered for greediness of their prey. As unhappy Solis descended, . . . suddenly a great multitude burst forth upon them. . . . Not one man escaped.[37]

This account and others like it contain the very elements of chance, surprise, and horror that help constitute the Savage Nation episode. In the accounts, Europeans arrive in an unknown country, unaware of the natives' cannibalism, just as Serena wanders into the Savage Nation's country "Fearlesse of ought, that mote her peace molest" (6.8.34). Often in the accounts, as cited above, the natives appear friendly; sometimes they are hidden from the Europeans' view. In either situation, the natives attack suddenly in a large group, surprising and overwhelming the Europeans. Serena gets a similar surprise when she awakens and the Savage Nation surrounds her. Her reaction to her first sight of the Savage Nation—"Her heart does quake, and deadly pallid hew / Benumbes her cheekes" (6.8.40)—also recalls descriptions in the accounts. Martire says, of the cannibals, "There is no man able to behold them, but he shall feel his bowels grate with a certain horror, nature hath endowed them with so terrible menacing, and cruel aspect" (70).

The most horrifying portrayal of cannibalism appears in Hans Staden's *Veritable History*. Perhaps because of this sensationalism, Staden's was the most popular of the later narratives of Native American cannibalism, reprinted in more than seventy editions, many of them illustrated.[38] Spenser may have read Staden's account and been struck by the description of his initial capture:

One day I was walking through the woods . . . , when I heard loud yells such as the savages make, and at once a company of them came running towards me and surrounded me. . . . They tore the clothes off my body, one taking the jerkin, another my hat, a third my shirt and so on. . . . [T]hey pretended to bite their arms as if it was me they were eating. . . . When they had brought me to their canoes they began to argue as some wanted to kill me on the spot and make a division, but at last the chief, who wanted to keep me, ordered that I should be taken home so that their wives might also see me and feast upon me.[39]

This scene resembles Serena's in a number of ways. Like Serena, Staden walks unsuspectingly into the cannibals' territory. The cannibals surround him with "loud yells such as savages make," just as the Savage Nation surrounds Serena "Whooping, and hallowing on euery part, / As if they would haue rent the brasen skies" (6.8.40). The cannibals tear Staden's clothes off, each one taking a different piece for himself; the Savage Nation tears Serena's clothes off, "The which amongst them they in peeces tear, / And of the pray each one a part doth beare" (6.8.41). Finally, the cannibals who capture Staden argue about whether to kill and eat him immediately or save him to eat later.[40] The Savage Nation holds a similar debate:

> Then gan they to deuize what course to take:
> Whether to slay her there vpon the place,
> Or suffer her out of her sleepe to wake,
> And then her eate attonce; or many meals to make.
>
> (6.8.37)

The accounts also provided details for Serena's rescue. Martire describes how Columbus defeats the cannibals a number of times, sometimes, like Calepine, rescuing prisoners who were about to be eaten (71, 78, 95). The superior firepower of the Europeans makes the cannibals' defeat inevitable—"our men so seared them with their guns that [the cannibals] fled immediately" (95)—but Martire also attributes this to the cannibals' essentially cowardly nature: "If they mistrust themselves to be the weaker part, they trust to their feet, and fly swifter than the wind" (149). Spenser's savages share this trait.

Calepine's righteous destruction of the Savage Nation recalls Martire's description of how Columbus will "waste and spoil the islands of the cannibals, . . . that those ravening wolves might no longer persecute and devour innocent sheep" (78). There are analogous statements elsewhere in the *Decades* and in other accounts.[41] Not only do the accounts contain similar details, they express a similar sentiment: Europeans have a moral duty to destroy the cannibals. Thus Calepine sends "damned souls to hell" (6.8.49) and rescues Serena, who has fallen into their hands "like a sheep astray" (6.8.36). Europeans must destroy the evil savages to save the innocent.

In *The Faerie Queene*, Spenser, like Martire, divides his savages into innocent primitives and vicious brutes. The Savage Nation fits into this last category, of course, as does the "wild and saluage man" (4.7.5). These characters are cannibals, and Spenser could easily connect their cannibalism to lust in the Savage Nation episode: the same connection already existed in the accounts of native America. By dwelling on the dismemberment of cannibal victims, the accounts also provided Spenser with a metaphor for the Savage Nation's visual violation of Serena.

Spenser, of course, did not need to read accounts of native America to find the distinction, used repeatedly in the *Faerie Queene*, between innocent and vicious savages. It was firmly established in western culture long before Europe encountered native America: in Arcadia, the shepherds of Virgil's eclogues piped and sang, and in Arcadia men worshipped the "Wolf-god Zeus" by eating the bowels of human sacrifices.[42] Accounts of native America did, however, reinforce the distinction between good and evil primitives. Europeans created a variety of representations of native America. Two extreme versions had a great influence on European culture: Native Americans as utter innocents, living "in the golden world," and Native Americans as utterly depraved, "inhuman cannibals."[43]

In his history of sixteenth-century nondramatic English literature, C. S. Lewis eloquently describes how these representations reinforced the European image of "Natural Man." He goes on to describe two myths that derive from this dual image of "Natural Man":

> America . . . affected not only imaginative but even philosophical thought. If it did not create, it impressed on our minds more strongly, the image of the Savage, or Natural Man. . . . The "Natural Man" is, of course, an ambivalent image. He may be conceived as ideally innocent. From that conception descend Montaigne's essay on cannibals, Gonzalo's commonwealth in the *Tempest,* the good "Salvage" in the *Faerie Queene* [6.4.5.6], Pope's "reign of God," and the primeval classless society of the Marxists. It is one of the great myths. On the other hand, he might be conceived as brutal, sub-

human: thence Caliban, the bad "Salvages" of the Faerie Queene [6.8], the state of nature as pictured by Hobbes, and the "Cave Man" of popular modern imagination. That is another great myth.[44]

While one may disagree with aspects of this description—some readers find Caliban heroic, for example—Lewis is certainly right that both myths surface in *The Faerie Queene*: the "ideally innocent" primitive in the Savage Man who rescues Serena (6.4.2–16) and the "brutal, sub-human" primitive in the Savage Nation from which she is rescued. Lewis could have cited other examples. For instance, in the canto following the Savage Nation episode, Meliboe praises the "simple sort of life, that shepheards lead" (6.9.33). There are also counterparts to the examples that Lewis does cite: in book 4, the subhuman "saluage man" (4.7.5), and in book 1, an innocent "saluage nation" (1.6.11).

The innocent Savage Nation is the antithesis of the Savage Nation in book 6: they do not try to rape a maiden, they rescue a maiden from rape (1.6.8). Like "good" Indians in the accounts, however, these "saluage people" (1.6.19) are mistaken in their religion, and just as Europeans try to convert "good" Indians, so Una tries to teach "truth" to the good Savage Nation (1.6.19).[45] These parallels do not necessarily mean that Spenser based the good Savage Nation on Native Americans—his good savages are fauns derived from classical mythology; their leader is the Roman god Sylvanus (1.6.7)—but both the accounts' "good" Native Americans and Spenser's good savages are "innocent" primitive.[46] Like encounters with "subhuman" primitives, encounters with innocent primitives demand a certain kind of action: an innocent savage should be instructed, just as a subhuman savage should be destroyed.

Spenser fulfills this last imperative with Belphoebe's slaying of the "wild and saluage man" (4.7.5), as well as with Calepine's destruction of the Savage Nation. Although they differ in many respects, both the Savage Nation and the "wild and saluage man" belong to the myth of the subhuman primitive. But while the Savage Nation is morally subhuman, the saluage man is literally subhuman:

> . . . no man, but onely like in shape
> And eke in stature higher by a span,
> All ouergrowne with haire, that could awhape
> An hardy hart, and his wide mouth did gape
> With huge great teeth, like to a tusked Bore:
> For he liu'd all on rauin and on rape

Of men and beasts; and fed on fleshly gore,
The signe whereof yet stain'd his bloudy lips afore.

(4.7.5)

Some scholars have argued the saluage man's "wide long eares," described in the next stanza, come from exploration narratives.[47] The stanza cited above shows, however, that the "saluage man" is an ogre derived from European folklore.

The saluage man's source differs from the Savage Nation's; nevertheless, they occupy the same space in Spenser's allegory. The saluage man plainly represents male lust. His club, his ivy wreath (4.7.7), even his facial features—"his huge great nose did grow, / Full dreadfully empurpled all with bloud" (4.7.6.5–9)[48]—all symbolize this role. The saluage man acts it out by kidnapping maidens and raping them. Cannibalism follows this violation:

. . . on the spoile of women he doth liue,
Whose bodies chast, when euer in his powre
He may them catch, vnable to gainestiue,
He with his shamefull lust doth first deflowre,
And afterwards themselues doth cruelly deuoure.

(4.7.12)

For Spenser, then, cannibalism becomes a symbol of lust.

Accounts of Native American cannibalism themselves link cannibalism with lust. For example, the widely distributed *Quatuor navigationes*[49] contains an incident that could have inspired the Savage Nation episode. This incident occurs on the third voyage, when Vespucci and his crew meet with some Brazilian natives. The native men send women, who seem frightened, to speak with the Europeans. To reassure them, Vespucci asks "a very agile and valiant youth" to speak with them alone. While the women "touch and feel" the young man, another woman creeps up behind him and knocks him unconscious. The women then tear him into pieces, which they roast and eat, while Vespucci and his men look on in horror.[50]

I have cited this incident to illustrate the sensationalism in early accounts of the New World, noting how they were filled with sex and cannibalism. Moreover, these features often appear in proximity. For example, in a crude translation of the *Mundus Novus*, Jan van Doesborch writes that Native American men hath conversation with the women . . . who that they first meet, is she his sister, his mother, his daughter, or any other kindred. And the women be very hot and disposed to lecherousness. And they eat also one another. The man eats his wife, his children, as we also have seen.[51]

The description implies that the sexual and cannibal appetites of Native Americans know no limits.

Just as the accounts' descriptions of Europeans as victims of Native American cannibalism may express anxieties about the European consumption of the Americas, so descriptions of unlimited Native American appetites may express anxieties about unrestrained European behavior in the Americas. Certainly, the connection between unlimited sexual and cannibal appetites appears repeatedly in the accounts. In the *Navigationes*, it gives an erotic tint to details in the cannibal incident cited above. Early in the *Navigationes*, the narrator tells us that Indian women are "lascivious beyond measure" and "showed an excessive desire for our company."[52] This description raises certain expectations, and when the narrator tells us that the young crewmember is to be left alone with a group of native women, we expect something different from what happens. Our expectation is reinforced by the narrator's description of how, before killing and eating him, the women "all began to touch and feel" the young man.

A woodcut from a German edition of the *Navigationes* highlights the eroticism of this passage.[53] The woodcut depicts a group of naked Indian men and one woman standing at the top of a rocky hill; the woman has her arms around a man's waist and looks up at his face. On their left, a naked Indian, his buttocks prominently displayed, crawls into a cave in the hill. In the foreground, Vespucci's young crewman stands fully clothed before three naked Indian women. The woman in the center is leaning back as she pulls the crewman toward her. Behind this group, another naked woman swings a club toward the crewman's head. The illustration could almost be an allegory, with the naked, cave-dwelling background figures representing the primitive nature of lust, and the foreground scene representing civilized man conquered by that lust.

The woodcut makes it appear that the Indian women are offering themselves sexually to Vespucci's young crewmember. The passage on which the scene is based is less explicit; nevertheless, it appears initially that the women are sexually interested in the young man. Only in retrospect do we realize that they were feeling him to see what kind of meal he would make. When the Savage Nation conducts a similar examination of

Serena, this examination also hints at sexual desire. The Savage Nation surrounds Serena: "round about her they them selues did place" (6.8.39). Spenser's cannibals do not feel Serena, but they do examine her visually, and "the daintest morsels chose" (6.8.39). This examination foreshadows Serena's visual violation two stanzas later; this time, the savages "view with lustfull fantasyes" (6.8.41) what they considered food earlier.

Parallels between the scenes reveal that Spenser is linking cannibalism and rape as different ways of consuming Serena's body. First, the Savage Nation regards the body as food:

> . . . of her dainty flesh they did deuize
> To make a common feast, and feed with gurmandize.
> So round about her they them selues did place
> Vpon the grasse, and diuersely dispose,
> As each thought best to spend the lingring space,
> Some with their eyes the daintest morsels chose;
> Some praise her paps, some praise her lips and nose.
>   (6.8.38–39)

Those savages praising parts of Serena's body are different from those choosing dainty morsels: her body is simultaneously being examined for beauty and taste. After they tear Serena's clothes off, the savages reexamine her body. Spenser lists the parts in a blazon stanza; the list concludes with "Those daintie parts, the dearlings of delight, / Which mote not be pro-phan'd of common eyes" (6.8.43). Spenser's use of the word *dainty* here recalls the "dainty flesh" and "daintest morsels" in the previous stanzas, when Serena's body was being regarded as food. And, just as before the Savages "deuize / To make a common feast," now they "deuize, / Thereof by force to take their beastly pleasure" (6.8.43).

Spenser's language reinforces the link between cannibalism and rape, but another parallel becomes clear only by considering how much these accounts dwell on the victims' dismemberment. This is true in almost every possible source I have cited for the Savage Nation episode: we find it in Staden's *Veritable History*, in the *Quatuor navigationes*, and in Martire's *Decades*,[54] and in most illustrations of American cannibals, many of which dwell exclusively on dismemberment. Against this background, the Savage Nation's stripping and ogling of Serena appear to be something more than a parody of Petrarchan conventions:[55] when Spenser's cannibals take off Serena's clothes—"which amongst themselves they in peeces teare, / And of the pray each one a part doth beare" (6.8.41)—and examine her body piece by piece (6.8.42–43), they visually dismember her.

By connecting this visual violation to cannibal feasts, Spenser draws on ideas—profoundly rooted in western culture—of civilization and savagery. Stephen Greenblatt has described how Spenser works with these ideas in the Bower of Bliss episode. He cites Freud's observation, in *Civilization and Its Discontents*, that "civilization is built up upon a renunciation of instinct,"[56] and goes on to read the destruction of the bower (2.12.83) as the elimination of a threat to "civility," a renunciation of erotic excess. He sees a "reiteration" of the episode in the sixteenth-century European destruction of Native American cultures. Europeans were enticed by the licentiousness they believed was part of Indian life, and like Guyon destroying the Bower, Europeans destroyed Native American cultures—in part, because those cultures attracted them.[57]

Both Greenblatt and I connect *Faerie Queene* episodes to the destruction of Native American cultures. He asserts a symbolic connection between the bower episode and European attacks on Native Americans: "Spenser's poem is one manifestation of a symbolic language that is inscribed by history on the bodies of living beings."[58] I have argued that Calepine's destruction of the Savage Nation is based on the European destruction of Native American cannibals. According to my reading, the author himself made this connection.

Let me conclude by suggesting that, in the Savage Nation episode, Spenser consciously uses American cannibals as part of his own symbolic language. Irish cannibals would not serve as well, because Spenser saw the Irish as part of European civilization, no matter how degenerate. Native Americans, on the other hand, were represented as lacking even the rudiments of civilization. Such a lack could be used to justify colonization, of course, but so could the Irish's degenerate civilization. Unlike a degenerate civilization, however, the *lack* of civilization could be used as a justification for genocide.

Spenser's use of Native American cannibalism is clarified by reevaluating the accounts in light of Freud's description of civilization as built upon "the renunciation of instinct." We have seen that the accounts associated Indians with cannibalism and incest. We have also seen that these features were cited together and that the connection between them resulted from the idea that Native Americans were not bound by "civilized" (European) norms. Freud would agree with this connection: in *The Future of an Illusion*, he describes incest and cannibalism as "instinctual wishes" that have been prohibited as part of the civilizing process.[59]

Even those who accept Freud's ideas about incest may find it difficult to believe that cannibalism is an "instinctual wish." Freud suggests a rea-

son for such a difficulty: among the "oldest instinctual wishes, . . . [c]anni-
balism alone seems to be universally proscribed and—to the non-psycho-
analytic view—to have been completely surmounted."[60] This description
is useful if we jettison its claims to universality. For Europeans, certainly,
customary cannibalism belongs to a very remote past. When, in the fif-
teenth and sixteenth centuries, Europeans encountered the practice in the
New World, they saw it as absolute proof that certain Native Americans
were "inhuman."[61] Cannibals were "other" in a way that even the most
licentious and incestuous Indians were not. When the accounts describe
cannibals, they never mention the possibility of reform, as they do when
they describe other Native Americans. The response to American cannibalism is inevitably an attempt to destroy its practitioners. In descriptions
of that destruction, Spenser thus found an ideal metaphor for the total
renunciation of lust necessary "to fashion a gentleman or noble person in
vertuous and gentle discipline."

NOTES

1. *Faerie Queene* quotations come from A. C. Hamilton's edition
(London: Longman, 1977).

2. Waldo F. McNeir, "The Sacrifice of Serena: *The Faerie Queene,*
VI.viii.31–51," in *Festschrift für Edgar Mertner,* ed. Bernhard Fabian and Ulrich
Suerbaum (Munich: Wilhelm Fink Verlag, 1969), 117.

3. Edmund Spenser, *A View of the Present State of Ireland,* in *Spenser's
Prose Works,* ed. Rúdolf Gottfried, vol. 11 of *The Works of Edmund Spenser: A
Variorum Edition,* ed. Frederick Morgan Padelford, Edwin Greenlaw and Charles
Grosvenor Osgood (Baltimore: Johns Hopkins UP, 1932–49), 46–158. I have
modernized the spelling in my quotations of prose. Unlike *The Faerie Queene,*
which was supposed to be a "famous antique history" (2.Pro.1), *A View* was not
meant to seem archaic: it describes the "present state" of Ireland. Nothing is
gained by leaving Spenser's spelling in its original form.

4. *View,* 158.

5. See, for example, the account, compiled by the two Richard Hakluyts,
of English cannibalism in Newfoundland ("The voyage of Master Hore and
divers other gentlemen to Newfoundland and Cape Breton," in *Hakluyt's Voyages,*
ed. Richard David, (Boston: Houghton Mifflin, 1981), 270–73).

6. *View,* 158.

7. Ibid. See also Andrew Hadfield, *Spenser's Irish Experience: Wilde Fruit
and Salvage Soyl* (Oxford: Clarendon Press, 1997), 66–67.

8. *View,* 153–54.

9. For Elizabethan ideas about the barbarous forebears of the Irish, see Walter J. Ong, "Spenser's *View* and the Tradition of the 'Wild' Irish," *Modern Language Quarterly* 3 (1942), 561–71.

10. Herodotus, trans. A. D. Godley, 4 vols. (London: William Heinemann Ltd., 1920), 4:64. For the absence of a source for the Gallic custom, see Rudolf Gottfried's note (Spenser, *View*, 343).

11. Eli Sagan, *Cannibalism: Human Aggression and Cultural Form* (New York: Harper & Row, 1974), 7.

12. *Divine Hunger: Cannibalism as a Cultural System* (Cambridge: Cambridge UP, 1986).

13. Sagan, 3–5.

14. We may rightfully doubt this claim; see Willy Maley, *Salvaging Spenser: Colonialism, Culture and Identity* (London: MacMillan, 1997), 11, 30, 42.

15. Sagan, 3, 25–26, 29–30; Sanday, 7.

16. Sagan, 22–23.

17. Strabo, *Geography*, trans. Horace Leonard Jones, 8 vols. (London: William Heinemann, 1923), 4.5.4, 2:259.

18. McNeir, "Sacrifice of Serena," 144–46.

19. Strabo, *Geography*, 4.5.4, 2:259.

20. See, for example, Hadfield, 177–80.

21. See Frederick J. Pohl, *Amerigo Vespucci, Pilot Major*, (New York: Columbia UP, 1944), 143–67.

22. Hans Staden, *Veritable history*, trans. Michael Alexander, in *Discovering the New World*, (London: London Editions, 1976), 91–121.

23. Lynn Glaser, *America on Paper: The First Hundred Years*, (Philadelphia: Associated Antiquaries, 1989), 156–63. Both accounts describe Nicolas Durand de Villegaignon's colony in Brazil; Léry's was written in response to Thevet's (ibid., 160). For a description of the colony and a comparison of the two writers, see Olive Patricia Dickason, *The Myth of the Savage, and the Beginnings of French Colonialism in the Americas* (Willowdale, Ontario: The University of Alberta Press, 1984), 183–92. See also Frank Lestringant, *Cannibals: The Discovery and Representation of the Cannibal from Columbus to Jules Verne* (Berkeley: University of California Press, 1997), 56–80, and Boies Penrose, *Travel and Discovery in the Renaissance*, (Cambridge: Harvard UP, 1952), 120.

24. Glaser reproduces two woodcuts illustrating cannibal scenes from the *Quatuor navigationes* and *Mundus Novus* (18, 142).

25. The map, known as Kuntsmann II, is a planisphere drawn between 1502 and 1503 (Germán Arciniegas, *Amerigo and the New World: The Life and Times of Amerigo Vespucci*, [New York: Alfred A. Knopf, 1955], 213–14).

26. Ibid., 214, n. 1. Glaser also describes and reproduces this illustration (15).

27. Alexander, *Discovering the New World*, 91–121.

28. Münster's work appeared in forty-six editions and six languages (Penrose, *Travel and Discovery*, 309). For reproductions of Münster's maps, see Glaser, 58–59, 61.

29. In *The Allegory of Love: A Study in Medieval Tradition* (1936; New York: Oxford UP, 1958). C. S. Lewis stresses the importance of popular material in *The Faerie Queene*: "What lies beneath the surface in Spenser's poem is the world of popular imagination: almost, a popular mythology" (ibid., 312).

30. Martire, *Decades*, in Arber, ed., *The First Three English Books on America*, 160; *Letters of Amerigo Vespucci*, ed. Clements R. Markham, (London: Hakluyt Society, 1894), 19, 45–46. For more on Spenser's sources for his American material, see Lois Whitney, "Spenser's Use of the Literature of Travel in *The Faerie Queene*," *Modern Philology* 19 (1921–22), 145.

31. Ibid., 6. Pietro Martire says that the Indians, "as well the women as men, are expert archers" (*The First Three English Books on America*, ed. Edward Arber, [Westminster: Archibald Constable and Co., 1895], 177).

32. Sebastian Münster, *Of the newe India, as it is knowen and found in these ourr dayes* [*Cosmographia Universalis*], trans. Richard Eden (London, 1553), in ibid., 30.

33. Gonzalo Fernandez de Oviedo y Valdés, *The Natural History of the West Indies* (1526), trans. Richard Eden (London, 1555), in ibid., 229.

34. Ibid., 113. See also ibid., 70, 177. Robert Ralston Cawley notes the connection between the arrows of Maleger and of the Indians (*The Voyagers and Elizabethan Drama*, [Boston and London: Modern Language Association of America, 1938], 367 n.183). Cawley also lists a number of accounts, including Münster's and Martire's, that contain references to the Indians' poisoned arrows (ibid., n.181).

35. For the parallel between Maleger and Antaeus, see Hamilton's note to stanzas 45–46 in the Longman edition. David Read uses Maleger's Indian elements to provide an American interpretation of the parallel between Maleger and Antaeus. Read relates the wrestling match between Arthur and Maleger to the European conquest of the Americas: according to Read, when Arthur lifts Maleger from the land, he is "performing a symbolic act of dispossession" ("Discovering an Empire: A Geographical Reading of Book II of the *Faerie Queene*" [Ph.D. diss., University of Chicago, 1987], 232).

36. Thomas Harriot, *A Briefe and True Report of the New Found Land of Virginia*, Facsimile of the 1590 edition published by Theodore de Bry and printed by Johann Wechel at Frankfurt-am-Main ed., (New York: Dover, 1972), 41.

37. Martire, 181. For the voyage of Juan de Solis, see Penrose, *Travel and Discovery*, 121.

38. Glaser, *America on Paper*, 156; Penrose, *Travel and Discovery*, 300. Spenser may even have seen Theodore de Bry's illustrated edition, which appeared in 1592.

39. *Discovering the New World*, 99.

40. W. Arens points to this argument as evidence that Staden's account may be fictitious. According to Arens, Staden could not have understood this debate if he had not yet learned the Tupinamba's language. Of course, Staden might have understood the cannibals' gestures (*The Man-Eating Myth: Anthropology and Anthropophagy* [New York: Oxford UP, 1979], 25–26).

41. For example, Martire describes how "one Johannes Poncius was sent forth . . . to destroy the cannibals . . . that the nations of the more humane and innocent people may at length live without fear of that pestiferous generation" (165).

42. Sir James George Frazer cites a number of sources for the Arcadian wolf cult, including Plato (*Republic*, viii, 565) and Pliny (*Nat. hist*, viii, 81). See *The Golden Bough: A Study in Magic and Religion*, part 3, *The Dying God* (London: Macmillan, Co., 1913), 83.

43. Martire, 165; Sir Walter Raleigh, "The discovery of the large, rich, and beautiful empire of Guiana, with a relation of the great and golden city of Manoa, which the Spaniards call El Dorado, and the provinces of Emeria, Aromaia, Amapaia, and other countries with the rivers adjoining," in *Hakluyt's Voyages*, 504.

44. C. S. Lewis, *English Literature in the Sixteenth Century, Excluding Drama*, (Oxford: Oxford UP, 1954), 17.

45. When these people worship Una, the scene is curiously reminiscent of one in *The Discovery of Guiana*. Sir Walter Raleigh claims that when he showed the Indians "Her Majesty's picture, . . . they so admired and honoured as it had been easy to have brought them idolatrous thereof" (457). If there is a relationship between the two scenes, it was Ralegh who was inspired by Spenser: the *Discovery* was published five years after the first three books of the *Faerie Queene*.

46. Numerous early accounts connect Native Americans to classical notions of Arcadia or the Golden Age, a connection that reappears when Montaigne creates the idea of the "noble savage" (*Oeuvres complètes* [Paris: Gallimard, 1962], 204–205).

47. Robert Ralston Cawley points to possible sources in Mandeville, Münster, and Hakluyt (*Unpathed Waters: Studies in the Influence of the Voyagers on Elizabethan Literature*, [Princeton, N.J.: Princeton UP, 1940], 107). See also Whitney, 146–47.

48. See Hamilton's note on the passage.

49. For a list of the various editions of the *Quatuor navigationes*, see Rudolf Hirsch, "Printed Reports on the Early Discoveries and Their Reception," in Fredi Chiappelli, ed. *First Images of America: The Impact of the New World on the Old*, (Berkeley: University of California Press, 1976), 2:538–40.

50. *Letters of Amerigo Vespucci*, 37–38.

51. Van Doesborch, *Of the newe lands*, in *First Three English Books*, xxvii.

52. *Letters of Amerigo Vespucci*, 8–9.

53. Olive Patricia Dickason reproduces the illustration in *Myth of the Savage* 7.

54. Staden, *Veritable History*, 110; *Letters of Amerigo Vespucci*, 38; Martire, *Decades*, 67, 130.

55. For this reading of the stanzas, see Harry Berger, Jr., *Revisionary Play: Studies in Spenserian Dynamics* (Berkeley: University of California Press, 1988), 228. It might be fruitful to explore the passage as a particularly violent "counter-discourse," similar to the "ugly beauty" counterdiscourse explored by Heather Dubrow in *Echoes of Desire: English Petrarchism and Its Counterdiscourses* (Ithaca: Cornell UP, 1995).

56. Sigmund Freud, *Civilization and Its Discontents*, trans. James Strachey (New York: Norton, 1962), 44, cited in Stephen Greenblatt, *Renaissance Self-Fashioning: From More to Shakespeare*, (Chicago: University of Chicago Press, 1980), 173.

57. Ibid., 179–84.

58. Ibid., 179. For a reading that sees the episode as specifically referring to events in the Americas, see Read, 164–216.

59. Sigmund Freud, *The Future of an Illusion*, trans. James Strachey (New York: Norton, 1961), 10.

60. Ibid., 11.

61. Ralegh, *Discovery of Guiana*, 504.

4

Robinson Crusoe Inc(orporates): Domestic Economy, Incest, and the Trope of Cannibalism

MINAZ JOOMA

By *Modesty in Discourse* I think it must of Necessity be understood, a Decency of Expression; particularly as our Discourse relates to Actions or Things . . . that are and ought to be . . . spoken of with reserve, and in Terms that may give no offence . . . and yet perhaps are of Necessity to be spoken to. . . . [S]uch Things . . . ought never to be spoken of at all, but when Necessity urges; and it were to be wished, that in a Christian and Modest Nation, where the Laws of Decency are expressly admitted as Rules of Life, all immodest Discourses were decry'd by universal Custom; and especially that Printing and Publishing such Things as are not to be read with . . . Decency, were effectually suppress'd. But as I have made that Subject a Part of this Work, I say no more of it here.

—Defoe, *Conjugal Lewdness*

In his discussion of cannibalism in *Robinson Crusoe*, E. Pearlman shows that several writers available to Defoe were fully aware that the consumption of human flesh by other humans was more than simply a food preference aberrant by European standards in a given period of history. Montaigne, who is probably the writer on cannibalism best known to modern readers, and whose *Essais* was first translated into English in 1603 by John Florio, writes of the symbolic and ceremonial functions of anthropophagy in his essay, "Of Cannibals": "[the] captor convokes a . . . gathering . . . [He and] his best friend . . . roast and eat [the captive] in common, and send bits of him to their absent friends. Not . . . for nourishment . . . but to signify an extreme revenge." Though himself a Catholic, Montaigne explored the symbolic richness of cannibalism to attack the cruelties perpetrated by his own culture in the name of the Church: he saw "more barbarity in eating a live than a dead man, in tearing on the rack . . . the body of a man still full of feeling, in roasting him piecemeal . . . under the cloak of piety . . . than in . . . eating him after he is dead."[1]

Modern anthropologists have, likewise, explored the figurative possibilities and the symbolic functions of cannibalism. Peggy Reeves Sanday, whose data demonstrate that over 56 percent of simple societies do *not* practice cannibalism, observes that sustaining a society primarily through cannibalism is impractical. The idea that cannibalism supplies food for everyday consumption is equally untenable for Pearlman; both deem this idea an ecological absurdity. While Sanday acknowledges that cannibalism can sometimes be a reaction to external conditions such as famine, she shows that even in societies where hunger is widespread, cannibalism is frequently not practiced.[2] Rather than viewing cannibalism in terms of food supply, Sanday conceives cannibalism, as anthropologist Mary Douglas conceives incest, as part of the larger framework of rituals and prohibitions that function as cultural signifiers. For Sanday, its ritual nature suggests that cannibalism, like incest, is a primordial metaphor for relations of domination and submission and for creating self- and social-consciousness; it is an ontological system consisting of "the myths, symbols, and rituals by which a people explore their relationship to the world, to other beings, and to being itself."[3]

The importance of Sanday's formulation to my discussion of *Robinson Crusoe* is clarified by Douglas's theory that ritualized behavior seeks to impose system on inherently untidy experience. Matter that humans cannot categorize clearly is experienced as disorderly, and so it arouses anxiety. According to Douglas, the primary function of ritual is to create order, and a semblance of order is attainable if differences—for example, between outside and inside, and male and female—are exaggerated. Because the body plays a central role in fundamental experiences, body symbolism is an especially emotive part of the common stock of symbols. Matter that straddles the bounds of the body, and body orifices where distinctions may break down easily, are deemed potentially polluting: each therefore generates fear. Although Douglas refers explicitly to substances (she names spittle, blood, milk, urine, and feces) that emanate from the body at vulnerable points, a parallel argument can be made for substances that enter and become part of the body. Such substances—particularly foods that pass from outside to inside the body—also blur lines of demarcation and so represent a similar threat to order. Sanday views ritual cannibalism in precisely these terms; since any substance being taken in has a foreign quality, there is a need to assimilate the foreign to the familiar in an acceptable manner. It is because Sanday believes that ritual cannibalism is intimately connected with a psychic concern with the orderly crossing of body boundaries that she sees it as a conceptual framework providing models for and of behavior and as a system for processing culturally encoded information.[4]

I believe that Sanday's conceptualization of cannibalism as an ontological system is extremely valuable for enlarging our understanding of Defoe's use of eating to broach the subject of power in *Robinson Crusoe*. While I do discuss actual eating and touch upon acts of anthropophagy in this novel, my broader argument is about the figurative use of consumption. I suggest that as metaphors of eating—and notably those of cannibalism—are used to represent relations of power, they disclose several eroticized domestic economies in *Robinson Crusoe*. In the discussion that follows, there is one temporary, but important, departure from Sanday. She marks the reproductive female body as the key ontological symbol in cannibalistic cultures typically dominated by competitive male individualism; cannibalism is a social aggression, associated with the oral phase of psychosexual development, directed at the mother.

For Sanday, cannibalism plays a primary role in the social construction of gender identity because there is an ongoing and violent repudiation of oral dependency on the mother in the psychological basis of patriarchal social structures. Before I turn to the issue of oral violence toward maternal bodies however, I first show the larger structure wherein some men exhibit a predatory violence toward other men. I contend that this violence is fundamentally incestuous. Furthermore, because oral aggression against female figures in *Robinson Crusoe* arises out of a previously established context of antagonistic relations between men, I focus attention on the intense competition for authority and power between male characters in the novel. This competition is repeatedly expressed through references to bodily control, orality, and consumption, all of which are linked together by the trope of cannibalism. As a result, the tropic fuction of cannibalism in the symbolic system of the text is to express the ideological anxiety generated by the expansion of the domestic to the worldly economy.

My discussion of *Robinson Crusoe* begins with a close look at strained relations between those who may eat and those who may be eaten in the novel. It should be noted that even though instances of actual cannibalism on Crusoe's island late in the narrative are memorable because of Crusoe's alarm and his fear of being destroyed, literal anthropophagy does not *establish* eater and eaten as metaphors for human relations. The later occurence of cannibalism clarifies mechanisms of power discernible in several domestic economies earlier in *Robinson Crusoe* including those that undergird extant domestic relations between fathers and sons in Crusoe's native England. An important feature of such father-son relationships is that parent and child possess different levels of power. The predatory quality of the father-son relation in *Robinson Crusoe* later enables and supports protocapitalist consumerism that emerges with colonialism in the period of mercantile expansion in which the work is set. Yet the question of power is more immediately associated with relations of consumption within families. Familial power dynamics emerge with what I refer to as the novel's politics of food or its politics of consumption, as it is first seen in Crusoe's father's house.

Crusoe's father, Kreutznaer, recommends the "middle state" as one that will allow his son to be appropriately nourished without exposure to "vicious living, luxury . . . extravagancies . . . hard labour, want of necessaries, and mean diet."[5] According to Kreutznaer, those who live the extremes suffer distemper and discomfort. It follows that Crusoe's acceptance of Kreutznaer's middle state would mean that he would not have to be "sold to the life of slavery for daily bread . . . but [could live] in easy circumstances . . . sensibly tasting the sweets of living without the bitter" (28–29). But just as Kreutznaer's gout-riddled condition undercuts his sermon on the virtues of temperance, so the ease with which Kreutznaer may withhold sustenance belies his apparent willingness to sustain Crusoe.[6] Kreutznaer's offer to place Crusoe under "no necessity to seek [his] bread" (29) is subject to certain conditions, for Kreutznaer also claims the power to withhold that other paternal blessing which would allow Crusoe to maintain himself outside his father's house. Having first warned Crusoe against rash actions, his father will undertake to

> do very kind things for me if I would stay and settle at home as he directed . . . he would not have so much hand in my misfortunes as to give me any encouragement to go away . . . [and] *if I did take this foolish step, God would not bless me*, and I would have leisure hereafter

to reflect upon having neglected his counsel when there might be none to assist in my recovery. (emphasis added, 29)

Given the fact that a retraction of paternal support and sustenance is threatened, figures of eating and nourishment in the early exchanges between Crusoe and Kreutznaer act as indicators of what it means to remain in the father's condition-bound house. If the son should disobey, as his errant brothers have before him, he will be doomed to a languishing state from which, starved of paternal approval in both senses, he might—like his brothers—never recover. The significance of the father's withdrawal of approval is encapsulated in two biblical sons whose fates are mapped out, like Crusoe's, through the metaphor of consumption. The captain on Crusoe's first nautical venture observes Crusoe's likeness to Jonah whose filial disobedience results in his being swallowed by a whale, and Crusoe fantasizes his own ultimate obedience to Kreutznaer and its reward of being feted and feasted like the returned Prodigal Son.

On the surface, the parables of the Prodigal and Jonah seem to offer the choices of obedience or disobedience, of reward or punishment, of being fed or being food. Jonah's fate of being entombed in the belly of the whale fits this model especially well. But the Prodigal's father's slaughter of the fatted calf conceals a sinister twist embedded in this particular father's power. Having wasted his substance (or, figuratively, consumed himself), the starving Prodigal is placed more thoroughly at his father's mercy. By receiving the Prodigal Son and feeding him, the parabolic father (of whom Crusoe believes his own father to be an emblem) would renew the capacity to dictate terms; he would renew the power to prey upon his charge's dependence. Even though departure from the father's house at one level signals a movement beyond paternal power, Kreutznaer's evocation of the omnipresent heavenly father suggests that such a removal creates at best an illusion of escape. The inevitability of the Prodigal's return and his ensuing obedience gives his father license to exact what price he might in the face of the child's involuntary dependency. By becoming his son's host—that is, by receiving him—Kreutznaer in a sense offers himself to the son for communion.

Yet while the concept of communion contains the promise of the reciprocity of host and guest, reciprocity is not offered here. In the son's communion with his father, unlike the communion with the Ur-father host of the religious ritual, the son accepts the kind of food that promises to convert the feeder into the form of "host" upon whom the father might live parasitically.[7] The son's return therefore enables a more thorough incorporation into the father's domestic economy and signals the father's authority over the members of his household. The Prodigal's parabolically prescribed return and the father's disposition to receive the son each underscore the father's power. Defoe's use of the Prodigal parable highlights the obligation that accompanies a child's acceptance of paternal sustenance; it shows that although filial obedience offers the promise of being fed, it also writes the child as metaphorical food—as a body available for the father's use. Here, the prerogative of consumption becomes the most prominent and alluring feature of the father's power over his son. The kind of paternalism that characterizes Kreutznaer's house clearly relies upon a debt nexus between the male parent who—from his comfortable "middle state"—makes provision for the members of his household; it forces a recognition of the invasive quality of paternal demands.[8]

As domestic relations in *Robinson Crusoe* are repeatedly concerned with the violation of bodily and psychic boundaries, the text's use of eating, purging, and being eaten become highly charged. Common to all three activities is the mouth, the site at which substances from the external world are incorporated into or, when necessary, ejected from, the body. Since the mouth and its functions plays such a crucial role in accepting the matter of one's being into the body and in rejecting what is deemed noxious,[9] the father's peculiarly oral violence toward the son (the blessing given or withheld and the injunction to live in the middle state) is oddly similar to the father's bread; each must be expelled before it is assimilated and before it possibly contaminates. At both literal and figurative levels, Kreutznaer's invasiveness must be purged before the son can begin to become his own master. It is fitting, therefore, that Crusoe's disobedience in going to sea awakens fears of being swallowed, and so losing being, and induces perpetual vomiting, swooning, and calentures which likewise threaten a loss of self. In the sense that the father-son relationship here is one in which the father seeks to assimilate the son, it is cannibalistic. In the sense that this cannibalistic relation exists between two close blood relatives as well as two members of a household that functions as a commensal family unit, it is also profoundly incestuous.

The power dynamic in Kreutznaer's house and the implications of its operation are taken up later in the novel in a second domestic economy. This economy emerges when Crusoe is enslaved by the captain of the Turkish rover. When Crusoe is captured and it becomes clear that he is to belong to the captain, persistent images of bodily invasion indicate that the fear of living in the new master's house arises from the threat of being physically possessed. The captain's claiming of Crusoe and the latter's enforced servility underline this threat. Crusoe is aboard a slave ship to increase his own material possessions when the Turkish ship attacks. He is alarmed by his transformation from merchant to "miserable slave," from master to minion. And Crusoe has, perhaps, good reason to be alarmed by these transformations when one considers the assumptions that he himself has brought to the role of the master. In his former position as plantation owner, for example, Crusoe has seen slave ownership as a way of amassing wealth and has viewed property with an eye to stock increase. Later in the narrative, when Crusoe laments the decisions that have led to his island sojourn, he discloses in a rhetorical question that it was specifically to expedite such increase that he first undertook the slaving mission:

> [W]hat business had I to leave a settled fortune, a well stocked plantation, improving and encreasing, to turn supra-cargo to Guinea, to fetch negroes, when patience and time would have so encreased our stock at home, that we could have bought them at our own door, from those whose business it was to fetch them? (199)

Although it is the plantation stock that is destined to increase, the notion of fetching human cargo that might be "purchased" at one's own door through one's own labors and through time expended at home is rather suggestive. It is especially so if juxtaposed with Crusoe's understanding of mastery elsewhere in the narrative. For when Crusoe describes mastery on the island as the state of having everything that he desires ("I had nothing to covet; for I had all that I was capable of enjoying; I was lord of the whole mannor" [139]), he attaches the perquisite of pleasure to the privileges and power of ownership. In so doing, Crusoe draws attention to another benefit that may be reaped by he who plants. In the light of Crusoe's definition of mastery, the plantation stock becomes akin to the human stock—African slaves—which might be, likewise, if euphemistically, "encreased" with time and patience expended at home. Precisely because the plantation passage fails to identify the most certain and direct method of increasing one's stock of slaves—sexual intercourse with slaves—it gestures toward the tacit sexual privileges of mastery which Defoe was elsewhere quite candid about.[10] Against the backdrop of Crusoe's definition of mastery as a pleasing admixture of power and the unobstructed enjoyment of all one covets, his recollection of the invasive Kreutznaer's "prophetick discourse" *en route* to the house of his captor and new master, the Turk, establishes a distinct point of similarity between their two houses.

The similarity between Kreutznaer's and the Turk's domestic arrangements in *Robinson Crusoe* is heightened when one considers that Turks were often linked with contemporary beliefs and growing fears (following a number of well-publicized prosecutions) about sodomitical practices.[11] The popular association of Turks with sodomy subtly, but unmistakeably, sexualizes Crusoe's situation as the slave of a Turk. The Turk's pointed separation of Crusoe from the crew, and his deliberate selection of Crusoe for domestic and personal uses are described in terms that connote their invasiveness: "overwhelmed" by his change of circumstances, Crusoe yields to the Turk as the crew of the slaver has previously been "obliged to yield" to the greater might of the rover. "[B]eing young and nimble and fit for [the Turk's] business," moreover, Crusoe is retained as a prize (41). But Crusoe's status as a chattel is indicated most strongly in the functions he must perform as domestic drudge and cabin boy. Lying first in the cabin of the master's docked larger vessel, Crusoe subsequently composes a third of the crew of the "pinnace," the Turk's pleasure vessel, with its odd suggestion of more than one other vehicle of male pleasure. In contemporary usage, pinnace was another name for a prostitute or mistress, but its phonemitical link to the male sexual organ is also curious. This pinnace is equipped with the accoutrements of merry-making; it also has a snug, low cabin in which there is room for the Turk "to lye, with a slave or two" (42). It is here that Crusoe is ordered to lie.

Crusoe's availability for domestic consumption is not the only significant point here. Also important is the text's reluctance to represent men as objects of male sexual pleasure except in the most oblique fashion. Such obliquity has created a lacuna around some aspects of male sexuality in *Robinson Crusoe* and caused several critics to speak of the text as being virtually devoid of the sexual theme. Certainly, Defoe does not deal with sexuality in *Robinson Crusoe* in the same way as he does in *Moll Flanders* or *Roxana*, in which novels female sexual desire is located centrally and in relation to heterosexual marital arrangements. Yet the alleged absence of the sexual theme in *Robinson Crusoe* is rather odd when one considers just how much of Defoe's writing—prose, poetry and prose fiction—is explicitly concerned with human sexual relations. Of the critics who do consider sexual arrangements in *Robinson Crusoe*, most assume that sexual desire is exclusively heterosexual desire. Hence the dearth of women in the work is summoned as evidence of the lack of sexual possibilities, or female figures are sought out, while the proliferation of men and groups of cohabiting men goes largely uncommented upon.[12]

The closure of all sexual possibilities other than the heterosexual requires the virtual divorce of *Robinson Crusoe* from the contemporary climate of sodomy trials, the activities of the Societies for the Reformation of Manners, criticism of homosexuality in courtly circles, raids on mollie houses, and documented concerns about sodomy in the Navy. And even if the work invites such closure, it ought to be noted that Defoe's writings before and after *Robinson Crusoe*, including his gleeful satire *The True Born Englishman*, attest to his awareness of the common concealment of sexual practices that social mores render unmentionable.[13]

Furthermore, in his treatise, *Conjugal Lewdness* (1727), from which I take my epigraph and in which Defoe makes much of the association between Turks and sodomy, Defoe relies upon a tacit understanding among his readers of mythical Turkish sexual practices to criticize the "unspeakable" conjugal practice of sodomy. Defoe strongly indicates that he disapproves of this practice and others that he makes an elaborate feint of not naming by asserting "that silence is occasioned . . . because the Wickedness is too gross to be reproved." He then praises the Turks for using signs instead of words: "I have observed the *Turks* . . . turning up the Slipper by which Signa[l] . . . the filthy Part might be expressed, without fouling the Mouth, or affronting the Ears of others."[14] Although the context of this short passage from *Conjugal Lewdness* is heterosexual marital practice, the point that it makes relies upon what is rejected; and what is strenuously rejected is the practice of sodomy associated, via the reference to Turks, with male homosexuality. Defoe's backhanded "compliment" to the Turks assumes that the reader shares Defoe's understanding of the nature of the absence to which such figures allude; it presumes that the reader concurs that what is absented by the Turkish custom is unspeakable because it is abhorrent.

Michel Foucault argues that such lacunae around the subject of male homosexuality often point to a denial of homoerotic potential. He suggests that because male power constituted through heterosexual relations is always polarized, polarities such as active command and passive compliance, dominator and dominated, and penetrator and penetrated mark one role as intrinsically honorable and the other its converse. When this model is transferred to two male partners, a conflict develops between an ethos which associates men with both the active and passive poles and the conception of all sexual intercourse in terms of male domination. To be an object of pleasure without giving up forever the high status accorded to men in the heterosexual matrix, the passive partner or "boy" must represent himself as capable of prevailing over others. He must either deny the passive role itself or deny the possibility that the passive role might afford pleasure. Denial affirms that such pleasure could not exist and prescribes that it ought not to be experienced. Where this is the case, desire becomes enshrouded by a tacit code of silence—an absence of what is socially and culturally awkward to name—and surrounded by taboo.[15]

In *Robinson Crusoe* the silence that envelopes master-slave sexual relations is particularly sonorous when one acknowledges the common understanding, contemporary and modern, of the sexual services that are frequently demanded of slaves. Orlando Patterson's study, *Slavery and Social Death*, indicates that in many parts of the Islamic world, and notably among Ottoman Turks in the seventeenth and eighteenth centuries, European slaves were especially prized. Patterson claims that homosexuality was common in parts of Morocco where boy markets were to be found and that the homosexual use of slaves remained an important aspect of Islamic slavery into the twentieth century. Paul Rycaut's *Present State of the Ottoman Empire* (1688) confirms that the homosexual use of servants and slaves was at least common enough to draw commentary from travelers who wrote about Turkish customs. Rycaut's prominence as secretary to Heneage Finch, the second Earl of Winchilsea, who was Ambassador to Turkey between 1661 and 1669, as well as his own five-year residence in Constantinople that he deemed his qualification to write on Turkish customs, lent his treatise a certain legitimacy. The impressive publication history of Rycaut's work and the popular attention that it continued to receive into the early eighteenth century suggest that Defoe's mention of Turks in the context of slavery would have been a subtle cue that contemporary readers would have been unlikely to have missed.[16]

Although I am not claiming that sodomitical acts actually take place either in the Turkish captain's house or aboard his pleasure vessel, I am suggesting two things. First, that the sexual consumption of domestic minions is established as considerably more than a possibility in *Robinson Crusoe*. More importantly, the pattern of master-slave power that parallels the father-son relationship of Kreutznaer and Crusoe, creates a predatory environment which requires that domestics at *all* levels and of both sexes are cast in terms of their availability to the master. This situation generates a domestic milieu that is at least partially homoerotic and intensely homosocial. Just as Crusoe exists as potential prey in his father's house, so he occupies a similar space within the Turk's domestic realm; the latter household replicates the conditions of the former because its boundaries include all that the master unequivocally owns and what he might consume by virtue of ownership. It is therefore apt that, as Crusoe makes his escape, he robs the Turkish master of his "pinnace" and that he does so only after he has first thrown the Turk's "manservant" overboard by "supriz[ing] him with my arm under his twist" (44). And it is entirely fitting that, in the course of stealing the pinnace, Crusoe also appropriates the Turk's "boy" as "[his] boy Xury"—his own, that is, to consume or to sell for sixty pieces of eight (54).

When Crusoe reproduces similar relations of consumption in the novel's third domestic economy, the relation of consumers to consumables from the point of his arrival on the island amplifies the connections between eating, power, and incestuous desire. Yet as these connections are amplified, they signal an important shift in the relations of eater and eaten that I have hitherto identified in *Robinson Crusoe*. At first, Crusoe experiences the island and its waters as invasive, as evidenced by the wealth of metaphors of ingestion and engulfment noted by many readers. However, if Crusoe quails at the thought of bodily annihilation through incorporation, then his power to resist annihilation and his shift to a position of strength is appropriately expressed in his impulse to devour rather than to be devoured. Such an impulse—directed toward consumable objects clearly identified as female—is amply displayed during Crusoe's lengthy island sojourn. The shift from Crusoe as prey to Crusoe as predator is striking in his removal of goods and foodstuffs from the stranded ship. As the salvaging process elaborates and extends the metaphor of anthropophagy, it identifies Crusoe as a consumer in the newly established domestic economy of the island.

When Crusoe is "delivered" on the shore in a symbolic rebirth, he is naked and hungry. The ship provides him with the means to assuage his immediate bodily needs. Because the ship offers food, "she" becomes, as Robert Erickson has observed, rather like a nurturing mother to Crusoe, who fills his pockets with biscuit from her copious supply.[17] The ship, with her bulbous upper forward deck providing sustenance, is like a nursing mother in one sense, yet with her "bulged" hold, she also resembles a pregnant woman. Although Erickson notes this resemblance, he stops short of the implications of Crusoe feeding on the laden ship. If the ship is like a pregnant woman, then does it not follow that feeding on the contents of her hold constitutes cannibalism? As Crusoe's repeated entries into the bowels of the ship conjure a graphic scene of mother violation, cannibalism, and incestuous desire become more thoroughly intertwined. Not only does Crusoe achieve his labored boarding of the ship in a naked state and with acknowledged physical difficulty, but his subsequent mutilation of the vessel which is recorded in his journal entry for May 7, 1659 ("the

beams being cut . . . the in-side of the hold lay . . . open") repeats the brutality of an earlier boarding of a similarly laden vessel. In a virtual reenact-
ment of the Turkish crew's assault on the trader where hacked decks and
rigging force the trader to yield her contents, Crusoe forces the stranded
vessel to submit her load; he hacks at the ship's ribs to get to her bowels.
Through his violence, Crusoe repudiates his dependence on the sustenance that the ship provides and replaces dependence with a brutal, eroticized command of her body.

Crusoe's subsequent use of the land echoes his treatment of the ship.
Following in the tradition of land as a nurturing mother established in
writings on New World settlement since the 1500s, the land first shelters
Crusoe by providing him with a new haven from the tempestuous element
after his vessel founders.[18] The land, which also nurtures Crusoe by providing him with food, rapidly develops into something other than a nour-
ishing mother figure when it acquires sensual appeal through a fecundity
that invites connotatively incestuous indulgence of the appetites: he finds
"[abundant] mellons upon the ground . . . [and] grapes upon the trees . . .
very ripe and rich" (113). Faintly dangerous because indulgence in her
fruits can bring on flux and fevers, the land nevertheless affords a "secret
kind of pleasure" and as Crusoe contemplates possession of her, he constructs himself as licensed to proceed by an age-old privilege: "this was all
my own . . . I was king and lord of all this country indefeasibly, and had a
right of possession . . . as complea[t] as any lord of a mannor in England"
(114). The fruits that Crusoe elsewhere wrests from the land as mother-
mistress through his plantation-style seeding of tracts for maximum yield,
enable the leisure necessary for the lordly enjoyment of his country-house
and sea-coast estates.

Because the wealth of the estates, each supported by its own plantation and cattle enclosures, depends upon the deliberate and purposeful
exploitation of the mother-mistress island, the cave that Crusoe finds in
the interior of the island acquires a double value. Erickson alludes to the
sexually suggestive nature of the "virginal cave made by no hands 'but
those of meer Nature' [that] marks Crusoe's farthest penetration into, or
'possession' of his kingdom."[19] The idea that the cave is virginal is, however, belied by the fact that its entrance is blocked by its previous occupant.
With his "loud sigh like that of an old man in pain," the "old he-goat, just
making his will . . . and gasping for life, and dying indeed of meer old age"
(183), resembles no one more closely than Crusoe's gouty, chamber-rid-
den father. The death of the goat releases to Crusoe, not a barren or
unseeded tract, but a cave pregnant with treasure. Nearly two-hundred

feet high and studded with what Crusoe believes to be diamonds, precious stones or gold, the womb-like enclosure becomes a "vault" that Crusoe will both disembowel and return to for safety.

As the systematic disembowelment of the maternal bodies of the land and the ship enables Crusoe's survival and his eventual domination of other men, it underlines the fact that Crusoe can *only* found his kingdom upon the mutilated and cannibalized body of the "mother" whereof he feeds. In each case, the son's libidinous violence toward the maternal body heralds his attempt at founding a domestic economy beyond the reach of his father's power but based, nevertheless, upon the relations of consumption established in the father's realm. If the rules governing eating in his father's house render Crusoe prey to his father's voracity, it is through a displacement of this subject position and through the enforced consumability of less powerful beings that Crusoe establishes his own domestic realm. The cannibalization of the mother ship and the plunder of the land signal—just as the use of lesser species and "savages" elsewhere signals—Crusoe's gustatory rite of passage into the ranks of those who consume rather than those who are consumed. The cannibal metaphor is deployed most disingenuously here: it evolves through successive transformations of appetite to render what Bartolovitch refers to as the "emergent subject of capital-to-be."[20]

It might be argued that Crusoe's utilization of the ship is justifiable given the dismal prospects that the island at first seems to offer for his survival. But Crusoe's thorough understanding elsewhere of what—besides subsistence—is at stake in the politics of consumption makes it difficult to dismiss his particular use of the stranded vessel. The stakes become more clearly defined in Crusoe's deliberate and extensive pursuit of female flesh. After mining another maternal body, a turtle filled with eggs, Crusoe learns that she-goats and their young may be had with brutal ease: he is apparently grieved when he kills a "she-goat which had a little kid". Although he says he hopes to tame the kid, it refuses to feed so Crusoe is "forced" to kill it and eat it himself (79).[21]

More interesting still—indeed a fascinating object lesson in the politics of food—is Crusoe's method of acquiring creatures for domestic use. On a separate occasion than the killing of the she-goat, he tethers a kid without food for several days within his compound. Crusoe then makes full use of his advantage. The kid is so tame with hunger that it follows him like a pet. As Crusoe continues to feed it, the kid "became so loving . . . gentle, and . . . fond, that it became . . . one of my domesticks also, and would never leave me afterwards" (124). Able simply through greater might to incorporate kids in the fleshly sense of eating them, Crusoe first effects a figurative incorporation which he casts as a benevolent domestication. Crusoe's feeding of the hungry kid in this passage (exactly as he will later nurture the cannibal he wants for companionship), makes the desired creature an integral part of his "little circle." As the flock from which Crusoe selects his food is ultimately spoken of as his "little family," the feeding *of* one's "domesticks" becomes collapsed into the lordly privilege of feeding *on* one's domestics, which—as one Modest Proposer has elsewhere suggested—is the age-old privilege of the powerful. Furthermore, because the majestic, paternalistic privilege of absolute command ("I could hang, draw, give liberty, and take it away, and no rebels among all my subjects" [157]) is exactly like the privilege of the butcher, it is only with the driest humor or the most gruesome irony that one can enjoy Crusoe's idyll and "smile to [see him] and [his] little family sit down to dinner" (157).

Like Kreutznaer before him, then, Crusoe uses his capacity to withhold food to keep about him a "family" upon which to feed; he institutes a form of endocannibalism when he gathers creatures to himself for later consumption. Crusoe's cannibalistic husbandry circumvents competition; it proclaims *his* license to eat through an incestuous familial economy the head of which has unrestricted access to its members.[22] It is as a son weaned from a "cannibal diet" with bread and milk, husbanded in more than one sense, and deeply indebted as a recipient of food and of life itself, that Friday enters this economy. The weaning of Friday is noteworthy because it repeats the stages of the goat-taming episode. Crusoe establishes his dominance and makes the goat and the Carib obey him by withholding the food that each can procure for himself and by replacing that food with food that Crusoe alone can supply. The weaning of Friday generates a dutiful son bound to glorify Crusoe and to do his bidding.[23] Yet the nurtured tractability of the colonial son resonates sinisterly with the cannibal trope because of the anological link created between goat and Carib by the taming and weaning episodes.

Before Friday's arrival on the island, Crusoe is agitated by his desire for a meet companion who will let him learn about himself: "my [violent] thoughts . . . set my blood into a ferment, and my pulse beat as high [as] in a feaver, meerly with the extraordinary fervour of my mind" (202). Exhausted by his own excitement, Crusoe falls asleep and dreams of Friday. Although Crusoe claims that his dream is unrelated to his mental agitation, the fact that he generates a companion for himself when he is in an excited, even frenzied, state, stresses the erotic appeal of Friday. Friday arrives on cue, like a new son conceived expressly to fulfil his father's desire, and he is twenty-six years of age just as Crusoe was when he was first "delivered" into his new life on the island. When Friday is encountered in the flesh in a meeting which virtually replays Crusoe's dream sequence, his difference from the other cannibals and likeness to Crusoe's race is striking. To Crusoe's waking eyes, "comely handsome" Friday has a very manly face and yet

> all the sweetness and softness of an European in his countenance. . . .
> His hair was long and black, not curled like wool; his forehead very
> high and large, and a great vivacity and sparkling sharpness in his
> eyes. . . . His face was round and plump; his nose small, not flat like
> the negroes, a very good mouth, thin lips, and his fine teeth well set,
> and white as ivory. (208)

The description of Friday's parts and features adopts the language of the blazon so that Friday is cast as at once Romantic love object, manly, and yet boyishly round. The combination of these effects gives the description a homoerotic quality that accentuates Friday's ripeness for consumption and supports Defoe's hints elsewhere that individualized erotic proclivities may be framed and practiced far from the strictures of one's native England. That sweet, plump Friday's appealing sensuality makes him potential prey is a point graphically made by Humphrey Richardson's modern novella, *The Sexual Life of Robinson Crusoe*. Richardson creates an episode in which Crusoe tries to rape Friday, and uses Crusoe's pleasing description of Friday to rationalize Crusoe's actions. Although the rape episode in Richardson's novella ends in participatory sodomy, this is of so violent a nature that it codifies Crusoe's strength and Friday's weakness in their respective positions of dominator and dominated. Because Friday is rendered as an assemblage of body parts in *Robinson Crusoe* moreover, the similarity between the cannibals' and the father-like Crusoe's potential uses for him is underscored.[24] The cannibals plan to use Friday for the ceremonial expression of the conquerors' power, for, as Friday explains and Crusoe translates, "they never eat any men but . . . [those] taken in battle" (224); even though Crusoe's consumption of Friday is figurative, it nevertheless addresses a power lust that is satiable through violent bodily domination.

Following the defeat of the cannibals at the time of Friday's so-called rescue, Crusoe—substituting goat for human flesh—also enacts the ritual of a victory feast.[25] The slaughter of a kid creates in Friday an abject submission exactly like that celebrated in the cannibal feast: "[Friday] . . .

kneeled down to me, and embrace[d] my knees . . . [his] meaning was to pray me not to kill him" (213). The rules governing the conquest, capture, and use of prisoners of war, as they are explained by Friday and tacitly adhered to by both the cannibals and Crusoe, dictate that he who spares life, gains the power to take life, and—by extension—he who spares life has the means to give life. Through a ritual which includes Crusoe's first gift of food to Friday and the ascription of a name, Crusoe articulates the reforming cannibal and his soon-to-be Christianized servant.[26] Crusoe gives meaning to Friday's gestures and speaks his servitude: "I made him know his name should be Friday . . . taught him to say Master, and then let him know, that was to be my name" (209). In the act of naming, Crusoe creates Friday anew by operating as though Friday has no language except dumb show, and no existence except through himself. By reinforcing this with a display of strength, Crusoe precludes Friday's resistence and defines him as a minion dependent on his master for survival. Friday's existence as son, servant, and "savage" is entirely subsumed into the existence of his "civilized" father-like master while Crusoe's satisfaction with his own position of authority is obscured.[27]

In the light of Crusoe's propensity to assimilate others and appropriate their value, his own fear of being literally consumed on the island can be viewed in two distinct ways, each associated with being invaded or colonized. At one level the existence of another person is a threat to the self, for, as Homer Obed Brown has pointed out, the very sight of the footprint destroys Crusoe's security and signals destruction rather than deliverance.[28] The cannibals in *Robinson Crusoe* do not, however, threaten mere destruction; they threaten "the worst kind of destruction" (200). If signs of the cannibals' presence threaten a loss of self, then an actual act of anthropophagy would provide irrefutable physical evidence that the most extreme subjection to another—and implicitly his system of values—had taken place. In fact, Crusoe's explanation for the killing of cannibals during the Spaniard's rescue shows that the murders have little to do with any immediate physical threat that the cannibals pose either to the Spaniard or to Crusoe himself. Crusoe's attack is triggered, despite his sometime resolution not to presume himself the executioner of God's justice, by the sight of the Spanish captive who is a European and whose first word upon rescue, though it is in the Latin form, is " 'Christianus' " (235). It is entirely consistent that, once Crusoe vomits the "disorder" occasioned by his first sight of a cannibal feast, he thanks God—*not* for *not* being the cannibals' next meal—but for his ontological separateness from them: "[I] gave God thanks that had cast my first lot in a part of the world where I was distinguished from such dreadful creatures as these" (172). Ironically, the anti-cannibal rhetoric here gains its force from a denial of the violence underlying the colonizing relationship and the projection of that violence onto its victim.[29]

In this sequence, as Crusoe later observes, cannibalism represents the complete loss of ontological being: "what would become of *me*, if *I* fell into the hands of the savages; or how should *I* escape from them, if they attempted *me* . . . " (emphases added, 201). Cannibalism is here the quintessential expression of what it is to be "mastered"—to be assimilated into an alien body without trace. Crusoe's earlier cannibalisation of several maternal bodies that yield food and supplies ultimately gives him the means to gain ascendency over the would-be cannibal victims, the cannibals themselves *and* all other potential marauders who might threaten his claim to the island and her resources. Crusoe's is mastery that is first learned through the politics of consumption in the father's house in his ostensibly civilized native country. Yet Crusoe is, ultimately, more ruthless and predatory than the so-called savages; he does not actually have to eat those he captures, for he incorporates them into a domestic economy made worldly—an economy in which those held captive by a monopoly on consumables are quietly compelled to do as the colonizer, Crusoe, desires.

NOTES

An earlier version of this chapter, "Robinson Crusoe Inc(orporates): Domestic Economy, Incest and the Trope of Cannibalism," first appeared in *LIT: Literature, Interpretation, Theory* 8.1 (1997): 61–81. I would like to thank Russell Angrisani for his careful reading of and suggestions for this revision.

My title evokes the interplay between the various meanings of *incorporation* including: to create uniformity, to put something into a body, to form a whole, to include as part of something, to form into an organization, and to create a legal constitution. Maggie Kilgour (*From Communion to Cannibalism: An Anatomy of Metaphors of Incorporation* [Princeton, N.J.: Princeton UP, 1990], 250 n.11) draws three forms from these more usual definitions of incorporation that are useful to my discussion of domestic economies in *Robinson Crusoe*: incarceration (to give form or body), consubstantiation (to join two bodies), and sublimation or cannibalism (one body's subsumption by another).

1. E. Pearlman, "Robinson Crusoe and the Cannibals," *Mosaic* 10 (1976): 50. Other writers on cannibalism available to Defoe include Richard Hakluyt, *Hakluyt's Voyages* (1600); Peter Martyr, *De nouo Orbe, or The History of the West Indies* (1612); Charles de Rochefort, *History of the Caribby-Islands,*

(1665). Michel Eyquem de Montaigne, "Of Cannibals," in *The Essays of Montaigne*, trans. E. J. Trenchmann, vol. 1 (London: Oxford UP, 1927), 209.

2. Peggy Reeves Sanday, *Divine Hunger: Cannibalism as a Cultural System* (Cambridge: Cambridge UP, 1986), 11.

3. Sanday, 31; Mary Douglas, *Purity and Danger: An Analysis of Concepts of Pollution* (New York: Frederick A. Praeger, 1966), xii, 21, 31.

4. Douglas, 4; Sanday, 31.

5. Daniel Defoe, *The Life and Adventures of Robinson Crusoe*, ed. Angus Ross (Harmondsworth, Middlesex: Penguin, 1965), 28. All subsequent references will be to this edition and page numbers will be given parenthetically in the text.

6. Ian Bell (*Defoe's Fiction* [Totowa, N.J.: Barnes and Noble, 1985], 83) notes that gout is traditionally associated with gluttony and venery. He links Kreutznaer with Defoe's identification of drunkenness as a German trait in *The True Born Englishman* and so with intemperance.

7. Kilgour, 15

8. Deborah Root (*Cannibal Culture: Art, Appropriation, and the Commodification of Difference* [Boulder, CO: Westview, 1996], 8–11) is especially incisive in her yoking of the prerogative to consume and power in emergent consumer cultures. For particularly lucid expositions of the culture of filial indebtedness, see Judith Lewis Herman, *Father-Daughter Incest* (Cambridge: Harvard UP, 1981), 129–43, and Florence Rush, *The Best Kept Secret: Sexual Abuse of Children* (Englewood Cliffs, N.J.: Prentice Hall, 1980), 176–82.

9. Paul Rozin ("Psychobiological Perspectives on Food Preferences and Avoidances," in *Food and Evolution: Toward a Theory of Human Food Habits*, ed. Marvin Harris and Eric B. Ross [Philadelphia: Temple UP, 1987]) describes the mouth as "the last site at which reversible decisions about acceptance or rejection can be made. Once swallow[ed] . . . the ingested substance is difficult to reject voluntarily" (182–83).

10. In *The True Born Englishman*, which also makes much of the figure of planting, Defoe shows that he was well-aware of the sexual abuses that frequently attend mastery. In this poem, he refers to "[t]hat Het'rogeneous *Thing, an Englishman*" as the product of the rapes perpetrated in successive invasions, conquests, and occupations of England (1.280–87). On economic and moral justifications for the slave trade, see David Dabydeen, "Eighteenth-century English Literature on Commerce and Slavery," *The Black Presence in English Literature*, ed. David Dabydeen (Manchester: Manchester UP, 1985), 28, 45. Charles Davenant's *An Essay Upon the Probable Methods of Making a People Gainers in the Ballance of Trade* (London, 1699), echoed by Defoe in *The Review* of February 3, 1713, is also useful on this point, as are Paula R. Backscheider, *Daniel Defoe: His Life* (Baltimore: Johns Hopkins UP, 1989), 438–41; Alan J. Downie, "Defoe, Imperialism, and the Travel Books Reconsidered," *YES* 13 (1983): 74–83; and

Carol Houlihan Flynn, *The Body in Swift and Defoe* (New York: Cambridge UP, 1990), 149–52.

11. Randolph Trumbach ("London's Sodomites: Homosexual Behavior and Western Culture in the Eighteenth Century." *Journal of Social History* 11.1 [1977]: 6) argues that as sodomy did not carry the same stigma in Islamic Turkey as it did in parts of Christian Europe, Turkey was seen as a "home" of sodomy. G. S. Rousseau ("The Pursuit of Homosexuality in the Eighteenth Century: 'Utterly Confused Category' and/or Rich Repository?" in *'Tis Nature's Fault: Unauthorized Sexuality During the Enlightenment*, ed. Robert Purks Maccubbin [New York: Cambridge UP, 1985], 132–68) claims that as popular myths about Turkish sexual behaviors generated tales of Ottoman homosexuality, the English came to link Turkey with the rise of sodomy. See also Dennis Rubini's, "Sexuality and Augustan England: Sodomy, Politics, Elite Circles, and Society," *Journal of Homosexuality* 16.1–2 (1988): 355–60, which considers different responses to sodomy within Christianity; and Arthur N. Gilbert's, "Buggery and the British Navy," *Journal of Social History* 10.1 (1976): 72–98, which examines prosecutions for buggery into the latter part of the century.

12. James Joyce noted the sexual apathy of Crusoe in a lecture on Defoe in Trieste in 1912. An English translation of this lecture is available in "Daniel Defoe," *Buffalo Studies* 1.1 (1964): 5–25. Eric Berne's brief discussion of *Robinson Crusoe* in his article, "The Psychological Structure of Space with some remarks on *Robinson Crusoe*," *The Psychoalytic Quarterly* 25 (1956): 549–67, offers some valuable insights on the links between sexuality and oral incorporative urges, but he does not connect these with homosexual desire. Leslie Fiedler (*Love and Death in the American Novel* [New York: Anchor Books, 1966], 366) sets *Robinson Crusoe* in a tradition of "pseudo-marriage" between men. He sees Friday as a stock comic racial and social inferior, and dismisses homoeroticism. Aydon Charlton ("The Appeal of *Robinson Crusoe*," *Sphinx* 2 [1974]: 21–37) traces the oral, anal, and sexual phases of psychosexual development in the work but goes little further. Robert A. Erickson ("Starting Over with *Robinson Crusoe*," *Studies in the Literary Imagination* 15.2 [1982]: 51–73) notes Crusoe's " 'womanless' condition" and the frequent charge of the work's "absence of sex" (52). Claiming the island and ship are mother figures, he considers only heterosexual desire. In "Orphaning the Family: The Role of Kinship in *Robinson Crusoe*," *ELH* 55.2 (1988): 381–419, Christopher Flint makes the provocative statement that "Friday seems to answer almost all of [Crusoe's] desires" (394), but he then works within a heterosexual matrix. Martin Gliserman ("*Robinson Crusoe*: The Vicisstudes of Greed—Cannibalism and Capitalism. Displaced Desire: Money, Mother, Eating, and Encirclements," *American Imago* 47.3–4 [1990]: 177–231) sees Crusoe's lust for money as a displaced desire for the mother. Ian Bell ("Crusoe's Women: Or, the Curious Incident of the Dog in the Night-Time," in *Robinson Crusoe: Myths and Metamorphoses*, ed. Lieve Spaas and Brian Stimpson [London: Macmillan, 1996], 37–38) concludes that *Robinson Crusoe* "places the

'buddies' in a wholly desexualised culture of their own not one where sexuality is rigorously suppressed." A notable exception to the trend is Humphrey Richardson's novella, *The Sexual Life of Robinson Crusoe* (Paris: Olympia, 1955). It is surprising that this work has received little scholarly and bibliographical notice because its graphic sexual violence invites analyses of hetero- and homo-erotic violence in *Robinson Crusoe* and, indeed, in Richardson's pornographic novella itself.

13. *The True Born Englishman*, 1:145–46.

14. Daniel Defoe, *Conjugal Lewdness; or, Matrimonial Whoredom. A Treatise concerning the Use and Abuse of the Marriage Bed* (1727; rpt., Gainsville, FL: Scholars' Facsimiles and Reprints, 1967), 385.

15. Michel Foucault, *The Use of Pleasure*, vol. 2 of *The History of Sexuality*, trans. Robert Hurley (New York: Vintage Books, 1990), 215, 220–23. Gilbert underlines Foucault's point when he observes the reluctance of alleged rape victims to come forward. To admit to sodomy in England in the latter part of the century, even as a nonconsenting partner, he suggests, was to expose oneself to the stigma of the sodomite, and—buggery being a capital offense—possibly to the death sentence (75, 77–78).

16. Orlando Patterson, *Slavery and Social Death: A Comparative Study* (Cambridge: Harvard UP, 1982), 421 n.18. Rycaut's *Present State* was published in 1668; by 1670 it was in its third edition. An abridged form was appended to Savage's "History of the Turks in 1701" and the work was translated into French (1670 and 1677), Polish (1678), and German (1694).

17. Erickson, 57

18. The image of land as a bountiful mother is evident in the works of Richard Hakluyt (1584), Robert Johnson (1609), John Smith (1616), John Hammond (1656), Robert Beverly (1705), and Robert Mountgomry (1717); it would have been very appealing to the mood of overseas investment in the first two decades of the eighteenth century. According to Annette Kolodny (*The Lay of the Land: Metaphors as Experience and History in American Life and Letters* [Chapel Hill, N.C.: University of North Carolina Press, 1975], 8–9, 12–22) the age-old idea of land-as-mother was revived by the "discovery" of America. She also notes that land subject to excessive demands was sometimes represented as a mother raped by her own children. On the use of the female form in eighteenth-century English erotica, see also Paul Gabriel Boucé, "Chthonic and Pelagic Metaphorization in Eighteenth-Century English Erotica," *Eighteenth-Century Life* 9.3 (1985): 202–17.

19. Erickson, 68.

20. Crystal Bartolovich, "Consumerism, or the Cultural Logic of Late Cannibalism," in *Cannibalism and the Colonial World*, ed. Francis Barker, Peter Hulme, and Margaret Iversen (Cambridge: Cambridge UP, 1998), 211–14, 223, 231.

21. Conversely, slaughtered male beasts, the "great lyon" and hungry leopard, are trophies signaling triumph over a "maneater"; they are "game indeed . . . but . . . no food" (49).

22. On this point, see Diane Armstrong, "The Myth of Cronus: Cannibal and Sign in *Robinson Crusoe*," *Eighteenth-Century Fiction* 4, no. 3 (1992): 218. Patterson groups the various meanings of the word *master* under four basic headings: a man with authority, as the captain of a sailing vessel; a teacher; a title or complimentary rank; a sign of superiority (334–35). These four categories demonstrate the ease with which brutal domination and pastoral edification can be conflated. Cf. Richard Braverman, "Crusoe's Legacy," *Studies in the Novel* 18.1 (1985): 1–26.

23. Pearlman observes that Friday is cast as a dutiful son if Crusoe's gifts of bread and milk are seen as weaning foods (50-52).

24. Edward D. Seeber notes similarities between Friday and the eponymous African of Aphra Behn's *Oroonoko, or, The Royal Slave* (1688). "Oroonoko and Crusoe's Man Friday," *Modern Language Quarterly* 12 (1951): 286–91. As Friday is *seen* as a collage of body parts and Oroonoko is *dismembered*, the two occupy different positions along a continuum of eroticized violence. On erotic violence in slave-master relationships, see Jessica Benjamin, "The Bonds of Love: Rational Violence and Erotic Domination," in *The Future of Difference*, ed. Hester Einstein and Alice Jardine (Boston: G. K. Hall, 1980), 41–70; also Richardson, 147–57.

25. Pearlman notes that Crusoe later admits that Friday probably would have escaped the cannibals altogether (53).

26. On naming as creation, see Lennard J. Davis, "The Facts of Events and the Event of Fact: New World Explorers and the Early Novel," *The Eighteenth Century: Theory and Interpretation* 32.3 (1991): 241–43, 246.

27. Patterson describes such relationships as parasitic. The master feeds on the minion's productivity; the minion, alienated from other sociocultural systems, is reduced to liminality (337). As Frank Lestringant (*Cannibals: the Discovery and Representation of the Cannibal from Columbus to Jules Verne*, trans. Rosemary Morris [Berkley: University of California Press, 1997) notes, in the context of the Catholic war against Caribs under Isabella in the sixteenth century, it was expedient to label peaceful peoples as anthropophagous in order to justify enslavement and eventual annihilation. The acceptability of the hypothesis of vengeance cannibalism to missionaries is discussed at some length by Lestringant. He suggests, as I do, that the real historical situation—the invasion of Carib lands by Europeans—is inverted in the weaning episode and that the "terror of being eaten justifies, in anticipation, the destruction of this unhuman humanity" (138). On this point, also refer to Root, 166–67.

28. Homer Obed Brown, "The Displaced Self in the Novels of Daniel Defoe" *ELH* 38 (1971): 571–72. Cf. Andrew Fleck, "Crusoe's Christianity,

Colonization and the Other," in *Christian Encounters with the Other*, ed. John C. Hawley (New York: New York UP, 1998), 74–89.

29. Peter Hulme, "Introduction: The Cannibal Scene," in *Cannibalism and the Colonial World*, ed. Francis Barker, Peter Hulme, and Margaret Iversen (Cambridge: Cambridge UP, 1998), 5, 14–15, 24. See also Gananath Obeyesekere, "Cannibal Feasts in Nineteenth-Century Fiji: Seamen's Yarns and the Ethnogrphic Imagination," in *Cannibalism and the Colonial World*, ed. Francis Barker, Peter Hulme, and Margaret Iversen (Cambridge: Cambridge UP, 1998), 186–88. Aparna Dharwadker ("Nation, Race, and the Ideology of Commerce in Defoe," *Eighteenth Century: Theory and Interpretation* 39.1 [1998]: 63–84) is particularly incisive on the matter of Crusoe's identity as a Christian colonialist when she suggests that Crusoe's perspective strategically erases differences between Europeans to render them as the "heterogeneous converse of the inferior races" (77).

5

Devouring the Disinherited: Familial Cannibalism in Maturin's *Melmoth the Wanderer*

JULIA M. WRIGHT

Among the variety of evils which distracted Ireland . . . one of the most perplexing and least remediable, was "the confusion worse confounded," in which a large portion of the landed property was involved. Five hundred years of successive forfeitures,—possessions held for ages by prescription, won by the sword and reconquered by the sword,—tenures obtained by force or usurped by fraud,—partitions of the soil carelessly made over to successive "adventurers, soldiers, patentees, and polatines," in grants, regrants, debentures, patents, commutations, and reprisals, gifts of "mitre land," consecrated by his holiness the Pope, and now conferred, by our sovereign lord the King.

—Sydney Morgan, *The O'Briens and the O'Flahertys* (London: Pandora, 1988 [1827], 49.

*M*elmoth the Wanderer (1820) by Charles Robert Maturin has long been regarded as one of the best works in the gothic tradition.[1] A convoluted interweaving of embedded tales about a demonic agent who tempts the miserable when they reach their nadir, it offers one of the more complex antiheroes of dark Romanticism. But this demonic agent, the eponymous protagonist of the novel, John Melmoth (the Wanderer), causes little of the novel's violence. The violence in the tale is primarily domestic: there are a few cases of stranger-to-stranger violence but innumerable incidents of infanticide, filicide, sororicide, parricide, and matricide. To add horror to horror, cannibalism sometimes figures in these murders, as familial intimacy is gothically distorted into the consumption of family flesh. This familial cannibalism is registered on a variety of levels. It appears in literal incidents of familial cannibalism, by implication in a tale in which the family's food is bought through the sale of the eldest son's blood, and as an emotionally charged trope through which the implicit violence of various forms of behavior can be exposed. Throughout, however, such cannibalism emerges, whether literally or figuratively, in the context of a crisis over property. Here Maturin follows his compatriot, Jonathan Swift, whose "Modest Proposal" uses cannibalism to figure the economic violence of colonialism and so expose its concealed physical violence.[2] But while Swift addresses the poor, Maturin directs his attention to aristocratic property, a subject hotly debated in the wake of the French Revolution and related to the controversy over the colonial intervention in indigenous lines of inheritance.

During the Romantic period, with the rising impact of the Industrial Revolution and an increasing dependence on imperial trade, the groundwork for a capitalist economy was laid over the remains of an aristocratic economy. While the latter was founded upon the conservation of property through the primogenitural transmission of a productive land base, the logic of the former emphasizes circulation rather than inheritance, consumption rather than conservation, and trade goods rather than land. These changes were not instituted silently, but amidst often-heated debates over the Rights of Man and the rights of empire, including, for instance, the Revolution controversy (with notable contributions from Edmund Burke, Mary Wollstonecraft, and Thomas Paine) and the discussion of the impeachment of Warren Hastings for his exploitation of Indians during his tenure at the East India Company (another controversy with notable contributions from Burke). The anxieties that this profound and all-encompassing economic transformation raised were often articulated in the gothic. Improper inheritances of aristocratic property are central to gothic novels from the first of the genre, Horace Walpole's *The Castle of Otranto* (1765), to Wilkie Collins's *The Woman in White* (1860) and Lawrence Norfolk's *Lemprière's Dictionary* (1991). As Jerrold E. Hogle notes, "The 'Gothic revival' occurs in a world of increasingly bourgeois 'free market' enterprise trying to look like a process sanctioned by more ancient imperatives yet also striving to regard the old icons as empty of meaning whenever they inhibit post-Renaissance Anglican acquisition."[3] Meaning itself becomes unstable with the erosion of "more ancient imperatives," particularly the distribution of wealth according to aristocratic affiliation, because of what Foucault terms "the symbolics of blood": "For a society in which the systems of alliance, the political form of the sovereign, the differentiation into orders and castes, and the value of descent lines were predominant; for a society in which famine, epidemics, and violence made death imminent, blood constituted one of the fundamental values. . . . blood was *a reality with a symbolic function*."[4] This transition from one economy to another was particularly fraught in colonial contexts; in Ireland, for instance, aristocratic estates were seized by "law" and force rather than eroded and partitioned by financial exigencies, leading to what Sydney Morgan terms, "the insecurity of property."[5] In *Melmoth the Wanderer*, Maturin engages this "insecurity of property" and "the symbolics of blood" through the gothic, offering familial cannibalism as a metaphor for violence to indigenous lines of inheritance.[6] The devouring of the dismembered familial body emerges as a powerful symbol for the evisceration of an hereditary economy by the consumption-based logic of the emergent capitalism of empire and for the imperial violation of the socioeconomic significance of blood.

Maturin's novel is not, however, programmatically anti-imperialist or conservative in its sanctification of lines of inheritance; anti-Catholicism is tempered by the occasional representation of a good Catholic, anticolonialism is complicated by the reproduction of colonial stereotypes, especially in relation to India, and the negative representation of disinheritance is not countered with a positive representation of inheritance. David Lloyd suggests that the perceived absence of an Irish novel-writing tradition (in the realist mode), that is comparable in quality to the British tradition derives from the "notion of a natural conjunction between stability and the novel form," while "subaltern history," following Antonio Gramsci, is understood as "episodic and fragmentary."[7] Lloyd invites us to read this kind of narrative as "another *mode* of narrative, rather than an incomplete one, of another *principle* of organization, rather than one yet to be unified," and to consider the mutually constitutive relations between the novel and "social conditions" in Ireland.[8] *Melmoth the Wanderer*, with its episodic, fragmented, and complex *emboîtement* structure, embodies such a narrative form while revealing the tensions that Lloyd traces.

In Maturin's novel, a proto-Dickensian heir, John Melmoth, leaves obscurity at college to visit a dying uncle in his bleak Irish estate to deal with the mundane tasks of meeting the servants, surveying the grounds, and following the well-established protocols which surround the dying and the inheriting. But then he suddenly falls through the floor of the traditional Irish genre of the so-called big house novel to land in the nightmare world of the gothic in which another John Melmoth, the Wanderer, is proprietor. Realism gives way to terror, linearity to fragmentation, the young hero to a proliferating series of heroes and heroines as well as a powerful antihero—and conservation to consumption. Maturin's novel focusses on an irreducible space of anxiety, relentlessly revisiting the moment of temptation, typically a crisis in which social values are tested by animal needs: "we could, in such a moment, feed on a parent, to gnaw out our passage into life and liberty, as sufferers in a wreck have been known to gnaw their own flesh" (267). There is no either/or in this anxiousness, no solution that can resolve it, because it derives from the inextricability of the individual from the social that is symbolized by the haunting of the body by the spirit. Georges Bataille suggests, "the spirit is so closely linked to the body as a thing that the body never ceases to be haunted, is never a thing except virtually, so much so that if death reduces it to the condition of a thing, the spirit is more present than ever."[9] This is the paradox from which the incidents of cannibalism in Maturin's novel derive their terror, and it is reflected not only in the representation of body and spirit but also in the representation of property and family and, in its colonial inflection, of the national land and its people. Nonritualistic cannibalism of the kind that appears in Maturin's novel represents the repudiation of blood's symbolic function.[10] In such cannibalism flesh and blood do not constitute the generative site of meaning; they are merely consumable objects, but consumable precisely because their meaning (as the sign of life, familial affiliation and nationality) is denied, their currency unrecognized.

CANNIBAL ECONOMIES: DEBATING RIGHTS IN THE ROMANTIC PERIOD

Before turning to Maturin's deployment of cannibalism to articulate the breakdown of stable, inheritable economies and the familial bonds with which they are linked, I wish to further situate Maturin's use of this metaphor in the context of the contemporary reinvention of, and debate over, the economic expression of aristocratic, national, and imperial interests. Maturin, an Anglo-Irish writer of Huguenot origins, uses cannibalism to engage Romantic-era debates that arise from crises over property raised by colonial unrest in the United States and Ireland and by radical agitation across the British Isles in the wake of the French Revolution, as well as the accelerating transition in Britain from a land-based hereditary economy to a commercial, capitalist one dependent on colonial possessions.[11] This economic transformation is variously articulated in literature of the Romantic period, often in tandem with particular claims about familial stability. In Jane Austen's *Mansfield Park*, for instance, the father is caught between familial pressures, which require his presence on the family estate to maintain order, and financial pressures, which require his presence in the colonial sugar plantations now subsidizing the family estate.[12]

These domestic economic changes necessarily transformed the imperial enterprise, as it was executed and represented from a British perspective. Comparing the Renaissance and Romantic eras in *Memoirs of Captain Rock* (1824), a critique of colonialism in Ireland, Thomas Moore, using the voice of an English editor, suggests that "There is no end to the resemblances between the two periods. The following passage is not more applicable to the English colonists of those days, than to the English capitalists of the present."[13] Renaissance imperialism focused on the naming of territorial possessions for the crown and the appropriation of raw currency in the form of gold, that is, on the accumulation of traditional signs of wealth outside of the circuit of market production (deeds to land), and only secondarily on some small, expensive trade goods (silk, spices). It was colonial in its violent establishment of title and settlements but not capitalist, in the sense that it did not seek to transform colonized peoples into a viable labor force or the land into the site of mass production (and consumption). Imperialism in the wake of the Industrial Revolution was more concerned with raw materials for a larger market (linen production in Ireland; cotton, sugar, and tea in other colonies) and the establishment of extensive commercial networks that required the involvement of the lower classes to provide company officers, laborers, and consumers. The chapter, "Of Colonies," in Adam Smith's influential and widely read study, *The Wealth of Nations* (1776), supported this new view of the imperial project, emphasizing commercial interests as well as the value of good relations between the imperial center and the inhabitants of the colonial periphery. Fredric Jameson's useful distinction between "the imperialist dynamic of capitalism proper" and "the wars of conquest of the various ancient empires"[14] can be understood in this context. The promotion of commercial activity in the colonies, through labor as well as resource-based industries that transformed the economic structure of the colonies and the imperial center, drew the population of the empire into a dependence on the colonial-commercial infrastructure. But to draw them into that infrastructure was to draw them out of indigenous economies, economies that in many cases (such as Ireland and India) were in part predicated on the hereditary distribution of wealth and power. Moore's distinction, between colonists and capitalists, thus marks the shift in emphasis from territorial acquisition and limited mercantilism to a commercialism that pervades the colonial economy. However, the comparison suggests a continuity between them, a continuity of prejudice: the passage Moore refers to begins, "Such conceptions had been formed of the state of Ireland and the disorders of its inhabitants. . . ."[15] In other words, the intolerance and derisive component of British imperial discourse remains constant while economic strategies change with the times.

Echoing this transformation of imperial practices, but reversing the political polarity of the hereditary-commercial binary, the rights of the aristocracy and "the rights of man" were hotly contested in the public domain. In general, the valorization of individual rights were associated with radicalism and the new commercial economies, and hereditary rights were favored by those who also sanctioned tradition and aristocratic privilege.[16] Burke thus describes tradition "us[ing] metaphors of genuine parentage and offspring—authentic bloodlines," positing and discussing at length in *Reflections on the Revolution in France* (1790), "the sacredness of an hereditary principle of succession in our government."[17] The radical position, which held that tradition was not a justification and that birth was not a qualification for rule, denied both the legitimacy of hereditary succession and the "family values" of the aristocracy. In *The Rights of Man* (1791–92), Paine writes,

> Mr Burke talks about what he calls an hereditary crown, as if it were some production of Nature; or as if, like Time, it had a power to operate, not only independently, but in spite of man; or as if it were a thing or a subject universally consented to. Alas! it has none of these properties, but is the reverse of them all. It is a thing in imagination, the propriety of which is more than doubted, and the legality of which in a few years will be denied.

> [T]o keep up a succession of this order for the purpose for which it was established, all the younger branches of those families were disinherited, and the law of *primogenitureship* set up. The nature and character of aristocracy shows itself to us in this law. It is a law against every law of nature, and Nature herself calls for its destruction. Establish family justice, and aristocracy falls.[18]

Paine thus argues that hegemonic forms of power are not founded upon the family but trammel upon it, turning the founding value of the Burkean view against it; nevertheless, in both cases, family and property are intertwined, as the structure of one validates the distribution of the other. The rising representation of imperial interests as commercial rather than territorial helped to conceal, for a British audience, the contradiction between the domestic entrenchment of aristocratic privilege and the imperial disinheritance of indigenous aristocracies.

Cannibalism was a recurring image in these complex and charged debates. Cannibalism had been used before, of course, as a powerful taboo that taints any social practice, or people, that it metaphorically touches. It enforces various social prohibitions in the folk tales published by the Brothers Grimm and serves a similar purpose in sensationalist literature and prints throughout the eighteenth and nineteenth centuries.[19] In the political controversies of the Romantic period, however, its usage is more focused; cannibalism often appears an evocative symbol for disinheritance, regardless of whether the inheritance is represented as one of universal human rights, aristocratic wealth and privilege, or the rights of citizenship in the nation of one's birth.[20] The radical Paine thus uses cannibalism to figure the disinheritance of younger children: "By the aristocratical law of primogenitureship, in a family of six children, five are exposed. Aristocracy has never had more than *one* child. The rest are begotten to be devoured. They are thrown to the cannibal for prey, and the natural parent prepares the unnatural repast."[21] Conversely, Paine's archnemesis, Burke, associates the French revolutionaries with cannibalism. According to Burke, in his "First Letter on a Regicide Peace" (1796), those who would negotiate with France "wait, it seems, until the sanguinary tyrant *Carnot*, shall have snorted away the fumes of the indigested blood of his sovereign . . . when sunk on the down of usurped pomp, he shall have sufficiently indulged his meditations with what Monarch he shall next glut his ravening maw."[22] In his *Reflections*, Burke represents cannibalistic behavior as the perverse inheritance of revolutionaries: referring to a theatrical representation of the "infamous massacre of St. Bartholomew," Burke complains that "they caused this very massacre to be acted on the stage for the diversion of the descendants of those who committed it. . . . [I]t was to teach them to persecute their own pastors. . . . It was to stimulate their cannibal appetites."[23]

While these rhetorical deployments of cannibalism lie on opposite sides of the political spectrum, they both target the same "unnatural" crimes—disinheritance and an abusive intervention in proper affections. For Paine, proper parental feeling is at odds with primogeniture and the conviction that all inherit, by descent from Adam and Eve, basic human rights; for Burke, "it is *natural*" to "look up with awe to kings," and kings inherit an inalienable right to monarchy.[24] In *Memoirs of Captain Rock*, Moore translates the image into the colonial context. After associating the colonial hegemony with the child-devouring giaour of William Beckford's *Vathek*, he writes,

> At length, in the year 1778, the fears of England—then suffering, in America, for her Saturnian propensity to devour her own off-spring—and the gradual increase of a national spirit in Ireland, concurred in removing the most obnoxious of the Penal statutes,—of those laws, which had so long excluded the great majority of the nation, from all interest or property in the soil on which they trod; and by which our rulers, having first plundered us of the estates and possessions of our forefathers, set an interdict on our acquisition of any more for our descendants.[25]

Moore thus links national and familial disinheritance to familial cannibalism, defining colonial economic violence as an unnatural, and counterproductive, appetite.[26] In *Melmoth the Wanderer*, Maturin echoes these debates, offering a sustained gothic articulation of their metaphor of cannibalism as well as the anxiety over property which that metaphor addresses.

CONSUMING THE DISINHERITED AND FAMILIAL BODY

Maturin evokes the colonial context most emphatically through the framing narrative of the novel, a narrative that is focused on the moment of colonial inheritance. While the novel is named after the Wanderer, the omnipresent character of the novel is actually another John Melmoth, the reader and auditor of the novel's tales in the fall of 1816 and the last descendant of the Wanderer's brother. There are two other Melmoths in the novel: the Wanderer's brother, an officer in Cromwell's army "who obtained a grant of lands, the confiscated property of an Irish family" (64) in the seventeenth century and founded the Melmoth line; young Melmoth's uncle, "old Melmoth" (53), a bigoted miser and inheritor of the officer's estate who dies at the opening of the novel. The officer is explicitly implicated in one of the most notorious barbarities in Ireland's colonial history, Cromwell's slaughter of the Irish and "planting" of his soldiers on confiscated lands, a strategic depopulation and repopulation, to secure the country as a colony of England. The four Melmoths thus include an agent of Cromwell's colonial agenda (the Wanderer's brother), a "stranger" (376) who travels the globe trying to conquer the weak (the Wanderer), the parsimonious landlord who withholds wealth from the native peasantry in order to pass on "considerable" property to his "sole heir" (58) (the uncle), and the new landlord who inherits both the wealth and the history of colonialism (the latest John Melmoth).[27] The moment of John Melmoth's inheritance of the "confiscated property" which his family has held for nearly two centuries is the setting for the narration of Maturin's various tales of greed, prejudice, domestic violence, and cannibalism. This pair of pairs also recalls Moore's comparison of the Romantic and Renaissance eras: the brothers live in the Renaissance, the setting of many of the novel's embedded tales; the nephew and uncle live in the Romantic period, the setting of the frame narrative and the rest of the embedded tales. Through the emboîtement structure, Maturin repeatedly invites the comparison of these two periods, suggesting similarities between the persecution of Protestants in Renaissance Spain and the persecution of Catholics in Ireland under the Penal Laws of the eighteenth century, or the greed of the Renaissance merchant, Aliaga, and that of Melmoth's uncle, while the frame narrative situates that comparison in the context of economic transition.

In his tales of cannibalistic behavior, Maturin follows in the footsteps of Swift's "A Modest Proposal" by collapsing the distance between exploiter and exploited through the removal of the intermediary economic steps between plenty and starvation. Maturin discards the abstractions of profit margins and monopolies, land enclosures, and labor conditions, or the implicit rebuke in contemporary graphic representations of fat factory owners and wasted workers, for the visceral clarity of one human being eating another. The first episode of literal cannibalism helps to clarify Maturin's use of the trope. Two lovers, an aristocrat "forced . . . to take the vows" because of his family's "fear of his contracting what is called a degrading marriage, i.e., of marrying a woman of inferior rank" (282) and the woman he wanted to marry, are caught in a monastery (they have used the standard gothic stratagem of disguising the woman as a young novice): they are discovered by a monk, a parricide who had sought refuge in the church and quickly became the henchman for the corrupt officials of the monastery. The parricide had killed his father in order to "inherit" his father's wealth more quickly and acts in a variety of ways to further familial violence and disinheritance, primarily by helping convent officials trap aristocrats forced to take vows, and thus disinherited, by their families.

While pretending to help the lovers escape, the parricide traps them in an underground cell. The Superior, "on fire at the insult offered to the sanctity of his convent" (288), nails the door shut and charges the parricide to guard them; gradually, they starve to death. This story is embedded in a nest of (dis)inheritances: it is relayed by the parricide to another disinherited aristocrat, Alonzo Monçada, as he pretends to help him escape from the monastery; Monçada then relays the story of his escape, including the parricide's narration, to the younger John Melmoth at the time of his inheritance.

Throughout his description of the lovers' suffering, the parricide uses the language of cannibalism to describe his sadistic pleasure as the couple starved to death. The parricide, who had earlier remarked, "*Emotions are my events*" (281), calls his delight "curiosity" rather than "cruelty," "that curiosity that . . . makes the most delicate female feast on groans and agonies" (289). Literal eating and imaginative cannibalism are quickly compared: "I was glad of the food he [another monk] left me, for I was hungry now, but I reserved the appetite of my soul for richer luxuries. I heard them talking within. While I was eating, I actually lived on the famine that was devouring them" (290). In the parricide's formulation, his noncorporeal appetite is at one remove from literal cannibalism—it feeds on the famine that feeds on the lovers. The parricide's division of his appetites recalls Bataille's distinction between two forms of consumption: "the use of the minimum necessary for the conservation of life and the continuation of individuals' productive activity in a given society" and "unproductive expenditures: luxury, mourning, war, cults, . . . games, spectacles, arts, perverse sexual activity," that is, "activities . . . which have no end beyond themselves."[28] The parricide has the power to choose between forms of consumption because he has access to both kinds of food, corporeal nourishment and the objects of sadistic desire (physical pain, emotional suffering, hunger). He assumes, moreover, that the first form of consumption is the guiding one even though the second is more emotionally satisfying than the mere "event" of eating; his pleasure derives, in part, from this assumption and his consequent interpretation of the sounds that he hears through the sealed door. He notes, for instance, that as "the agony of hunger increased . . . [t]hey were rapidly becoming objects of hostility to each other,—oh what a feast to me!" (291). Finally, his imaginative feasting is iterated literally by the imprisoned monk: "It was on the fourth night that I heard the shriek of the wretched female,—her lover, in the agony of hunger, had fastened his teeth in her shoulder" (291).

In such scenes, the novel offers a gothic inflection of Bataille's "notion of expenditure," in which "expenditure" refers to the form of "unproductive" consumption that exceeds the necessities of life. Expenditure is predicated on loss—"a *loss* that must be as great as possible in order for that activity to take on its true meaning," whether "one sacrifices a fortune" to buy a diamond or participates in "a bloody wasting of men and animals in *sacrifice*."[29] In Maturin's novel, such "expenditure" demands a sacrifice of flesh and its "true meaning" is revealed in that sacrifice. The cannibalistic lust of the parricide is situated through the revelations of loss that greet the parricide when he opens the cell. First, he describes the cannibalistic failures of the imprisoned monk. He had left no more than "a slight scar" on his lover's shoulder—even "the rabid despair of famine had produced no farther outrage"—and could not even go through with a final attempt at self-cannibalism (292). The parricide's surrogate, the one who was to literally feed on the woman while the parricide fed imaginatively on her consumption, is thus revealed to be a failed cannibal, offering the illusion of cannibalistic violence to the hungry parricide but not, the parricide now knows, the reality. This revelation of counterfeit cannibalism voids the significance of the event for the monk: his starving "brother" refused the food that he, well-fed, desired and so contradicted the basis for the parricide's lust, namely, that the lovers were descending from idealistic love to a violence that reduces the other to "thinghood" in the desperate repudiation of the consciousness that inhabits the flesh.[30] Second, and more powerfully, the parricide recognizes the female victim—his only sister. In a cascade of losses, the meaning of his "expenditure" is transformed: he has not only feasted on illusory cannibalism but so alienated himself from family and society in the egotistic pursuit of his own excessive desires that he has murdered a father for his gold and a sister for her screams. As he repeats, in narration, the moment of the discovery, the parricide exchanges his identification with the would-be cannibal for one with the cannibalized victim, his expenditure for his loss, and his devouring mouth for an unproductive voice: " 'she was my own sister,—my only one,—and I had heard her voice grow fainter and fainter. I had heard—'and his own voice grew fainter—it ceased" (293). The parricide's greed, for gold and for his cannibalistic feast, is intimately linked to familial violence; familial violence registers excess, and the parricide's violent nightmares and feelings of loss mark the haunting of that excess by the familial feeling he had tried to deny.

This cannibalistic scene is foreshadowed and refracted through a series of allusions to cannibalism in the preceding pages. The parricide's auditor, Monçada, in telling this story to John Melmoth, repeatedly uses cannibalism to describe his fears during their escape attempt, particularly his fear of the parricide. He regrets being "driven to trust his life and liberation to hands that reeked with a father's blood" (265), to someone "with a yawn that distended like the jaws of an Ogre preparing for his cannibal feast" (279). He worries that the parricide is a demon who will force him to participate in a satanic version of communion, and imagines "being forced to witness the unnatural revels of a diabolical feast,—of seeing the rotting flesh distributed,—of drinking the dead corrupted blood" (265). But then, instead of demonizing the parricide, Monçada imagines the point at which he would himself commit such a crime:

> I was all physical feeling,—all intense corporeal agony, and God only knows, and man only can feel, how that agony can absorb and annihilate all other feeling within us,—how we could, in such a moment, feed on a parent, to gnaw out our passage into life and liberty, as sufferers in a wreck have been known to gnaw their own flesh, for the support of that existence which the unnatural morsel was diminishing at every agonizing bite. (267)

As the will of the flesh to survive subsumes first the noncorporeal and then the corporeal ("all other feeling" and then "their own flesh"), cannibalism is represented as a natural response that is enabled by the consumption of the self by the will to survive. Maturin thus compares the parricide's perverse cannibalism, a cannibalism based on unnatural sadistic desires, with a form of nonperverse cannibalism, that is, a cannibalism based on the natural urge to survive, on the inevitable choice of cannibalism over self-annihilation. Both feed on the flesh of relatives, but one from the desire for a kind of "unproductive" consumption, in Bataille's phrase, and the other from the pressure of necessity. It is here that Maturin rounds out Swift's premise; that is, while Swift figures the rich as cannibals, feeding on the bodies of the poor indirectly through economic inequity, Maturin suggests that that economic inequity leads to bodies so starved that they duplicate, with even more directness, that violence. This is the locus of the gothic horror of Maturin's novel, namely, the possibility that anyone who is starved will be driven to cannibalism, and the degree to which starvation is produced by institutions over which individuals have little or no control. Moreover, as Steven Bruhm suggests, "the self in Romantic fiction seems to know itself only through acquaintance with physical agony"[31]; that is, Monçada's physical extremity leads to an epiphany about his own capacity for cannibalism that undermines his previous confidence that it is the province only of such monsters as the parricide.

In "The Tale of Guzman's Family," Maturin repeats the parricide's transformation of flesh wasted away by starvation into flesh cannibalistically consumed, but more directly links it to disinheritance, describing a family's fall into the cannibalistic extremity that Monçada fears. In this tale, the eldest son of the Walbergs, Everhard, secretly sells his blood to buy food for his impoverished family. He repeatedly returns to the home with an abundance of food and an increasingly wasted body, an unread image of the cannibalistic exchange of the familial body for the family's food:

> "Squabbling about your supper?" cried Everhard, bursting among them with a wild and feeble laugh,—"Why, here's enough for to-morrow—and to-morrow." And he flung indeed ample means for two days' subsistence on the table, but he looked *paler and paler*. The hungry family devoured the hoard, and forgot to ask the cause of his increasing paleness, and obviously diminished strength. (549; Maturin's emphasis)

The father discovers the "horrible secret" (552) when Everhard's wounds burst open in the night and a doctor has to be called to treat him. At a moment of greater extremity, he tells the others, "My son sells his blood to a surgeon, to save us from perishing! My daughter trembles on the verge of prostitution, to procure us a meal" (554–55). The association of the selling of blood with the prostitution of the daughter emphasizes the commodification of the (familial) body to which poverty has driven them. But it also recalls the context of disinheritance in the tale. The Guzman of the tale's title is a wealthy man without an heir; his sister, Ines Walberg, is summoned, with her impoverished family, from Germany to Spain by Guzman who "proclaim[s] them heirs to all his vast riches" (526). After a brief period in which they live in luxury at Guzman's expense, they are disinherited: the estate, at Guzman's death, is instead transferred to the church. The Walbergs, unable to secure work in their professions because of their displacement from Germany and religious persecution in Spain, lapse into deeper and deeper poverty and increasingly perilous hunger. At first, they share their food, with the adults sometimes sacrificing their share to the children, but then the adults begin to snatch portions from the children, with the father becoming particularly violent, until domestic peace is, after Everhard's partial consumption and the father's attempt to murder his family, magically restored with their rightful inheritance.

This tale, with its awkward resolution, crystallizes the economic violence that Maturin marks with cannibalism. The body of the eldest son, the usual heir under the law of primogeniture, as well as the reproductive body of the daughter, mark what Foucault terms the transition from "*a symbolics of blood* to *an analytics of sexuality*,"[32] as Everhard is driven to near-death by the last gasps of the former and the daughter verges on the inauguration of the latter. But they specifically become, on their disinheritance, consumable commodities rather than the vehicles for the genealogical transmission of property. On their restoration to inheritance, this commodification is halted: in Maturin's economics, hereditary property staves off the ravenous maw of the commercial. Inheritance is oriented toward amicable conservation rather than gothic devouring: familial property conserves familial flesh and proper familial relations, with the gothic corollary that disinheritance is tied to the cannibalistic consumption of familial flesh and familial violence. Disinheritance, to return to Bataille's concept of haunting, repudiates the familial dimension of property; it turns familial property, including the body, into commodities and currency, breaking it into a divisible assemblage of things that can circulate freely among individuals, independent of familial affiliation.

COLONIAL CONSUMPTION AND IMPERIAL PREDATION

Melmoth the Wanderer stands at the terrifying still point of this churning world. A "disinherited child of nature" (424), he searches the globe for an heir to his hellish estate, for someone who is willing to take his place and so permit his release from immortal restlessness. With his body rendered immutable by an absolute damnation that can only be resolved by an equal exchange, the Wanderer exemplifies the economy of inheritance in which the property is conserved and the son is to simply replace the father. His quest is, in a sense, an attempt to perpetuate that economy, but the Wanderer's damnation remains eternally conservative:

> The secret of my destiny rests with myself. If all that fear has invented, and credulity believed of me be true, to what does it amount? That if my crimes have exceeded those of mortality, so will my punishment. I have been on earth a terror, but not an evil to its inhabitants. None can participate in my destiny but with his own consent—*none have consented*—none can be involved in its tremen-

dous penalties, but by participation. I alone must sustain the penalty. (696)

The Wanderer, in Bataille's phrase, "balances *accounts*,"[33] but the balance is restored vertically, between man and God, or between spirit and Spirit, rather than unevenly inflected horizontally, between human beings, or, to follow Bataille, between one inspirited body and another. The Wanderer marks the hereditary economy which haunts the commercial rather than activates the violence of the latter against the former; he has sold his soul, and is trapped irrevocably between the two economies. While the estate he would pass on is far from desirable, it must be passed on; it cannot be sold, exchanged for currency, or divided. But at the same time, he is unable to access that solution because he is himself "disinherited" and has no power to designate an heir. He haunts the passage of another estate's inheritance but cannot himself enter that circuit. This is why he often appears when the two economies are in conflict, such as when Aliaga must choose between parental responsibility and commercial interest. At such moments, he attempts to take advantage of his victim's location between the two conflicting economies to seduce another into the immutable damnation and violence of the between-space. Moreover, the Wanderer's occupation of that space situates his function as the novel's commentator on economic affairs; his most comprehensive analysis of such matters appears in the description of European culture he presents to Immalee (401–12).

The Wanderer's literal haunting of his brother's descendants not only marks his marginal position in relation to hereditary economies but also calls attention to Maturin's representation of the Wanderer as an imperial figure—an appropriate ghost for a colonial estate. As many have noted, the Wanderer is another avatar of that seductive hero of Romanticism, the Miltonic Satan. But the Miltonic Satan, as Maturin's contemporaries recognized, is an imperial figure: William Hazlitt, for instance, writes, "Satan is not the principle of malignity, or of the abstract love of evil—but of the abstract love of power. . . . After such a conflict as his, and such a defeat, to retreat in order, to rally, to make terms, to exist at all, is something; but he does more than this—he founds a new empire in hell, and from it conquers this new world."[34] This imperialist taint is closely identified with the Wanderer's damnation: at the climactic conclusion of his tale, the Wanderer transforms a priest's command, "go, cursing and to curse," into the reply, "I go conquering and to conquer" (676). The Wanderer's empire is a hell in which a history of improper property relations is collapsed into a single time and space:

> In other cases, the possession of the territory is the security for the man,—but here the man is the security for the everlasting possession of the territory. . . . Listen to me while I announce to you the wealth, the population, the magnificence of that region to which I will endower you. The rulers of the earth are there—all of them. There be the heroes, and the sovereigns, and the tyrants. There are their riches, and pomp, and power. . . . There are . . . all those nameless and name-undeserving barbarians, who, under various titles and claims, ravaged and ruined the earth they came to conquer. (460–61)

Inverting the dominant imperial paradigm, Maturin identifies the European colonizers as the "barbarians" and, more to the point, represents them as exploitative and as interlopers. "Nameless," they have no legitimate title to the land that they "ravaged and ruined"—they disinherit. In this passage, Maturin specifically targets the Western imperial disinheritance of indigenous aristocracies during the Renaissance imperial land grab, alluding in particular to the Catholic church's role in the competition for imperial acquisitions: "There be also those triple-crowned chieftains of the West, who hide their shorn heads under a diadem, and for every hair they shave, demand the life of a sovereign—who, pretending to humility, trample on power—whose title is Servant of servants—and whose claim and recognizance is, Lord of lords" (461).[35] This allusive passage is clear in its critique: imperialists who claim to be Christian intervene in the indigenous aristocratic distribution of power, "demand[ing] the life of a sovereign" and "trampl[ing] on power."

In his representation of India—a thinly coded representation of Ireland under colonial rule rather than an informed representation of the part of India under European domination—Maturin continues this reversal of dominant characterizations of Europeans in the imperial context. Rather than representing them as civilizing agents or settlers of underused territory, Maturin instead characterizes them as marauders who turn a land of plenty into a waste land and an "inoffensive" indigenous people into a population that is starved, hopeless, and hostile to the mercenary and proselytizing colonizers:

> he could watch the vessels as they floated by, and, from the skiff to the huge trader, be sure that every one bore its freight of woe and

crime. There came on the European vessels full of the passions and crimes of another world,—of its sateless cupidity, remorseless cruelty, its intelligence, all awake and ministrant in the cause of its evil passions. . . . He saw them approach to traffic for "gold, and silver, and the souls of men;"—to grasp, with breathless rapacity, the gems and precious produce of those luxuriant climates, and deny the inhabitants the rice that supported their inoffensive existence;—to discharge the load of their crimes, their lust and their avarice, and after ravaging the land, and plundering the natives, depart, leaving behind them famine, despair and execration. (400)

Rather than an Eden of limitless goods, India is a land of limited resources in which to consume its "precious produce" is to indirectly consume its inhabitants by denying them the food that sustains their flesh. It is this scene of colonial consumption that the pseudo-imperial Wanderer watches "as a tiger views a forest abounding with prey" (400)—the only figure for whom food is plentiful. He then turns to Immalee, the daughter of a Spanish merchant, shipwrecked during a trade voyage and raised in isolation from society in the idyllic natural world of an island near India, and tells her about Europe in terms that represent this colonial predation as typical of European culture. On being told that Europeans eat meat, the vegetarian

> Immalee shuddered at the mention of animal food, as the most delicate European would at the mention of a cannibal feast. . . . "Some," said he [the Wanderer], by way of consolation, "have a taste by no means so sophisticated,—they content themselves at their need with the flesh of their fellow-creatures; and as human life is always miserable, and animal life never so, (except from elementary causes), one would imagine this the most humane and salutary way of at once gratifying the appetite, and diminishing the mass of human suffering." (401)

Here, as excessive power again slides into cannibalism, it is difficult not to hear echoes of Swift's "A Modest Proposal." Swift makes similar calculations in which cannibalism at once "gratif[ies] the appetite" and "diminish[es] the mass of human suffering," and, like Maturin, uses cannibalism as a figure for the exploitation of one class by another: "I grant this food [i.e., infants] will be somewhat dear, and therefore very proper for the landlords, who, as they have already devoured most of the parents, seem to have the best title to the children."[36] The figuring of those who economically prey on human beings as cannibals inscribes the colonial exploitation of Irish tenants and Indians into the ultimate cultural taboo, as well as reverses racist and classist models in which the Other of the ruling class was accused of perpetrating horrors of cruelty and bestiality. But it does so not only for the horror of cannibalism but for its content, allowing for a visceral representation of the effects of excessive consumption in a closed or limited economy in which property must be conserved rather than consumed. In this sense, *Melmoth the Wanderer* has much to do with the tradition of vampire novels which, as Carol Senf notes, represents aristocrats cannabilistically feeding on the blood of those whom they exploit.[37]

Melmoth thus introduces Europe to Immalee as a culture in which figurative cannibalism and predatory violence are, ultimately, the consequences of a social system that (recalling Paine) allows "an unequal division of the means of existence" (403) in contradistinction to "the united family of nature" (402). Immalee is ultimately destroyed because she is transported from this "family of nature" into her European family; that family, because of its financial concerns, fails to protect her. Immalee's brother avoids contemplating her resistance to a forced marriage because the marriage will raise his standard of living, while Immalee's father, Aliaga, ignores Melmoth's warnings about Immalee's danger because of his urge to prevent "the probable failure of a [financial] house" (654). Aliaga is also the recipient of "The Tale of Guzman's Family," but falls asleep during its narration and fails to heed its warning. After Immalee's marriage to, and pregnancy by, Melmoth is revealed, and his demonic nature is understood, Melmoth berates Aliaga, "Wretched old man—you were warned—but you neglected the warning—I adjured you to save your daughter—*I best* knew her danger—you saved your gold—now estimate the value of the dross you grasped, and the precious ore you dropt!" (676). The merchant, who had accumulated part of his wealth by exploiting India in the way that the narrator of "The Tale of the Indians" so vehemently excoriates, is thus accused of trading money for his "Indian" daughter's life and soul— echoing the commodification of flesh in other cannibalistic episodes in the novel, including "The Tale of Guzman's Family." Aliaga's parental neglect causes the death of his son, daughter, and grandchild—infanticide by greed. Moreover, these deaths end the family line, leaving no heirs to the fortune for which Aliaga sacrificed so much.

Immediately after the recitation of "The Tale of Guzman's Family," the Wanderer berates Aliaga for accusing him of being an agent of Satan: " 'You yourself, Senhor, who, of course, as an orthodox and inveterate

Catholic, must abhor the enemy of mankind, have often acted as his agent.' . . . [Aliaga] devoutly disavowed his ever having been an agent of the enemy of man. 'Will you dare to say so? . . . Have you never in trade overreached a dealer, or banquetted on the spoils of your starving debtor?'" (568). Once again, Maturin, like Swift, identifies cannibalism with economic violence. Like Monçada's turn from representing the parricide as a cannibal to imagining himself as a parricidal cannibal, Melmoth's identification of the merchant as "the enemy of mankind" complicates the easy association of cannibalism with the Other. Aliaga's mercantile-motivated neglect not only resonates with the Wanderer's representation of European culture—particularly since the Wanderer's warnings circulate around images of cannibalism—but also mirrors the parricide's crimes. Both are guilty of figurative cannibalism and allowed their lust for gold, an excess beyond the properly distributed inheritance, to supersede their familial feelings, leading to the deaths of their relatives, including an innocent daughter whose body is victimized because of their misplaced vigilance.

HAUNTING THE NATIONAL BODY

Cannibalism derives its terror from its treatment of the body as a thing to be consumed, and the observer's recognition that, to repeat Bataille, "the spirit is so closely linked to the body as a thing that the body never ceases to be haunted, is never a thing except virtually."[38] I suggested earlier that this paradox is reflected not only in the representation of body and spirit, but also in the representation of property and family, and of nation and national identity, in Maturin's novel. The Wanderer haunts the confiscated Irish estate, appearing at the moment of inheritance to each succeeding generation. This is, in many regards, a common case of haunting, but as I have already implied, this haunting symbolizes the repression of the effects of imperial predation, the refusal to see the physical violence of colonial economic violence. The Wanderer is not linked to the land, but to the mismanaged and confiscated land; to use Tom Dunne's phrase, the Melmoth estate is "haunted by history."[39] The parsimonious uncle from whom John Melmoth inherits lays waste to that land, consuming its life until only dregs are left, and he insistently tries to destroy the spirit of the confiscated estate, denying the signification of its haunting and suppressing the evidence of it.

The Wanderer is introduced to John Melmoth initially through his ghostly appearance at the time of his uncle's death; moreover, he is introduced as a figure pushed to the margins, shut away, by the abusive land-lord. The Wanderer is named in an informal codicil in the uncle's will; this supplementary text is explicitly marginal, and implicitly connected to the history of Irish oppression. During the reading of the will,

> the attorney . . . added, "There are some words here, at the corner of the parchment, which do not appear to be part of the will." . . . "I enjoin my nephew and heir, John Melmoth, to remove, destroy, or cause to be destroyed, the portrait inscribed J. Melmoth, 1646, hanging in my closet. I also enjoin him to search for a manuscript . . . in the third and lowest left-hand drawer of the mahogany chest standing under the portrait,—it is among some papers of no value, such as manuscript sermons, and pamphlets on the improvement of Ireland, and such stuff; he will distinguish it by its being tied round with black tape. . . . He may read it if he will;—I think he had better not." (58)

Maturin is careful with his details: "sinister" is derived from the Latin for "on the left hand," so his placement of the manuscript bound by "black tape" in the "lowest left-hand drawer" anticipates the contents of that manuscript, the Wanderer's misdeeds. The manuscript's existence is noted in the margins of the paper and the legal document; it is situated at the lowest edge of the desk which borders the portrait, encircled by a black ribbon, surrounded by "trivia" that foreshadows the manuscript's contents and contextualizes them. The ignored and unread "pamphlets on the improvement of Ireland" frame a manuscript which begins the series of tales that are ostensibly about the Wanderer but, as they focus on him, detail abuses of power, particularly acts of disinheritance, in colonized and colonizing countries throughout the age of European imperial expansion.

The imperial past is thus presented as something which, though repressed, will be passed on to the next generation—it is bound up with the land that has been confiscated but never "improved," and is passed on with it upon inheritance. When the young John Melmoth inherits his substantial estate, he consequently surveys not the grounds and buildings he now owns but the demonic history of his family. As Dunne suggests, "Melmoth may combine elements of Faust, Mephistopheles, and the Wandering Jew, but it should be remembered that he also belonged to an Irish Cromwellian colonist family which he continued to haunt and whose concern to escape the burdens of its history paralleled and was reflected in his doomed attempts to lift the curse of immortality."[40] This reflection extends to the estate itself, hellishly barren and mismanaged: "There was not a tree or shrub on the lawn; . . . a few sheep were picking their scanty food amid the pebblestones, thistles, and hard mould, through which a few blades of grass made their rare and squalid appearance" (44). In the words of Milton's *Lycidas*, "The hungry Sheep look up, and are not fed."[41] Colonial predation, as in the representation of India, has laid waste to the land, and the conquering Wanderer hovers over it as a reminder of how it became waste.

At the end of the novel, cannibalism strikes the Wanderer's auditors, the latest heir of the Irish estate and the disinherited Monçada. After the close of the Wanderer's narration, knowing that the Wanderer is soon to be dragged to hell, they "passed the remainder of that day without even thinking of food, from that intense and burning anxiety that seemed to prey on their very vitals" (701), as eating is once again supplanted by being eaten. But while the parricide, the Walbergs, Aliaga, and other European merchants feast on the famine of others, John Melmoth and Monçada have internalized the cannibalistic process: they have chosen to fast (recalling the inclusion of the body's consumption of itself during fasting in the definition of autophagy), and their own anxieties "prey on their very vitals." Maturin thus closes the circle again. Cannibalism, in both the passive form of famine and the active form of devouring, is reflected back toward the source rather than outward toward another. The only exchange in the last sentence of the novel lies outside of the circuit of production and consumption: "Melmoth and Monçada exchanged looks of silent and unutterable horror" (703). Trading identical "objects" ("looks of silent and unutterable horror") within the closed economy of a mutual glance, leaves no surplus, no deficit—and no violence. Like the parricide at the moment he relives his recognition of loss, they are silenced, but not absolved. The tales of Melmoth the Wanderer have left the new estate-owner with not only the "confiscated property" and the Wanderer's name, but the disturbing history of both, leaving him, like Coleridge's wedding guest, "A sadder and a wiser man."[42] At the moment of inheritance, John Melmoth is not incorporated into a social elite, as he would be in most English novels of the period, but unwillingly, and inextricably, implicated in a colonial history of disinheritance and cannibalistic predation.

At the end of the novel, the Wanderer is dragged through doors and corridors and then estate grounds until he is thrown from a coastal rock, expelled from Ireland as forcibly as his brother had entered it. But his presence still haunts the colonial estate. Traces of the violence which expelled the Wanderer remain: "These traces were exceedingly plain" (702) and lead to the last physical mark of the Wanderer's passing, a handkerchief left on a "crag" at the ocean's edge (703). In the final lines, Maturin easily mingles these marks of the violence of the Wanderer's trail with images of wasted land and poverty. He makes the implications of their conjunction clear by using such loaded terms as "down-trodden" and representing the land as the site only of violence:

> They traced the footmarks distinctly through the narrow gravel walk, which was terminated by a broken fence, and opened on a heathy field which spread half-way up a rock whose summit overlooked the sea. The weather had been rainy, and they could trace the steps distinctly through that heathy field. They ascended the rock together.
>
> Early as it was, the cottagers, who were poor fishermen residing on the shore, were all up, and assuring Melmoth and his companion [Monçada] that they had been disturbed and terrified the preceding night by sounds which they could not describe. . . .
>
> Through the furze that clothed this rock, almost to its summit, there was a kind of tract as if a person had dragged, or been dragged, his way through it—a down-trodden track, over which no footsteps but those of one impelled by force had ever passed. (702)

At the end of this novel of cannibalistic consumption and disinheritance, Ireland lies, like the parricide's sister, starved to death with marks of violence on its shoulder.[43]

Gorily anticipating Marx's concept of alienated labor, cannibalism in Maturin's novel marks the substitution of proprietorial conservation, through primogenitural inheritance, with commodified individuals, and it does so with particular reference to the disinheritance of indigenous peoples through the imposition of a commercial-imperial economy. Against the violence of consumption, Maturin offers conservation as a force of stability, balance, and containment, but offers it only to mark its vulnerability. While the Wanderer is cast out of Ireland at the novel's close, and the new heir internalizes rather than conceals and repudiates the history which haunts the family estate, Maturin offers no utopian vision of a reformed landlord, decolonization, or a wasted estate bursting once again into life. Rather than offering metaphors of incorporation, such as those discussed by Maggie Kilgour, cannibalism marks expulsion from a stable economy into one so unstable and unregulated that violence governs its relations. While there is "insecurity of property," as Morgan puts it, there is only economic inequity and corrupt power. Implicitly recalling the confiscations under the Penal Laws in Ireland, the Wanderer declares,

> you might starve for this day's meal, while proving your right to a property which must incontestibly be yours, on the condition of your being able to fast on a few years, and survive to enjoy it—and that, finally, with the sentiments of all upright men, the opinions of the judges of the land, and the fullest conviction of your own conscience in your favor, you cannot obtain the possession of what you and all feel to be your own, while your antagonist can start an objection, purchase a fraud, or invent a lie. So pleadings go on, and years are wasted, and property consumed, and hearts broken. (407–08)

While the Wanderer's body is cast out of Ireland, echoing the ending of Lewis's *The Monk* in fulfilling the gothic requirement of the demon's destruction, his economic assessment stands without contradiction and is supported by the narratives of the text, tale after tale in which "property [was] consumed, and hearts broken." It is here that Maturin refuses the moral closure of English gothic novels. While the surface of the novel, the Wanderer-as-demonic-agent plot, is resolved, its recurring subtext of colonial seizure and disinheritance, of familial violence and cannibalism, strains against resolution or absolution.

NOTES

1. All references to the novel cite Charles Maturin, *Melmoth the Wanderer: A Tale*, ed. Alethea Hayter (Markham: Penguin, 1984); page references are incorporated parenthetically into the text.

2. Maturin alludes to the title of Swift's work as well as its content. A madman in one of the embedded narratives is the author of a "modest proposal" " 'for the spreading of Christianity in foreign parts . . .' This modest proposal was, to convert the Turkish ambassadors . . . by offering them their choice of being strangled on the spot, or becoming Christians" (89).

3. Jerrold E. Hogle, "*Frankenstein* as Neo-Gothic: From the Ghost of the Counterfeit to the Monster of Abjection," *Romanticism, History, and the Possibilities of Genre: Re-forming Literature, 1789–1837*, ed. Tilottama Rajan and Julia M. Wright (Cambridge: Cambridge UP, 1998), 190.

4. Michel Foucault, *The History of Sexuality*, vol. 1, trans. Robert Hurley (New York: Vintage, 1990), 147–48.

5. Morgan, 50. In *The Wild Irish Girl* (1806), written under her premarital name, Sydney Owenson, Morgan offers a solution resonant of Hogle's description of gothic novels' economic coordinates: recognizing the injustice of the disinheritance of Irish aristocrats, the English protagonist who will inherit a seized Irish estate marries the last descendant of the family from whom it was taken, transferring genealogical legitimacy to the landowner and restoring the semblance of economic power to the indigenous aristocracy. Maturin was much indebted to Morgan's work and directly alludes to that debt in the title of his novel, *The Wild Irish Boy*.

6. For a provocative discussion of the novel's engagement with emergent capitalism in relation to gendered subject positions and homophobia, see Margot Gayle Backus's *The Gothic Family Romance: Heterosexuality, Child Sacrifice, and the Anglo-Irish Colonial Order* (Durham, N.C.: Duke UP, 1999).

7. David Lloyd, *Anomalous States: Irish Writing and the Post-Colonial Moment* (Durham, N.C.: Duke UP, 1993), 130, 127.

8. Lloyd, 127, 131.

9. Georges Bataille, *The Theory of Religion*, trans. Robert Hurley (New York: Zone Books, 1992), 40.

10. By using the term, *nonritualistic cannibalism*, I exclude forms of cannibalism in which ritual and belief invest the consumption of flesh with meaning, as in the consumption of a particular organ to appropriate the quality associated with it.

11. I use the term *commercial*, and occasionally *mercantilism*, rather than the more familiar *capitalist* because of the emphasis of the former terms on trade and mass consumption, issues more relevant to Maturin's use of cannibalism than such capitalist concepts as venture capital, labor, and profit margins, and because there are shades of anachronism in using such a strongly Marxist-inflected term in pre-1850 contexts.

12. For a discussion of *Mansfield Park* in this context, see Edward W. Said, *Culture and Imperialism* (New York: Vintage, 1994), esp. 80–97. Maria Edgeworth's "Lame Jervas," Eliza Fenwick's *Secresy*, and Matthew G. Lewis's "The Anaconda" are just a few other texts in which this domestic dependence on colonial wealth is represented.

13. Thomas Moore, *The Memoirs of Captain Rock*, 2nd ed. (London: Longman, Hurst, Rees, Orme, Brown, and Green, 1824; rpt. New York: AMS Press, 1978), 30 n.

14. Fredric Jameson, "Modernism and Imperialism," *Nationalism, Colonialism and Literature*, ed. Seamus Deane (Minneapolis: University of Minnesota Press, 1990), 46.

15. Moore, 30–31 n.

16. This political overlapping between domestic debates about rights and imperial practices accounts for apparent contradictions in the history of British colonialism, as in, for instance, the participation of Dissenting radicals in proselytization efforts in India and the defense of the Indian aristocracy's rights by conservatives such as Edmund Burke.

17. Steven Blakemore, "Revolution in Representation: Burke's *Reflections on the Revolution in France*," *Eighteenth-Century Life* 15 (1991): 9; Edmund Burke, *Reflections on the Revolution in France* (1790), ed. Conor Cruise O'Brien (Markham: Penguin, 1986), 105.

18. Thomas Paine, *Rights of Man* (1791–92), ed. Henry Collins (Markham: Penguin, 1983), 144, 104.

19. Repeatedly in the fairy tales collected by the Grimms, for instance, the protagonist who trusts a stranger (that is, someone other than a blood relative) is threatened with cannibalism: the bride in "The Robber Bridegroom" discovers that her fiancé robs, kills, and then cannibalizes his brides; in "The Juniper Tree," the evil stepmother makes a stew of her stepson and feeds him to his father; in "Hansel and Gretel," the children accept an old woman's hospitality only to discover that "she would kill, cook, and eat" any children who did so (Jacob Grimm and Wilhelm Grimm, *The Complete Fairy Tales of the Brothers Grimm*, trans. Jack Zipes [Toronto: Bantam, 1987], 62). On cannibalism in popular prints and literature of the eighteenth and early nineteenth century, see Howard Stone, *The Night Side of Dickens: Cannibalism, Passion, Necessity* (Columbus: Ohio State UP, 1994), esp. part 1. For a discussion of nineteenth-century representations of cannibalism in the specific context of emerging racist discourses, see H. L. Malchow, *Gothic Images of Race in Nineteenth-Century Britain* (Stanford, Calif.: Stanford UP, 1996), chap. 2; and Peter J. Kitson, "'The Eucharist of Hell'; or, Eating People is Right: Romantic Representations of Cannibalism," *Romanticism on the Net* 17 (February 2000) <http://users.ox.ac.uk/~scat0385/17cannibalism.html>.

20. For a broader examination of metaphors of cannibalism in British Romantic discourse, see Kitson.

21. Paine, 104.

22. Burke, "First Letter on a Regicide Peace" (1796), vol. 9 of *The Writings and Speeches of Edmund Burke*, ed. R. B. McDowell and William B. Todd (Oxford: Clarendon, 1991), 206.

23. Burke, *Reflections*, 249.

24. Burke, *Reflections*, 182.

25. Moore, 162, 224.

26. Moore also conflates Asia, the United States, and Ireland in this passage, but such conflations are common in Irish anti-imperialist discourse of the period. In such texts, colonized nations are often represented, implicitly or explicitly, as iterations of Ireland; to a degree, this representation is well-founded and revealing, since Ireland was the laboratory in which the English, and later the British, first tested various colonial mechanisms. However, such writers also

repeat the British failure to distinguish between colonies and cultures in meaningful terms. Maturin's novel exhibits both the benefits and the problems of such a conflation.

27. The relationship between *Melmoth* and Ireland's colonial condition has been briefly noted by a number of critics. See, e.g., Backus, 113–26; Alok Bhalla, *The Cartographers of Hell: Essays on the Gothic Novel and the Social History of England* (New Delhi: Sterling, 1991), 62; Tom Dunne, "Haunted by History: Irish Romantic Writing 1800–1850," *Romanticism in National Context*, ed. Roy Porter and Mikuláš Teich (New York: Cambridge UP, 1988), 81–82; Dale Kramer, *Charles Robert Maturin* (New York: Twayne, 1973), 12; and Julian Moynahan, *Anglo-Irish: The Literary Imagination in a Hyphenated Culture* (Princeton, N.J.: Princeton UP, 1995), 117.

28. Georges Bataille, "The Notion of Expenditure," trans. Allan Stoekl, *Visions of Excess: Selected Writings, 1927–1939*, ed. Allan Stoekl (Minneapolis: University of Minnesota Press, 1985), 118.

29. Bataille, "The Notion of Expenditure," 118–19.

30. Bataille, *Theory of Religion*, 40.m

31. Steven Bruhm, *Gothic Bodies: The Politics of Pain in Romantic Fiction* (Philadelphia: Univ. of Pennsylvania Press, 1994), 147.

32. Foucault, 148, original emphasis.

33. Bataille, "The Notion of Expenditure," 125 original emphasis.

34. William Hazlitt, *Lectures on the English Poets* (Toronto: Oxford UP, 1952), 97. For a generative discussion of Satan's imperialism, see J. Martin Evans, *Milton's Imperial Epic: Paradise Lost and the Discourse of Colonialism* (Ithaca: Cornell UP, 1996).

35. This passage offers a clear allusion to papal involvement in Renaissance imperialism, including, for instance, a series of papal bulls and the Treaty of Tordesillas (1494) under Alexander VI which partitioned the regions of the globe not under Christian rule (that is, uncolonized, from a Western perspective) and divided the spoils between Spain (the setting for many of the novel's embedded tales) and Portugal. Since the pope wears a triple crown, the phrase, "triple-crowned chieftains of the west," is almost certainly a reference to rulers of such Catholic countries acting imperially under the sanction of the pope and the claim of a Christian mission.

36. Jonathan Swift, "A Modest Proposal," *Irish Tracts, 1728–1733*, ed. Herbert Davis (Oxford: Basil Blackwell, 1989), 490. The "modest proposal" in Maturin's novel is "'for the spreading of Christianity in foreign parts. . . .' This modest proposal was, to convert the Turkish ambassadors . . . by offering them their choice of being strangled on the spot, or becoming Christians" (89).

37. Maggie Kilgour notes the relation between cannibalism and vampirism in *From Communion to Cannibalism: An Anatomy of Metaphors of Incorporation* (Princeton, N.J.: Princeton UP, 1990), 172-73. While Kilgour emphasizes the mock-communion in Dracula "tak[ing] on the role of Christ,

offering his own breast and blood to Mina," 173, vampirism thrived as a metaphor for economic exploitation. Carol A. Senf argues that the nineteenth-century vampire is used "as a kind of social metaphor, a way of illustrating political oppression," and often represented as an aristocrat with an aristocrat's power, *The Vampire in Nineteenth-Century English Literature* (Bowling Green, Ohio: Bowling Green State UP, 1988), 22, 41–42. For example, Sheridan Le Fanu and Bram Stoker—both Irish authors, like Moore, Burke, Swift and Maturin—wrote two of the most important nineteenth-century vampire tales, "Carmilla" and *Dracula*, and their vampires are aristocrats with ungentle attitudes toward the lower classes.

38. Bataille, 40.

39. Dunne, 68.

40. Dunne, 81–82.

41. John Milton, *Lycidas*, in *John Milton: Complete Poems and Major Prose*, ed. Merritt Y. Hughes (New York: Odyssey, 1957), line 125. Maturin's description of the Irish estate repeatedly echoes *Lycidas*.

42. Samuel Taylor Coleridge, "The Rime of the Ancient Mariner," *Coleridge: Poems*, ed. John Beer (Toronto: Dent, 1982), line 624.

43. This parallel is especially apt if one considers the recurring trope, in various national tales of the period (including *The Wild Irish Girl*), of marriage between a man who represents colonial power and a woman who represents the conquered land. Such marriages allegorically suggest harmony between landowner and land, but the scoring of the land, like the lover's teethmarks in the woman's shoulder, offers a gothic inversion of such easy assurances.

6

Are You Being Served? Cannibalism, Class, and Victorian Melodrama

KRISTEN GUEST

The war of the poor against the rich will be the most bloodthirsty the world has ever seen.

—Friedrich Engels, *The Condition of the Working Class in England*, trans. W. O. Hendersen and W. H. Chalmer (Oxford: Basil Blackwell, 1971 [1845]), 334.

How innocent, how guileless, is the man who never dreams that there are cannibals in London! Why, society is beset by anthopophagi. One cannot walk the streets without rubbing coats with men-eaters; cannibals duly entered; consumers of human flesh and blood according to the statutes.

—Douglas Jerrold, "The Debtor and the Creditor," in *The Writings of Douglas Jerrold*, 8 vol. (London: Bradbury and Evans, 1851–58), 5: 244.

> The history of the world, my sweet, . . .
> Is who gets eaten and who gets to eat, . . .
> How comforting for just once to know, . . .
> That those above will serve those down below.

—Stephen Sondheim, *Sweeney Todd, the Demon Barber of Fleet Street*, book by Hugh Wheeler (New York: Dodd, Mead and Company, 1979), 102.

Cannibalism has traditionally been viewed as a powerful signifier of the boundary between civilization and barbarism, an opposition which, once established, underwrites enterprises of religious, economic, and cultural colonization or, alternatively, ostracism and exclusion from organs of political and social power. Historically, this opposition has been invoked, most often through rumors or vague unsubstantiated charges, to describe marginal populations as diverse as Jews and the Irish, as well as indigenous populations of the New World. That charges of cannibalism are common to these otherwise disparate groups would seem to give credence to Montaigne's observation that "everyone calls barbarism that which is not his own usage."[1] Relativist critiques aside, the opposition between civilization and savagery expressed in the notion of cannibalism has frequently been evoked to define a threatening other that must either be assimilated or annihilated. While it is evoked to justify extreme actions by designating absolute difference, however, this opposition ironically suggests the uncanny relatedness between the body of the self and the body of the other. In this respect, as Maggie Kilgour suggests, even as cannibalism "depends upon and enforces an absolute division between inside and outside" it also "dissolv[es] the structure it appears to produce."[2]

Montaigne's point, that attempts to construct an opposition between civilized self and barbaric other bring us face to face with the inescapable problem of our shared status as human beings, is now often echoed by modern anthropologists, historians, and literary critics. In his consideration of cannibalism in a colonial context, for example, Gananath Obeyesekere explores how the discourse of cannibalism is constituted by the fears and desires excited by encounters with the other. For Obeyesekere, it is not difference but the "theme of a common humanity that binds British and Maoris" in the dialectical construction of cannibalism.[3] He further suggests that cannibalism does not polarize self and other so much as it allows both colonizer and colonized to engage in fantasies about a savage other who is really a projection of the self.[4] By focusing on the problematic overlap between "civilization" and "savagery," Obeyesekere effectively challenges the binary differentiation of self and other that underwrites much colonial practice. Insofar as he concludes that cannibalism evokes anxieties about the self/other distinction because it confronts us with the specter of a common humanity, Obeyesekere significantly advances attempts to challenge formulations of a racialized other.

While this line of thought has proven valuable for revisionary scholarship on cannibalism in the New World, however, little attention has so far been paid to the "borderline" cases that take place within an Old World context. Here, ethnic groups such as the Jews and the Irish, as well as marginalized populations such as criminals, the insane, and the poor have been subject to the same charges of cannibalism and barbarism as aboriginal groups and thereby defined as an incipient threat to civilization that must be checked by the dominant culture. In his critical survey of representations of the cannibal, Frank Lestringant argues that such charges became increasingly common in western society after the end of the Enlightenment as Montaigne's ideal of the noble savage was gradually replaced by a vision of the cannibal as degenerate.[5] For Lestringant, such shifts in the image of the cannibal suggest the "inability to make sense of anthropophagy" experienced by an increasingly scientific and industrialized west.[6] While changing visions of the cannibal are certainly indicative of the historical growth of scientific determinism, however, they also suggest our growing fear of, and attempts to manage, the degenerate as an uncanny force within ourselves.

The fear that the other might be a reflection of our self is active in representations of socially marginal groups as cannibals. In fact, if we apply Obeyesekere's postcolonial logic to marginal groups within western culture, the idea of a "common humanity" becomes more apparent and more problematic. Unlike the colonial subject who is racially and culturally distinct from the colonizer, the "borderline" other shares significant physical attributes with the dominant population. In western culture in particular, dominant and marginal groups often participate in a common cultural and linguistic context and may even share a related racial heritage. Despite their similarities, however, it is partially through the definition and exclusion of marginal groups that the dominant population consolidates its power. As a result, marginal groups can neither be dismissed as "irredeemable savages" nor comfortably assimilated to prevailing norms. The central problem with the "borderline" case in mainstream culture is therefore that, unlike the racial other of colonial discourse, marginal ethnic or social groups in a European context are problematic "others" whose participation in western culture vexes attempts to define them in oppositional terms. In the latter part of the nineteenth century, for example, scientists tried to categorize and codify visual markers of difference by studying ethnic groups as well as criminals, the insane, and the poor in the hope of establishing physical typologies that would help them identify and contain the threat of otherness.[7] Despite these attempts to definitively map difference, however, the fear of a threatening and invisible other was pervasive throughout the fin de siècle in both England and Europe.

In England, in particular, this fear was manifest in metaphors that drew a conscious parallel between the savagery of its colonies and its lower classes. Years before Conrad's *Heart of Darkness* appeared, in fact, Salvation Army General Charles Booth made the comparison in his *In Darkest England and the Way Out*. For critics of London's slums the pervasive and invisible "other" was the poverty-stricken tenant of the East End whose plight formed one of the most powerful concerns in dominant Victorian society. As T. H. Huxley remarked, the Polynesian savage "in his most primitive condition" was "not half so savage, so unclean, so irreclaimable as the tenant of a tenement in an East London slum."[8] This ongoing impulse to construct the poor as other emerged with a particular sense of urgency in early Victorian England, where the idea of a Britain divided from within was succinctly expressed in Disraeli's famous description of:

> Two nations; between whom there is no intercourse and no sympathy; who are as ignorant of each other's habits, thoughts, and feelings, as if they were dwellers in different zones or inhabitants of different planets; who are formed by a different breeding, are fed by a different food, are ordered by different manners, and are not governed by the same laws.[9]

When Disraeli penned this passage in 1845, the specter of class division evoked considerable anxiety for middle-class Victorians, many of whom feared that frustrated lower-class trade unionists and chartists would rise up to destroy the forces of "civilization" embodied by private property. Ranging themselves against this "savage" threat, the middle classes engaged in a variety of responses to poverty including Poor Law legislation, sanitary studies, Malthusian population theory, and statistical analysis, all of which helped construct physical and conceptual boundaries between the lower classes and dominant culture. Even as they developed scientific models for rationalizing and containing the threat of poverty, however, middle-class Victorians also engaged in tactics of limited assimilation with respect to the lower classes and so reproduced their colonizing mission on the home front.

In their attitudes toward the poor, the middle class often reproduced the colonial logic of assimilation by attempting to "convert" the lower classes to their own standards of respectability. The idea of respectability, as Walter Houghton points out, was a key component of the bourgeois worldview associated with moral and physical order, piety, self-control, and cleanliness.[10] By adopting these values, the poor putatively gained the approval of the mainstream classes as well as the dim prospect of social mobility. The idea of respectability was therefore useful to the dominant class because it disseminated middle-class domestic values among the poor, diffusing the threat they represented even as it rearticulated the existing hierarchy. While it performed crucial ideological work for the dominant classes, respectability was attractive to the poor only insofar as it demonstrated how permeable the apparently fixed boundaries between classes were. After all, if one could aspire to behave like one's social superiors one could also aspire to enjoy the attendant privileges of their rank, including full membership in the public sphere through universal manhood suffrage. In this respect, the middle classes' bid to assimilate the lower classes to their own system of values was accompanied by an attendant anxiety to reinforce the class distinctions that divided them, and thus to maintain their own social power.

Within this cultural context, the lower classes therefore assumed a peculiar "borderline" status, inculcated with middle-class values on the one hand and vilified as a threat on the other. While the lower classes were viewed as "savages" in relation to the civilizing norm of bourgeois existence, however, the colonizing model adopted by the middle classes also evoked the uncomfortable parallel between cannibalism and consumerism. As Douglas Jerrold observed, "respectable society" was itself cannibalistic. "To read of the sufferings of one class, and the avarice, the tyranny, the pocket cannibalism of the other," he wrote, "makes one almost wonder that the world should go on."[11]

Among mainstream middle-class Victorian writers, none exemplified the two-fold fear of being consumed and the fear of consuming another like Charles Dickens. While several critics have noted that Dickens's anxiety about being eaten stemmed from childhood fears aroused by the sensationalistic tales told by his nurse,[12] James E. Marlow has astutely pointed out that Dickens's early fear of being eaten was gradually replaced by a larger fear—fueled by reports of survival cannibalism from the Franklin expedition—that civilized men could commit acts of cannibalism. Dickens's sense of the uncomfortable fit between capitalism and the middle-class virtues of enterprising benevolence (both in the colonies and at home) is expressed in his persistent use of cannibal metaphors that describe a world in which human beings are envisioned as objects of consumption.[13] Appropriately enough, given the rapid rise of "consumer" culture at the time, Dickens's cannibalistic metaphors remind us that the real "other" may in fact be the capitalist down the street. Thus, as Marlow argues, it is the "civilized" values that Sir John Franklin represented for Dickens—of "enterprise, will and energy"—which make his reputed cannibalism so terrible. From Dickens's perspective, if Franklin "could be brought to the level of the lowest savage in a vain struggle for survival, there would be no hope that normal Englishmen would not choose to survive at whatever costs."[14] Dickens's position is thus one in which the division between "civilization," or benevolence, and "savagery" always threatens to collapse into the kind of cultural relativism based on custom that Montaigne describes. More importantly, his intense anxieties about cannibalizing and being cannibalized reflect the contradictions implicit in Victorian attitudes toward the lower classes.

Dickens's two-fold fear of eating or being eaten may, in fact, echo one of the greatest anxieties confronting middle-class Victorians: for whom the affluence of empire contrasted sharply with the seemingly insoluble "poverty question," and the specter of starving masses formed a stark contrast to the affluent middle-class consumers whose appetites their labor served. Ironically, given the fact that for lower-class Victorians, the problem of acquiring sufficient food was a constant source of anxiety throughout the "Hungry Forties," the fear of *being* consumed most often devolved on mainstream consumers. For the well-fed middle classes, there was the fear of being metaphorically swallowed into the toiling masses—losing status through social ruin or economic disaster—or of being literally overpowered by the voracious Luddite or Chartist masses that broke machines and burned crops. In the symbolic imagination of this class, social and political tensions were reflected in the competitive capitalist ethos of "eat or be eaten" and the fear inspired by this ethos was projected on the laboring masses who came to represent the literal threat of cannibalism. Here the difficulty of maintaining an opposition between self and other becomes highly problematic once the idea of cannibalism is evoked, for even as it functions as a marker of difference cannibalism also carries the reminder of how similar we are. For the dominant classes in Victorian England, then, attempts to define the poor as "savage" other inevitably raised questions about their own position as consumers.

For the masses, conversely, questions about cannibalistic consumption were most often expressed in a sensationalism that seemed to revel in the tension between transgression and humor with a Rabelaisian disregard for the boundaries of good taste. Typical among the lower classes were jibes aimed at vendors of foodstuffs. According to one of Henry Mayhew's interviewees, "People, when I go into houses, . . . often begin crying, 'Meeyow,' or 'Bow-wow-wow.'"[15] This type of joke was often taken to sensationalistic extremes through rumors of cannibalism. Thus, Peter Haining notes a successful libel case prosecuted in early nineteenth-century London, in which a sausage maker recovered damages from the publisher of a broadside ballad for insinuating that he incorporated human flesh in his wares,[16] while Thomas Erle's memoirs recount the story of the vendor "who went the way of all piemen," and subsequently "afforded room for surmising that the expression that the deceased had 'gone the way of all flesh' was pregnant with unusual significance."[17] In what follows, I suggest that the horror evoked by stories of cannibalistic transgression served a function among lower-class theater audiences that transcended the entertainment value of sensationalism. For lower-class Victorians, representations of cannibalism did not help constitute the boundaries of "civilization" so much as they offered the frission of an escapist "what if," in which audiences simultaneously identified with the horror of the act *and* evoked a model of reverse assimilation that could parodically translate the norms of middle-class behavior into an alternative script for social interaction. By highlighting the disjunction between mainstream constructions of a self/other relationship founded on class and turning the colonial model of assimilation to its own advantage, the lower classes could highlight the systemic inequality of Victorian social structure. Far from generating anxiety for the Victorian poor, then, cannibalism worked to level the hierarchical terms that defined social identity in middle class culture.

"INTERNAL EVIDENCE": CANNIBALISM AND MELODRAMA

Perhaps the most compelling example of how the parallel between cannibalism and consumer culture was represented by lower-class Victorians occurs in the 1847 stage treatment of the Sweeney Todd story. Initially serialized in *The People's Periodical and Family Library* (1846) under the title *The String of Pearls: A Romance*, the story of Sweeney Todd was adapted for the stage by George Dibdin Pitt in 1847. Aimed almost exclusively at the lower-class audiences of the popular Royal Britannia Theatre in the East End of London, *The String of Pearls* presents a sensational and highly melodramatic picture of the "Barber Fiend of Fleet Street" who robs and murders his clients and then disposes of their corpses by recycling them through the pie shop next door. The story of Sweeney Todd has many possible sources in popular legend—among them the story of Sawney Beane (a Scottish cannibal), as well as numerous French versions which include, variously, murderous female barbers from the reign of Charles II, and a barber of the French Revolution era.[18] Although each of these source stories has its roots in the sensational broadside tradition, all are pointedly moral fables in which the barber's transgression is punished by a coercive state power such as the king or the police. However, in Victorian England—where versions of these tales were recirculated through the Penny press—the Sweeney Todd story was adapted for theatrical presentation as a melodrama to slightly different ends, with the Barber taking his own life to avoid punishment by the law.

While earlier versions of the Sweeney Todd story reinforce the value of an existing political hierarchy, the Victorian play's use of cannibalism calls this hierarchy into question. In part, this revision was a reflection of melodrama's interest in linking class to a transcendent moral code by associating poverty with "good" and wealth with "evil." In early examples of the genre, this meant that lower-class characters were pitted against aristocratic villains. When the middle class consolidated its political power in the Reform Act of 1832, however, aristocrats were often replaced by middle-class villains who helped focus a critique of the dominant culture's values.[19] Because of its apparently apolitical stance, critics have often regarded melodrama as a straightforward affirmation of simplistic values.[20] In the case of the Sweeney Todd story, however, we may see how melodrama helps reinforce the emerging distinction between private sentiment and public action that allowed the middle classes to separate themselves politically and socially from the lower classes. Far from shifting interest from class to the individual as some critics have averred,[21] melodrama articulates a lower-class response to bourgeois ideology. In fact, given the lower class's powerlessness to participate in the accepted public sphere of politics, the theater came to function as an alternative venue in which this group could express its frustration with the dominant culture.

In theater history, the pressures of individualism made themselves felt in the first decade of the nineteenth century when the Covent Garden Theatre—one of the two theaters in London legally sanctioned by royal patent to perform drama—was rebuilt and its prices raised. The resulting "OP" ("old price") wars were not just a reaction against higher prices; rather, they were a collective response to the experience of class stratification imposed on audiences by the prohibitively high admission prices and architecture of the new theater, which, to outraged patrons, seemed to enforce "the absolute seclusion of a PRIVILEGED ORDER from all *vulgar contact.*"[22] While public battles raged over changes to the "legitimate" theaters, the legal monopoly of the patent theaters was being silently undercut by taverns, saloons, and "illegitimate" theaters that began staging melodramas in order to get around the law. "Melo-drama," a French import that had come to prominence during the Revolution, soon found new footing in England where managers used its musical interludes to circumvent limitations on dramatic performance imposed by the patents. Illegitimate theaters subsequently stimulated the growth of distinctly lower-class forms of entertainment—particularly melodrama, whose popularity skyrocketed, eventually even displacing much "high" drama from the legitimate theaters. One such saloon-turned-theater was the Royal Britannia, located in Hoxton, which began staging musical entertainments in 1841 and subsequently became a recognized theater after the patent laws were repealed in 1843.

Unlike Covent Garden, the Royal Britannia catered to a working-class audience. "Besides prowlers and idlers" suggests Dickens's Uncommercial Traveller, "we were mechanics, dock-laborers, costermongers, petty tradesmen, small clerks, milliners, stay-makers, shoe-binders, slop-workers, poor workers in a hundred highways and byways."[23] Given that this type of audience prevailed, the Britannia retained an egalitarian character even after it was enlarged and remodeled in 1858. Further to the democratic nature of the theater's design, Dickens's Traveller emphasizes that, unlike the patent theaters and the Royal Italian Opera, the Britannia "has been constructed from the ground to the roof, with a careful reference to sight and sound in every corner."[24] Prices, too, reflected its accessibility, ranging from sixpence for a place in the upper stalls to one shilling for a reserved seat.[25] Also unlike the patent theaters—which were increasingly designed to segregate audience members according to class—the Britannia was a theater in which the seating arrangements reinforced one's sense of the drama as a collective experience. "We had all come together in a place where our convenience was well consulted," he suggests, "and where we were well looked after, to enjoy an evening's entertainment in common."[26] Thus, as the Traveller tells us, blandly understating the custom of Victorian audiences to interact vocally with plays, melodrama had the effect of consolidating a collective public response: "We all agreed (for the time) that honesty was the best policy, and we were as hard as iron upon Vice, and we wouldn't hear of Villainy getting on in the world—no, not on any consideration whatever."[27]

In Dickens's brief description of the relationship between audience and theatrical space at the Royal Britannia, we may see how the moral polarities of melodrama served to reinforce the spectator's sense of drama as a collective experience and the theater as an alternative public sphere in which mainstream morality was accepted "for the time" as a common point of reference. In effect, the simplicity of the sentiment evoked at the theater enabled audiences to partake of a common—if only fleetingly held—opinion and so be united as a community. Even as he satirizes the habits of lower-class theater patrons, then, Dickens drives home the importance of the theater as a communal space by drawing attention to the intimate relationship between the audience's opinion of the plays and the widespread consumption of sandwiches, "as substantial as was consistent with portability and as cheap as possible":

> we could never weep so comfortably as when our tears fell on our sandwich; we could never laugh so heartily as when we choked with sandwich; Virtue never looked so beautiful or Vice so deformed as when we paused, sandwich in hand, to consider what would come of the resolution of Wickedness in boots, to sever Innocence in flowered chintz from Honest Industry in striped stockings.[28]

Dickens's irony aside, the fact that this communal feast brings together two modes of consumption—the literal consumption of food and the metaphoric consumption of entertainment—suggests how popular melodrama served the lower classes in ways that are not reflected in dismissive appraisals of it as "mere" entertainment or in formulations that see it strictly in terms of middle-class notions of individualism. Further to this point one could argue that, far from reinforcing the mainstream conception of middle-class individualism—in which persons with superior talent and energy rise through their efforts—Victorian melodrama for the working classes focused instead on the more radical notion of individualism as a signifier of equality.

In its thematic use of polarities between good and evil, rich and poor, innocence and experience, the stage treatment of the Sweeney Todd story clearly falls within the tradition of popular stage melodrama. The play begins with Sweeney the "demon barber" undertaking to murder Mark Ingestere, who has just returned from the colonies with a priceless string of pearls for his sweetheart, who he can now afford to marry. In the course of his attempt to rob and murder Ingestere, Sweeney commits a series of acts that leave no room for us to doubt his character. However, despite the fact that he intimidates and lies to control those around him, Sweeney's plans are foiled by Jarvis Williams, the comedic baker who turns detective to expose the deceiving barber. In the final scene, Sweeney turns his razor against his own throat rather than submit to the law, and the young lovers are reunited as Ingestere emerges, unharmed, from the cellar beneath

Sweeney's shop. Like most melodramas of its period, *The String of Pearls* introduces extremes of moral transgression only to contain them by evoking a worldview in which good triumphs. Despite its apparent optimism about the power of innocence to conquer evil, however, the story of Sweeney Todd also introduces an uncomfortable sense of overlap between these apparently opposing terms by evoking a common trait—consumerism—that unites the villainous Sweeney and the valorous Ingestere. Both Sweeney and Ingestere are economic individualists able to turn circumstances to their advantage. While Ingestere moves up the ranks to captain a ship and garner colonial riches in India, however, Sweeney capitalizes on his innocuous position as a barber to rob and murder his patrons. Even so, the two are linked by association as capitalist "consumers" and the hero's surname—Ingestere—identifies him as an "ingester" of goods whose "capital" is embodied in the same string of colonial pearls that make him a target for Sweeney's consuming greed.

These implicit tensions between Ingestere and Sweeney are explicitly addressed through the act of cannibalism that occurs at a central moment in the play. The highly formulaic plotline typical of melodrama turns, in *The String of Pearls*, on the sensational discovery that Sweeney's victims have been converted into meat for Mrs. Lovett's pie shop. In *Letters From a Theatrical Scene-Painter*, Thomas Erle describes this situation as "a series of effects . . . produced by successive discoveries in the pies of what may be called 'internal evidence' of the true nature of their ingredients."[29] As Erle suggests, the process of discovery begins with a hair, which "is not viewed as a circumstance of much gravity, since it is a matter of common experience that long hairs have an intrusive tendency which induces them to present themselves in combinations with most alimentary substances." From the hair, we proceed to "a thumbnail:"

> which appears to give rise to some indistinct, but uneasy, misgivings in the breast of the consumer. He pursues his meal with reflective hesitation, and with a zest which has now been obviously impaired by the operation of disquieting mental influences. The startling revelation of a brass button attached to a fragment of material substance of some kind or other which bears the aspect of having once formed a constituent portion of somebody or other's leather breeches, proves what is called a 'staggerer,' and brings the repast to an abrupt and uncomfortable conclusion. The terrors of the scene culminate in the discovery of a full and detailed account of the whole matter set forth on the paper in which the pies had been wrapped.

The plot of "The String of Pearls" thus introduces cannibalism as a horrific dupe practiced on Mrs. Lovett's unwitting customers, a dupe which not only moves us from the familiar to the radically other—as an ordinary occurrence takes on ghastly dimensions—but also explores the collapse of familiar self and alien other by appealing to the idea of "common humanity" on a visceral level. Here, in effect, the moral opposition of good and evil that underpins the standard melodramatic plot is subordinated to a different binary register in a central dramatic "situation" that reverses the usual terms of the civilization/savagery pairing by making the "cannibal" an innocent victim of reckless consumerism.

The sensationalistic effect of watching Jarvis discover that he has been duped into an act of cannibalism under discomfortingly familiar circumstances was undoubtedly the primary goal of the proprietors of the Hoxton Britannia Theatre. The process of reading the "internal evidence" of the pies turns on the fact that we experience dawning knowledge along with the victim of the hoax and so relies, in effect, on our common experience of having ingested food products on faith. "The uncomfortable atmosphere of suspicion and distrust which already envelops the rations of opaque slime and gristle commonly known as mutton pies is amply sufficient of itself," Thomas Erle reminds us in his account of the play, "without the addition of further misgivings which might be suggested by *The Barber Fiend*."[30] By introducing cannibalism as an uncanny echo of a commonplace event, Pitt binds the audience's sympathies to the inadvertent cannibal who is also the victim of a vicious system of consumerism that knowingly sets out to deceive him. In this case it is not the cannibal consumer who poses a threat to civilization but rather the treacherous shopkeeper who values human life at so much per pound. Thus, through this reversal of the mainstream view of the lower classes as threatening other, the designation of the poor as cannibalistic "savages," is contested by the play's representation of unwitting "cannibals" as *victims* of capitalistic greed.

For patrons of the Royal Britannia, the play's reference to the adulteration of foodstuff would have struck a familiar note, as the lower classes were often at the mercy of unscrupulous shopkeepers throughout the early Victorian period.[31] Mrs. Lovett epitomizes the capitalist ethos when she explains the markup on a twopenny pie which consists of "a farthingsworth" of meat "and not an iota more" and "a halfpennyworth" of flour from Miller Brown, who, the interlocutor points out, "has nearby his mill certain cavities in the earth containing a certain white substance known as chalk" (37). The substitution of "fillers" in staple products such as flour, sugar, butter, coffee, and tea was, as Friedrich Engels suggests, a practice undertaken "with scandalous disregard for the ultimate consumer." As well, he points out, meat was typically "lean, old, tough, and partially tainted:" "It is the produce either of animals which have died a natural death or of sick animals which have been slaughtered."[32] For meat pie vendors, substandard meat was easily disguised by grinding and seasoning, as Henry Mayhew suggests in *London Labour and the London Poor*. "Piemen generally are not very particular about the flavor of the meat they buy," he tells us, "as they can season it up into anything."[33] In *The String of Pearls*, however, the cannibalization of Sweeney's victims takes corrupt shopkeeping to its most gruesome conclusion in order to demonstrate how economic individualism impacts on all of humanity, morally and physically. Significantly, Mrs. Lovett's customers are not just members of the lower classes; rather, they constitute a virtual cross-section of humanity. Thus, lawyers, clerks, shopkeepers, and laborers all flock together to partake of pies whose contents are similarly heterogeneous. This common "ground" of humanity not only demonstrates the problems implicit in attempts to designate the poor as other, but also invokes the melodramatic logic of good and evil to condemn a shopocracy that injures its customers through deceit.

Commonly evoked by the middle classes to define an ethnological other, cannibalism is thus turned to completely different ends in *The String of Pearls*, where it appeals to the human body as the final indicator of where, on a visceral level, one may begin to define what "common humanity" means. In this respect, Pitt's play challenges attempts to distinguish between classes based on a self/other model of difference by evoking the "internal evidence" of sameness—to borrow Erle's terms. In mounting this sort of critique, Pitt uses melodrama—the representational register of sentiment—as a way to evoke an emotional response to questions generally considered from a purely utilitarian perspective. By mapping the melodramatic opposition between good and evil onto the opposition between civilization and savagery and then applying this logic to shopkeepers rather than the poor, Pitt draws our attention to the moral questions at stake in the public sphere of business. In doing so, he counters the utilitarian discourse of the public sphere with an appeal to sentiment that reverses the threat posed by the emergence of the poor as a borderline "other." This critique of the traditional tendency to conflate the distinction between good and evil with the distinction between civilization and savagery not only gives the lower classes a common point of identification, it also implicitly criticizes the moral pretensions of middle-class individualism. Unlike mainstream representations of cannibalism—which typically invite us to examine with horror the actions of a depraved other—Sweeney Todd's sensationalistic effect relies on our identification with the act and, by implication, with a particular position on equality.

WHO IS SERVING WHOM? CANNIBALISTIC DOUBLE-TALK

The complex interrelationship between the moral absolutism of melodrama and the impulse to segregate self and other is addressed directly in Pitt's treatment of cannibalism in *The String of Pearls*, where melodrama challenges the underlying assumptions of middle-class individualism. Here, through a reversal of traditional definitions of self and other, the audience is encouraged to identify with the literal "cannibals" of the piece while the duplicity of shopkeepers stands in as a form of metaphoric cannibalism morally and physically dangerous to humanity. The play further takes up this theme through the character of the Demon Barber himself: a cold-blooded utilitarian who affects a sentimental side in order to deceive those around him. In this respect, Sweeney's duplicity—like the deceiving contents of Mrs. Lovett's pies—functions as an implicit commentary on the disjunction of public and private identity central to middle-class identity. Using the conventions of popular melodrama to challenge the contradictions implicit in bourgeois endorsements of laissez-faire economics and political inequality on the one hand and sentimental appeals to common humanity on the other, Pitt explores the rift between public and private ways of conceptualizing (and rationalizing) class difference.

In *The String of Pearls*, we see how melodrama can be used to contest a dominant middle-class political identity by drawing our attention to the contradictions implicit in this position. The fact that the ideal of open competition favored by the dominant classes was not consonant with the private virtue of sentiment was, as Friedrich Engels pointed out in 1844, a paradox worthy of discussion. Specifically, Engels noted that while the bourgeoisie "have all sorts of so-called 'private virtues,'" in their public lives "Every single human quality with which they are endowed is grossly debased by selfish greed and love of gain."[34] Sweeney himself is a caricature of middle-class economic acquisitiveness whose first action in the play is to try and cheat Ezekiel Smith, a skilled laborer, out of his fee. Smith has just completed building and installing the revolving barber chair that Sweeney will use to dispose of his victims, but rather than pay Smith on demand, Sweeney declares he is being "robbed." To this, Smith declares, "No robbery, Mr. Todd, only my just reward for labour" (9). Sweeney and Smith proceed to act out in microcosm the nineteenth-century relationship between labor and capital, haggling over the intangible value of work. Finally concluding that he dislikes Smith's "method of grabbing money," Sweeney resolves to "shave him close, shave him very close indeed" and pushes a doomed Smith into his chair (10). Even as this conversation between Sweeney and Smith sets up the economic focus of the play, it also clearly establishes that Sweeney's primary motivation in murdering people is greed. By his own confession he is a capitalist who subordinates all human values to his love of cash, even as he appropriates the language of sentiment to mask his actions. "When a boy," Sweeney tells us, "the thirst of avarice was first awakened by the fair gift of a farthing—that farthing soon became a pound—that pound a hundred pounds—so to a thousand pounds until I said to myself, I will possess a hundred thousand pounds."[35]

While Sweeney's attitude toward money makes him the perfect economic utilitarian, he achieves upward mobility by masking this impulse with an apparently overriding concern for the well-being of others. Appropriating the ethos of the sentimental middle class, Sweeney is the soul of benevolence when in the company of others. Thus, for example he answers the entreaties of his apprentice's mother—who earnestly reminds Sweeney "not to work 'im too 'ard" because "'E comes of a very 'dellikite' family"—by invoking the rhetoric of private sentiment (12). "I doubt if you would find a kinder more considerate employer in the length and breadth of London, let alone here in Fleet Street" he tells her, "I will treat your boy Tobias as I would my own son, my own flesh and blood" (13). Here, boundaries between public and private life are collapsed as Sweeney conflates the roles of employer and father. Yet, as appealing as this image may be, its real function is to deceive Tobias's mother, whose desire to emulate middle-class notions of respectability—expressed in the claim that her family is physically "dellikite"—places her son in jeopardy. Under the sentimental appeal to a "family" relationship, Tobias is subsequently bound as Sweeney's apprentice. No bargain, this, as Sweeney reminds Tobias when they are alone:

> Now remember this Tobias Ragg, remember it well. You are my apprentice and you have had of me board, lodging and washing . . . Save that you will take your meals at home, that you don't sleep here and that your mother gets up your linen. Now are you not a fortunate, happy dog? (13)

Sweeney's ability to deceive those around him thus turns on his ability to assume a mask of sentiment in order to cover up his real intentions. In his business dealings, too, Sweeney finds others like himself. Accordingly, when Tobias solves the mystery of the missing customers, Sweeney has him committed to an insane asylum run by Jonas Fogg, a keeper as duplicitous as himself. On the surface the exchange between Sweeney and Fogg is couched in the language of professional concern and private sentiment, yet most of what they say carries a sinister double meaning:

FOGG: Does he rave?

TODD: Oh yes, he does, and about the most absurd nonsense in the world. In fact, to hear him one would think that instead of being one of the most humane of men I was, in point of fact, an absolute murderer.

FOGG: A murderer?

TODD: Yes, a murderer to all intents and purposes a murderer. I ask you, Mr. Fogg, could anything in the world be more absurd than such an accusation? I, Sweeney Todd, who have the milk of human kindness flowing in every vein, who would not harm a single hair of the meanest of God's creatures.

FOGG: Quite, quite.

TODD: I, who would stoop to help the lame dog over the stile. Why my very appearance ought to be sufficient to convince anybody at once of my sweet and considerate disposition.

FOGG: As you say, Mr. Todd. Absurd that any person could mistake the sort of man you really are. (60)

Here, Fogg's bland response that it is "absurd" anyone could "mistake the sort of man you really are" undercuts Sweeney's protestations of goodwill. Subsequently, we learn that Fogg, too, is ruled by self-interest as the two men come to an "understanding" that Tobias will "die like Simkins . . . suddenly" (60). Always practical in these matters, Sweeney declares that this "is decidedly the best way, because it saves a good deal of trouble and annoyance to friends and relations, as well as preventing expense" (60). As a matter of course, Sweeney represents himself as a concerned and soft-hearted employer while exploiting, threatening, and abusing his apprentice; similarly, he murders his partner, Mrs. Lovett, even as he cajoles her with talk of sympathy and understanding. More importantly, Sweeney engages in an assumed rhetoric of cheerful solicitation with his customers—expressed in an often-repeated offer to "polish you off"—which conflates a posture of servitude with an incipient threat.

More than any other aspect of the play, Sweeney's dealings with his customers reflect the duplicity of his character. He affects the desire to serve only to turn this offer against the customer who unwittingly becomes an object of consumption. By engaging in a species of rhetorical prevarication Sweeney's solicitous promise to "polish you off" turns against the customers he would serve—much like the revolving barber chair used to dispense with his unwitting victims. As a result, Sweeney's love of money leads him to view his fellow men purely in terms of their commodity value; once he has robbed his victims, they are duly meted out to the customers of Mrs. Lovett's pie shop in "farthingsworth" portions. For Sweeney, the rhetoric of sentiment, like the rhetoric of servitude, becomes an elaborate form of double-talk in which the possibility of alien otherness lurking within seemingly benign familiarity is explored as a correlative of middle-class acquisitiveness. In his characterization of Sweeney, Pitt departs from the melodramatic convention of making the villain an aristocrat or powerful member of the bourgeoisie, characterizing him instead as an economic utilitarian rising from the lower orders in a perverted version of Smilesian self-help. In this respect Sweeney feeds his lust for personal gain by converting his customers into objects of consumption, espousing a coolly utilitarian view of circumstances worthy of the narrator of Swift's "A Modest Proposal" as he does. *The String of Pearls* thus uses the sensationalistic effect of cannibalism to knit together the double-talk of the Barber Fiend with a critique of what, to lower class audiences, was a hypocritical and duplicitous middle class.

By appealing to the moral and ethical assumptions that underpin the bourgeois ideal of the private individual, Pitt problematizes the middle-class construction of the lower class as barbaric other. In Sweeney Todd's Fleet Street, it is not the masses who constitute the threat of barbarity but rather the middle-class proprietors whose affectations of respectability and sentiment mask a calculating rationality that values human life at so much per pound. Sweeney himself emerges as the barber "barbarian" who resides in Fleet Street—the economic heart of the British empire—a man whose love of money leads him to turn against those he would serve. This representation of middle-class hypocrisy helps frame an alternate vision of society using the vocabulary of melodrama to reverse perceptions of the lower class as a scientifically quantified threat and place it instead as a victim of an economically driven dominant class. Despite this critique, however, the end of the *The String of Pearls* does not merely put forward a corrective reading to counter middle-class fantasies of the poor as other. Rather, the story of Sweeney Todd sets up a model of reverse assimilation through which the lower classes identify with cannibalism, not as an indicator of savagery, but as a way to challenge the binary distinctions characteristic of dominant culture.

If, ultimately, the lower-class audiences of *The String of Pearls* are presented with a critique of middle-class economic individualism through Pitt's portrayal of the Demon Barber and his "other" Mark Ingestere, they are also given a more successful example of how the cannibalistic ethos of the play might serve them in the example of Jarvis Williams. Jarvis, who shows up at Mrs. Lovett's pie shop looking for "a situation" in the second act, carries out the comic business of the piece, but he also provides an alternative social script for viewers. Unlike Ingestere and Sweeney—who adopt the values of bourgeois culture wholesale in order to get ahead—or Mrs. Ragg—who is assimilated to the abstract values of middle-class culture—Jarvis adapts the roles and languages of mainstream culture to his own ends. Thus while Sweeney affects a mask of sentiment to hide his real motivation, Jarvis recognizes "it's the conduct, it ain't the toggery that makes the gentleman" (48). Jarvis is, indeed, a man of action, breaking out of Mrs. Lovett's cellar bakery, rescuing Tobias from Jonas Fogg's asylum, and finally tracking Sweeney to his shop, where he turns the tables on the Barber by forcing him into his own chair. "As Shakespeare says," Jarvis exclaims, "we'll hoist him with his own petard" (84). While Jarvis is clearly on the side of good, however, he is not aligned with a fixed moral code. Thus Jarvis has neither the individualistic work ethic characteristic of Sweeney and Ingestere nor the fixed moral values associated with melodrama. Instead, he appeals to Mrs. Lovett for "some *light* employment" (48) and resists Tobias's plea that he not kill Sweeney because "'twould be murder" (84). In this respect, Jarvis represents a point of identification for the audience, and fittingly enough, it is he—the inadvertent cannibal, with whom the audience is identified—who expresses the cannibalistic alternative to assimilation by the dominant class. Throughout the play, Jarvis appropriates and adapts the language of mainstream culture for his own ends, as when he tells Tobias that "kiebosh" is "a word of Greek extraction, signifying the upset of the apple-cart" and "bunk" is "another Greek word and means G.O." (64). Jarvis's relationship to mainstream society is comic, yet it also demonstrates how dominant forms and representations can be assimilated to express an alternative to existing social scripts.

While *The String of Pearls* offers us an alternative view of cannibalism as a framework for expressing lower-class experience, it also demonstrates the problems implicit in political critiques based on tactics of assimilation. "Jarvis," for all his individual appeal, remains reliant on the norms he appropriates as do Sweeney, Ingestere, and Mrs. Ragg. Similarly, while theaters offered symbolic spaces in which lower-class audiences were free to imagine themselves released from the constraints of political reality, they also reinscribed the social distinctions endorsed by dominant culture. However, melodrama—as Elaine Hadley reminds us—is a duplicitous form, "both cannily subvert[ing] and unwittingly adopt[ing]" the institutionalized values it evokes.[36] Through its duplicitous participation in mainstream economies, then, melodrama, like cannibalism, draws our attention to the unstable boundaries between private and public spheres and allows us—as it did the Victorian lower classes—to imagine something beyond normative ideological positions.

NOTES

1. Michel de Montaigne, "Of Cannibals," *The Essays of Michel de Montaigne*, vol. 1, trans. Jacob Zeitlin (New York: Knopf, 1934), 181.

2. Maggie Kilgour, *From Communion to Cannibalism: An Anatomy of Metaphors of Incorporation* (Princeton, N.J.: Princeton UP, 1990), 4.

3. Gananath Obeysekere, "'British Cannibals:' Contemplation of an Event in the Death and Resurrection of James Cook, Explorer" in *Critical Inquiry* 15 (summer 1992): 638.

4. Obeyesekere, 653. For an excellent extended discussion of the tensions between literal and metaphoric representations of cannibalism in the tradition of western humanism see Maggie Kilgour, *From Communion to Cannibalism*.

5. Frank Lestringant, *Cannibals: The Discovery and Representation of the Cannibal From Columbus to Jules Verne*, trans. Rosemary Morris (Berkeley: University of California Press, 1997), 5.

6. Lestringant, 5.

7. The photographic typologies of Cesare Lombroso and Jean Martin Charcot are exemplary of this trend. For highly useful accounts of this movement, see Daniel Pick, *Faces of Degeneration: A European Disorder, 1848–1918* (Cambridge: Cambridge UP, 1993); Sander Gilman, *Difference and Pathology: Stereotypes of Sexuality, Race, and Madness* (Ithaca, N.Y.: Cornell UP, 1985); and Sander Gilman, *The Jew's Body* (New York: Routledge, 1991).

8. Quoted in Asa Briggs, *Victorian Cities* (Harmondsworth, Middlesex: Penguin, 1990, reprint), 315.

9. Benjamin Disraeli, *Sybil, or the Two Nations*, originally published in 1845 (Harmondsworth, Middlesex: Penguin, 1980), 96.

10. Walter Houghton, *The Victorian Frame of Mind* (New Haven, Conn.: Yale UP, 1957), 184–85.

11. Quoted in James E. Marlow, "English Cannibalism: Dickens After 1859," *Studies in English Literature* 23(1983): 650. Angus Easson makes a similar argument in "From Terror to Terror: Dickens, Carlyle and Cannibalism" in *Reflections on Revolution: Images of Romanticism*, ed. Alison Yarrington and Kelvin Everest (New York: Routledge, 1993), 96–111.

12. For an extensive discussion of the impact of Dickens's childhood experiences and his fear of cannibalism on his literary work, see Harry Stone, *The Night Side Of Dickens: Cannibalism, Passion, Necessity* (Columbus: Ohio State UP, 1994), 12–77. Marlow also makes the point, 648–49,

13. For an exhaustive description of cannibal imagery in Dickens's works see section 1 of Harry Stone's *The Night Side of Dickens*.

14. Marlow, 651–52. Anxieties about maintaining a strict division between "civilization" and "savagery" were strongly in evidence throughout the Victorian period as cases of survival cannibalism came to the forefront of the public imagination through journalistic tales of doomed explorers and shipwrecks. The Franklin case was just one such event, as were the later wrecks of the *Medusa* and the *Mignonette*. For a fascinating account of the court case involving survival cannibalism on the *Mignonette*, see A. W. Brian Simpson, *Cannibalism and the Common Law* (Chicago: University of Chicago Press, 1984).

15. Henry Mayhew, *London Labour and the London Poor, Selections*, ed. Victor Neuberg (Harmondsworth, Middlesex: Penguin, 1985), 95.

16. Peter Haining, *The Mystery and Horrible Murders of Sweeney Todd: The Demon Barber of Fleet Street* (London: Frederick Muller, 1979), 22.

17. Excerpt from Erle's 1880 *Letters From a Theatrical Scene-Painter* included in *The Golden Age of Melodrama: Twelve Nineteenth-Century Melodramas*, ed. Michael Kilgarriff (London: Wolfe, 1974), 270.

18. For more on sources for the Sweeney Todd story, see Peter Haining, *The Mystery and Horrible Murders of Sweeney Todd: The Demon Barber of Fleet Street* (London: Frederick Muller, 1979), 89–98; and E. S. Turner, *Boys Will Be Boys* (London: Michael Joseph, 1948), 38–39.

19. In "Victorian Melodrama and the Performance of Poverty," I take up this question in detail. See *Victorian Literature and Culture* 27/2 (summer 1999): 443–56.

20. Peter Brooks discusses the binary moral structure of melodrama in *The Melodramatic Imagination* (New Haven, Conn.: Yale UP, 1976), 15–17.

21. See, for example, M. Willson Disher, *Melodrama: Plots That Thrilled* (London: Rockcliff: 1954), xiii; Michael Booth, *English Melodrama* (London: Herbert Jenkins, 1965), 14; and Brooks, 11–12.

22. James Boaden, *The Life of John Philip Kemble*, quoted by Elaine Hadley in *Melodramatic Tactics: Theatricalized Dissent in the English Marketplace, 1800–1885* (Stanford, Calif.: Stanford UP, 1995), 40. Hadley's discussion of the motivation behind the OP wars in chap. 2 of *Melodramatic Tactics* is excellent, as is Marc Baer's more extended treatment in *Theatre and Disorder In Late Georgian London* (Oxford: Clarendon Press, 1992).

23. Charles Dickens, *The Uncommercial Traveller*, originally published 1861 (London: Chapman and Hall, 1907), 34. While Dickens's Uncommercial Traveller is a fictional persona, his descriptions of the Royal Britannia accord with Thomas Erle's description of this venue in *Letters From a Theatrical Scene Painter* (1880), as well as with another fictionalized account, A. L. Crawford's *Sam and Sallie* (1933).

24. Dickens, 32–33.

25. Haining, 77.

26. Dickens, 34.

27. Dickens, 36.

28. Dickens, 36–37.

29. Excerpt in Kilgarriff, 263-64.

30. Kilgarriff, 270.

31. In *The Condition of the Working Class in England*, trans. W. O. Henderson and W. H. Chaloner, (Oxford: Basil Blackwell, 1971), Friedrich Engels—whose primary aim is to condemn the British middle classes—examines the relationships between food quality, availability, and workers' hours and pay schedules, noting that the lower classes are "in no position to be particular," 82–83. Engels's findings are confirmed by Edwin Chadwick's conservative *Report on the Sanitary Condition of the Labouring Population of Great Britain*, originally published in 1842 (Edinburgh: Edinburgh UP, 1965), 311–14, as well as by Henry Mayhew's journalistic survey in *London Labour and the London Poor* (1851–52), 15–16, 68–100.

32. Engels, 80.

33. Mayhew, 96.

34. Engels, 311.

35. George Dibden Pitt, *Sweeney Todd*, adapted by Brian J. Burton (Birmingham: Combridge Jackson, 1962), 21. All published versions of *A String of Pearls* derive from the 1883 Dick's Acting Edition. Subsequent references are to Burton's adaptation and will be included in the text.

36. Hadley, 12.

7

From Caliban to Cronus: A Critique of Cannibalism as Metaphor for Cuban Revolutionary Culture

SANTIAGO COLÁS

Talking about cannibalism in Latin America means talking about the word much more than the thing. The word itself was coined by Christopher Columbus during his first voyage to the Caribbean in 1492, with the thing nowhere in sight. It seems he heard, or rather thought he heard, his native guides refer to a ferocious, man-eating people of the West Indies, as *canibales* ("cannibals"). Turns out they said *caribes* ("Caribs"), but no matter. Columbus filed his report, without ever having laid eyes on a scene of humans eating human flesh, and the word *canibales* began its long adventure through the modern European languages with the definition "man-eating savages" stuck to it like a bad habit.[1] The word did some hard work for Europeans in the centuries that followed, figuring prominently in the rhetorical justification for their genocidal annihilation of the native peoples they encountered in the New World. After all, if those people were cannibals, humans who ate other human beings, weren't they beyond salvation? Didn't their very continued existence threaten the coherence of the Europeans' civilizing mission in the Americas?

Cannibalism might have been nothing more than an episode in the long and sad marriage between European misnaming and European violence in the New World. Might have been, that is, had the negative value assigned the word—though never its meaning—not been forcefully and eloquently contested by New World writers. Confronting the European image of an aggressive, barbarous native, these writers saw not a threat but rather a word that summed up an equally long history of New World resistance to violent imposition of European norms upon the region. Where Europeans saw a savage threat, these writers recognized European fear and vulnerability. They found in cannibalism the limits to Europe's capacity to contain, assimilate, or indeed, destroy the resistant societies of the region.

Already in the 1920s, a group of Brazilian poets and artists rallied behind the *Manifiesto antropófago* of Oswald de Andrade. They looked to turn the European yarns of man-eating savages from a source of shame and embarrassment into a revered pedigree of fearless anti-imperialist violence. To be sure, these Brazilian poets didn't eat any European poets. Not really, but then, as I said, the story of cannibalism in Latin America is always more the story of the word than of the thing. No, they were speaking figuratively. They were calling for a cannibalism of European cultural norms. The Brazilian *anthropofagist* poets saw in the history of Latin American culture a slavish consumption and obedient regurgitation of European models in art and literature—a cultural force-feeding *ad nauseum*. And they sought to transform that act of consumption into an aggressive, willful means of nourishment, strength, and creativity.[2]

The Brazilian *anthropofagists*, however, were an avant-garde cultural group, isolated from any accompanying anti-imperialist mass movement through which their artistic practices might have struck roots in reality and for which these practices might have served as some kind of galvanizing symbol. Like their counterparts in the European avant-garde, the social potential they hoped to unlock was preempted by the emergence of local varieties of anticommunist fascism. Only after World War II, when revolutionary independence movements rose up and took power in Africa and Asia, did their vision gain a second life. The nations of Latin America had gained independence from Spain and Portugal, with few exceptions, in the early nineteenth century. Nevertheless, their national histories had unfolded under the vigilant, often violent, control of English and United States imperialism. Because of this, anti-imperialism elsewhere in the Third World struck a chord among the many Latin Americans aware that their miserable material conditions derived from the same imperialist yoke being sloughed off by people elsewhere in the Third World. The apex of this postwar, self-conscious movement in Latin America was reached in Cuba, in 1959, with the seizing of power by Fidel Castro's revolutionary

26th of July Movement. While decolonization continued in Africa throughout the 1960s, the Cuban revolution inspired other revolutionary anti-imperialist movements throughout Latin America, including Brazil, where a new generation of Brazilian artists, especially filmmakers, found inspiration in the work of the *anthropofagist* poets of the 1920s.

Meanwhile, at the end of the 1960s, in a development not directly influenced by the Brazilians, a group of Caribbean writers, perhaps infused with the fervor of mass revolutionary movements in their region, took up their pens to transform the European images of cannibalism that had so long defined the area's people. The immediate foil for this effort was Shakespeare's *Tempest*, written in 1611. Shakespeare's last play, and apparently informed by reports of the New World circulating in the England of his time, *The Tempest* centered around the efforts of Prospero, a former Duke of Milan usurped by his brother, to regain his power from his base of operations on a tropical island suspiciously resembling those of the West Indies. That island already had two inhabitants when Prospero and his daughter Miranda arrived, twelve years before the start of the play's action. Ariel, an immigrant like Prospero himself, is a fairy spirit with magical powers whom Prospero freed from a witch's hex upon his arrival. In return, Ariel serves Prospero as his indentured servant, performing a variety of magical functions in the hope of one day gaining the freedom Prospero has promised him. The only native inhabitant of the island is Caliban, son of that same witch. Somehow deformed and not quite human-looking, Caliban, who possesses a survivalist's intimate knowledge of the island's natural resources, is—in the long tradition of European colonialism— enslaved by Prospero and taught to use language.

It was Caliban that modern Caribbean writers sought to assume as their symbol of revolutionary anti-imperialist culture. And the model, indeed, seemed a perfect one. To begin with, Caliban's name is an anagram of cannibal. Since "cannibal" had been Columbus' misnomer for the Carib natives of the West Indies, Caliban seemed to these writers a figure for their own ancestors. Beyond this, however, they found in Caliban's rebelliousness—he plots, unsuccessfully, Prospero's assassination—a symbol for the insurgency of their own time. Finally, and perhaps most pertinently to these writers, Caliban, in a famous exchange, formulated perhaps the first instance of Caribbean cultural anti-imperialism. Reminded by Prospero, in the course of a threatening harangue, that he owes his use of language to the former, Caliban replies: "You taught me language, and my profit on't / Is, I know how to curse. The red plague rid you / For learning me your language!"[3] This perfectly summed up both the history of European cultural imperialism and the preferred stance of revolutionary intellectuals to that history. There was, to be sure, no unlearning the language of Prospero, but perhaps, like the Brazilian *anthropofagists* before them, that language could be turned against him. What better place to begin than with Shakespeare, the very epitome of western civilization? And what better place to begin in Shakespeare than *The Tempest*, wherein Shakespeare himself offered the ammunition for such a turnabout? In this way, the Caribbean rewritings of *The Tempest*—to which I will be referring as "Calibanism"—both called for the assumption of Caliban as a symbol of Caribbean insurgency and exemplified that attitude and practice for which they called.

The Martinican poet Aimé Césaire's *Une Tempête: Adaptation de "La Tempête" de Shakespeare pour un théâtre nègre* (A Tempest: Adaptation of "The Tempest" by Shakespeare by a Negro Theatre) was written in 1969. In the same year, the Barbadian Edward Brathwaite dedicated a poem in his volume *Islands* to Caliban. And in Cuba, the poet and essayist Roberto Fernández Retamar published an essay "Cuba hasta Fidel" ["Cuba until Fidel"], which identified Cuban revolutionary culture with Caliban. Two years later, inspired by post World War II political developments, including, of course, the Cuban revolution and by the emergence of a pan-Caribbean cultural consciousness exemplified by the Calibanist writing of the late 1960s, Retamar elaborated the work of this 1969 essay into a short book entitled *Calibán: Apuntes sobre la cultura en nuestra América* (Caliban: Notes Toward a Discussion of Culture in Our America).

Retamar's book ends with an abrupt shift from description to prescription, from a history of Calibanist culture in Latin America to a proposal for the transformation of intellectual activity in the revolution. Referring to revolutionary fighter Ernesto "Che" Guevara's 1959 address at the University of Las Villas, Retamar writes: "He proposed to Ariel, through his own most luminous and sublime [*aéreo*] example if ever there was one, that he seek from Caliban the honor of a place in his rebellious and glorious ranks."[4] By this point in the book, we've learned already that, in Retamar's *dramatis personae*, Caliban represents the rebellious *mestizo* masses of Latin America, and Ariel the region's intellectuals, fluttering nervously between fearful submission to the will of imperial masters and humble subordination to their fellow-slaves, the revolutionary majority. In that case, Retamar proposes that intellectuals place their skills in the interests of the revolutionary masses.

With this proposal, Retamar self-consciously renews the challenge issued by Marx at the beginning of the revolutionary marxist tradition in the eleventh of his famous theses "Concerning Feuerbach": "The philosophers have only *interpreted* the world, in various ways; the point is to change it."[5] Retamar, like Marx before him, calls on intellectuals to become active and practical. And though Marx does not there explicitly invoke revolution, we know that for an intellectual to change the world, in his eyes, meant, to join "the revolutionary class, the class that holds the future in its hands."[6] For Retamar too the precondition for a transformation of intellectual activity was to repudiate the bourgeois imperial master and humble themselves before the class of the future. Only with this change in attitude and class affiliation could intellectuals begin to transform the product of their activity from interpretation to real, concrete social change. Marx and Retamar outline the conditions necessary for intellectuals to go beyond producing texts and to start producing real human freedom.

In a fairly straightforward way, Retamar joined his Caribbean counterparts, Césaire and Brathwaite, in adopting the imperialist representation of Caliban and turning it to anti-imperialist ends. Retamar's final vision can be seen as a rewriting of the end of Shakespeare's *Tempest*. That text, of course, ends with the success of Prospero's plan for regaining his dukedom. As for Caliban, his hopes for freedom are dashed when Ariel snitches and then gratefully accepts the long-awaited freedom offered by Prospero in return for his intelligence work. Retamar thus, as might be expected, cannibalizes Shakespeare in the name of revolutionary culture. In so doing, he formally fills the prescription with which his text ends. Or does he?

Actually, Retamar's meal doesn't go down so easily. One might say his eyes were too big for his stomach, or something along those lines. For though Shakespeare's *Tempest* provides the metaphorical main course of *Caliban*, Retamar helps himself to numerous other selections from the menu of Latin American cultural history. Foremost among these are Guevara and that other great hero from the pantheon of the Cuban revolution, the late nineteenth century poet, journalist, and revolutionary fighter José Martí. Their importance to Retamar may well seem predictable given their ideological weight in the propaganda of the Cuban revolution. But their role can be justified on more substantive grounds as well. Martí and Guevara both embodied precisely the vision with which Retamar ends his text. Both were white, middle-class intellectuals who, at a certain moment, subordinated the traditional aims of intellectual life to the urgent demands of a mass revolutionary movement. But as such, one might expect that Retamar's use of them would be less cannibalistic, in the aggressive, subversive sense of the term, than his approach to Shakespeare.

In fact, however, Retamar can't seem to keep his appetite under control. As Retamar notes in the section leading up to his final passage, Martí wrote, in his 1891 essay *Nuestra América* (Our America), that "The European university must yield to the American university."[7] Elsewhere in the same text, Martí asserted that "the imported book has been vanquished in America by the natural man."[8] Retamar, earlier in *Caliban*, reconstructed these two passages as equivalents, speaking of Martí's "violent rejection of the imposition of Prospero ('the European university [,] . . . the European book[,] . . . the Yankee book'), which *must yield* to the reality of Caliban ('the [Latin] American university[,] . . . the Latin American enigma')."[9] There is, the reader may have noticed, a slight slip—whose significance I shall discuss below—in Retamar's gloss on Martí's two passages. Where Martí claimed that the "imported book" *already* had been vanquished by the natural man in Latin America, Retamar's coupling of the two passages and his omissions (marked by the ellipsis in his own text), connects the two terms of the equation via the imperative ("must yield") that Martí only uses in reference to the European and American university. There is, moreover, a slip in his own transposition of this dual equation into the final passage of the book, in which the "European university" is represented not by Prospero, as earlier, but rather by Ariel.

As for Guevara, while it is true that, in citing his university address, Retamar refers to his exemplary character, he describes it, curiously enough given the web of *Tempest* references, as "*aéreo*" (translated as "sublime" but carrying primary meanings of "aerial" or, figuratively, "elevated"). To affirm what we might think of as the Arielist dimension of Guevara's life's work in the midst of affirming the latter's Calibanist humility seems striking. With regard to both Guevara and Martí, the significance and force of their call for a practical intellectual work can only be grasped in the context of their embodiment of that call. Both lived as thinkers—though neither only as a thinker—and died as revolutionaries. Though tragic, and by no means essential, it is their deaths, or at least the practical revolutionary activity which led to their deaths that confers on their *words*, their *texts*, a transformative potential. Through their lives they literally transformed the aim of intellectual activity from the production of texts to the production of human freedom.

The problem, as I said, appears to be that Retamar's cannibalism goes too far. In adding Martí and Guevara into his revolutionary recipe, Retamar devours precisely what was revolutionary in their lives: namely, the unity of theory and practice, or that aspect of their lives' activity that went beyond their texts. If Martí and Guevara lived to end the text, or to transform it into revolutionary practice, then Retamar, no doubt unwittingly and in the service of the most laudable of themes, formally transforms their revolutionary practice into a text. In this sense, the end of Retamar's *Caliban* is now, paradoxically, also the end of Caliban, as a figure for the revolutionary transformation of intellectual practice. He goes from the indigestible, intractable revolutionary force before which intellectual Ariel has only the choice of betrayal or affiliation to an entirely unpalatable second course. Like those Warner Brothers cartoons in which Wile E. Coyote looks at the racing, elusive roadrunner and freezes him in his imagination as a plucked, beheaded platter of poultry, the intransigent Caliban has been literally transformed into mere food for thought.

But it may not be Retamar's fault after all. It may be that cannibalism isn't such a healthy regimen for revolutionary cultures. To begin with, insofar as cannibalism comes to stand for a *critical* and *active* interpretive practice it depends upon the illusion of a degraded alternative: something like passive, slavish consumption and imitation. This is what the Brazilian *anthropofagists* thought they were supplanting with their new aesthetic in the 1920s, and it is what the Caribbean Calibanists thought they were ending in the 1960s. But as Retamar's own citation of Martí and Guevara suggests, even the most humble and reverentially intended quotation involves, at least on an unconscious level, an aggressive, possessive rewriting; a remaking of the original text in one's own image. The difference lies, in that case, not between cannibalism and consumption but between consumption that self-consciously emphasizes its transformative relationship to the consumed and consumption that complacently or naively accepts its illusion of pure imitation. But in both cases, one can no more read a literary text and leave it unaffected by the process than one can be said to have eaten a meal without digesting it.

But in its other attractive dimension as well, cannibalism leaves something to be desired where revolutionary culture is concerned. For coexisting with the aggressive, active resistance implicit in the eating of one's enemy goes a wishful identification, a desire to be the enemy, or at the very least a desire to take on his or her perceived strengths.[10] Moreover, whatever desires *drive* cannibalism, its material effect, in fact, is to blur the boundaries separating the cannibal and his or her victim. The food and the cannibal literally become one. The difficulties that this dynamic presents for a political or cultural project predicated on the firm distinction between imperialist oppressors and heroic revolutionaries should be obvious. That such distinctions are not so stable as we might like already seems clear from the shifting categories in Retamar's work, in which for example

Guevara appears first under the heading of Caliban (14) and later as the greatest Ariel that ever lived (45).[11] And it may be revealed in the apparently casual slip in Retamar's double use of Martí's quote about the European and American universities. In Retamar's text, via the recurrent citation, Prospero is replaced by Ariel. But since Ariel should seek to identify with Caliban, then does the substitution mean that Prospero too should seek to identify with Caliban? Finally it's hard to know what makes Caliban distinct as Caliban anymore once he's eaten everyone on the island.[12] And indeed, this is precisely the conclusion we drew from Retamar's text: that by the end of it, Caliban has vanished, and its hard to tell who ate who.

But the popularity of so ill-suited a metaphor among anti-imperialist intellectuals in this period must have been something other than just a careless mistake. And so, indeed, it was. Cannibalism became the choice metaphor precisely because (and not in spite of) its internal ambivalences and contradictions. For these last permitted the expression, in the midst of the most ringing black-and-white denunciations of imperialist culture and calls for anti-imperialist cultural resistance, of the ambivalence that necessarily accompanies the intellectual writing in the situation of Third-World revolution. In that case, we might say that where cannibalism may not be so healthy for revolutionary culture, it may be just what the doctor ordered for intellectuals in a revolutionary situation.

Consider Retamar's performance at the 1968 Cultural Congress of Havana, a gathering of major intellectuals and artists from around the globe. Retamar presided over the commission on the "responsibility of intellectuals with respect to the problems of the underdeveloped world." Retamar was confronted with the thorny—but apparently not particularly troubling—presence of the Trinidadian marxist C. L. R. James, who openly criticized the luxurious treatment of delegates to the congress and the exclusive nature of the meeting. James proposed, moreover, "that all intellectuals, those from the developed world as well as those from the underdeveloped world, should be firmly discouraged, and in fact abolished as a force" and, later, "that the function of this Congress is that intellectuals should prepare the way for the abolition of the intellectuals as an embodiment of culture."[13] This certainly sounds as though it should be Calibanist music to Retamar's ears. Retamar, however, could only lamely respond, with the anonymity and passivity of bureaucracy, "the Preparatory Committee of the Congress cannot, at this late stage, hope to reform the situation" and that "a redefinition of the intellectual could not be undertaken in the Commmission." Only a year later Retamar would write "Cuba hasta Fidel," one of the three Caribbean Calibanist works that would inspire his own *Caliban* in 1971. To understand Retamar's ambivalence as something other than personal idiosyncrasy, or worse, hypocrisy, it is important to grasp the nature of the problem of intellectual culture in the Cuban revolution in fuller dimension, both historically and in terms of the military and political discourse on which it modeled itself.

Ambivalence characterized the rhetoric of revolutionary leaders in every sphere nearly from the beginning, and was particularly marked in the sphere of revolutionary intellectual culture.[14] For example, in his June 1961 "Words to the Intellectuals" ("Palabras a los intelectuales"), Fidel Castro defined the two necessary, and in his view inseparable, axes of revolutionary art: that it should be produced "for the great exploited masses of the people" (since for a revolutionary, "whatever is good for them will be good for us; whatever is noble, useful, beautiful for them will be noble, useful, beautiful for us") and that it should be produced with the future in mind.[15] Castro envisioned an intellectual revolutionary vanguard, modeled on the military and political revolutionary vanguard (e.g., 279) which would identify its interests with those of the people, indeed, which was essentially defined by its identification with the people.[16] At the same time, Castro explained that the people's cultural level was very low and that the revolutionary intellectual should try to make "all cultural manifestations reach the people" just as the revolutionary government was trying to bring "material goods" to people that had only known "hunger." The young Karl Marx may have captured the double logic of Castro's discourse in his reproach to Hegel: "it is of no use to pretend that the gulf does not exist when we prove the contrary by the very act of leaping over it."[17] Just as with *Caliban* the overt pretension that intellectuals must identify with the revolutionary masses conceals (and then elsewhere reveals) a relief in knowing that, in fact, intellectuals are not identical to those masses.

In Castro's case, over and beyond the fact that he draws a formal circle within which only intellectuals are admitted (just like the organizers of the Cultural Congress), invariably the "we" as grammatical subject refers to the revolutionaries (and those intellectuals—Ariels—who want to join the revolution); meanwhile, "the people"—Caliban—who are supposed to be the subject of the revolution become the predicate whose essence it is to need to be led. They are the poor in economic terms, the disenfranchised in political terms, and the ignorant or coarse in cultural terms. It is those people who appear as "the great unredeemed mass" in the climactic paragraphs of "History Will Absolve Me" ("La historia me absolverá"), Castro's closing argument in his defense at his 1953 trial for the raid of the

Moncada army barracks (37).[18] They appear again as the target of the condescending moral and political arrogance of *foquismo*, the military theory enshrined as mythology by Che Guevara and Régis Debray, according to which an already purified guerrilla *foco* (focal point) gets as far away from the people as possible to light a spark of revolutionary consciousness in some remote rural province.[19] In this way, the degradation of "the people" as an inert mass that requires a catalyst becomes the necessary, and unconsciously desired, precondition for revolutionary transformation—a precondition that had to remain hidden from the revolutionary vanguard to ensure they would carry out their mission. As Guevara wrote in his instruction manual for guerrilla fighters, "The peasant must always be helped technically, economically, morally, and culturally. The guerrilla fighter will be a sort of guiding angel who has fallen into the zone."[20]

A fetish—as in Marx's fetishism of the commodity—springs from the need to repress, to remain ignorant of, or to misrecognize conditions of production, in this case, those of the revolutionary vanguard itself.[21] Here, the fetishized object is the future as the "end" of Castro's speech (in every sense of the "end"), just as the future was the repository into which Castro dramatically placed his own fate in 1953—"Condemn me, no matter, history will absolve me!"[22] It is also the future to which, in 1965, Che Guevara deferred mass participation in the government of the revolution: "A new generation is being born. The party is a vanguard organization. The best workers are proposed by their fellow workers for admission into it. It is a minority, but it has great authority because of the quality of its cadres. Our aspiration is that the party will become a mass party, but only when the masses have reached the level of the vanguard."[23] Castro delivered the fate of the entire Third World to this future in his 1967 speech "Waves of the Future": "OLAS is the interpreter of tomorrow's history, interpreter of the future, because OLAS is a wave of the future, symbol of the revolutionary waves sweeping a continent of 250 million. This continent is pregnant with revolution. Sooner or later, it will be born. Its birth may be more or less complicated, but it is inevitable."[24] And were the continent to die during this delivery, it would have been in the noble service of advancing the patrilineage. The future once again becomes a fetishized object—both "sensuous and suprasensible." In reality, the product of human sensuous activity in the present, the future in its fetishized form becomes a (pre-)destination, a suprasensible god to which must be sacrificed whatever does not measure up in the present. Finally, this same future appears, not only in Retamar's shift to the prescriptive mode at the end of *Caliban*, but in his cannibalizing transformation of Martí's declaration that the imported book *had already been* vanquished by the natural man in Latin America into a double wish for the future: that the European university and the imported book should yield to the American university—not to the natural man, by the way. Words to the intellectuals, indeed.

But if the early rhetoric of the revolution safely deposited a real transformation of the relationship between vanguard and mass in an as-yet unrealized future, how did these same figures deal with the simple passage of time, with the actual historical unfolding of the future in the present? On January 2, 1968, in the midst of the Cultural Congress of Havana, Fidel Castro delivered a speech with two crucial, apparently disconnected, but in fact closely related, announcements: the first introduced gasoline rationing and the second declared 1968 to be the "Year of the Heroic Guerrilla." Both statements, and the fact that they were made in the same speech, were symptomatic of dimensions of the Cuban revolution of complex importance to establishing the context in which Retamar conceived his Calibanism.

To understand this relationship it is necessary to go back to October 1962.[25] By this time, the United States government's diplomatic, economic, and military assault on Cuba was in full swing, and Cuba had already established its alliance with the Soviet Union which, Cuba hoped, would both help to defend Cuba against American aggression and take up the economic slack caused by the American trade embargo. But because the Soviets had failed to consult Castro in their resolution of the missile crisis, and because that resolution, in effect, diminished Soviet defensive support of Cuba, October 1962 marks the beginning of a period in which Cuba sought to assert its autonomy from the Soviet Union.

The principal lever employed for this push-away was guerrilla warfare. Between 1962 and 1968, Cuba actively promoted and supported guerrilla movements throughout the Third World and Latin America. Havana became the headquarters for Third-World armed revolutionary insurgency. Thus, the first Tricontinental Congress, held in Havana January 3–15, 1966, produced two new international organizations: the Organización de Solidaridad de los Pueblos de Africa, Asia y América Latina (OPSAAAL) and the Organización Latino Americana de Solidaridad (OLAS). Castro's government supplied guerrilla groups in Latin America with arms, money, and aid. Because the Soviets had been seeking to develop relations with Latin American governments so as to ensure good working environments for their communist parties in the region, Cuba's actions directly antagonized the superpower.

The antagonism was deepened in March 1967 when Castro criticized the Soviet-bloc nations for maintaining diplomatic and economic relations with Latin American governments. Later, Castro rejected a Soviet request to attend the first OLAS conference in July 1967. Meanwhile, in April, the Cuban government published Che Guevara's "Message to the Tricontinental," which while obviously primarily attacking United States' imperialism, also was aimed at the passivity of the Soviets and their communist parties in the Third World. Che famously called for "two, three, many Vietnams."[26] Indeed Che's earlier outspoken criticism of the Soviet's quietist policy toward the Third World undoubtedly exacerbated tensions and contributed to his leaving Cuba to advance the project of Third World revolution and led to his attempt, with Castro's support, to establish a *foco*, or cell, in Bolivia in late 1966.

Foquismo theory offered a strategy whereby a tremendously outnumbered and outarmed rebel guerrilla group could win a military victory over the armed forces of the state, even where "objective" conditions for revolution were not yet present. It rested on the beliefs, first, that throughout the Third World, a repressed rural peasantry (more than an urban proletariat) would provide the mass support for the revolution and, second, that military operations by a small vanguard could bring about such "objective" conditions. The *foco* installs itself in the "wildest and most impenetrable places."[27] Only after a "fortunate blow" is struck, does the *foco* begin to propagandize among the peasants, articulating their immediate needs and demands with the larger exigencies of the national revolution. It may have been true, as we shall see, that this image—of the *foco* as a self-igniting spark rapidly setting an entire nation afire—was a mythologization of the actual process of the Cuban revolutionary struggle. Nevertheless, it was a symbolic image that provided for very real effects in terms of dramatizing the agency of the Third-World subject. Cuba's emerging importance as one center—perhaps along with Vietnam—of what George Katsiaficas has called "the global imagination of the New Left"[28] seemed guaranteed.

But Cuba's dramatic attempts to establish its independence from the Soviets were severely set back by two events in late 1967. First, the Soviets, incensed with the intractability of their Latin American ally, turned a slowdown in their own domestic production of oil into the disciplinary mechanism of a cutback in deliveries to Cuba. Then, on October 8, 1967, Guevara was captured by United States–trained Bolivian rangers. The next day he was executed. While Castro still had one more barb for the Soviets—the expulsion to Moscow of Aníbal Escalante and eight other members of the Communist Party for "microfactionalist activities," economic realities prevailed, and Castro was forced to capitulate, by with-drawing support for the Latin American guerrillas, on the one hand and, on the other hand, supporting the Soviet invasion of Czechoslovakia in the wake of the Prague Spring.

These are the threads of historical events that Castro knotted together in his double announcement on January 2, 1968. The initiation of gasoline rationing, while couched in the rhetoric of defending the revo-lution and Cuban autonomy, tacitly acknowledged Cuba's economic dependence on the Soviets. That it should have been the major substance of a speech marking the ninth anniversary of the revolution only under-scores the inevitable importance to Castro of these economic links. At the same time, the declaration of 1968 as the "Year of the Heroic Guerrilla," while honoring Che and symbolically extending his legacy and thus fur-ther defying the Soviets, was at the same time, again tacitly, an acknowl-edgment that the celebrated illusion of a *foquista* Latin American revolution had been punctured. The government's own repudiation of guerrilla warfare on the continent only drove home, with the force of materiality, that acknowledgment.

I am anxious, in this era when smirking I-told-you-so's to marxism have become the vogue on both the left and the right, among intellectuals and in the popular press, to situate my own criticism of Retamar's utopian Calibanist vision. The quarter century that has passed since the publica-tion of *Caliban* has seen fierce right-wing military regimes and paramili-tary death squads, the triumph and decline of the Sandinista revolution in Nicaragua, the redemocratization of most of the region under the aegis of United States–sponsored free trade zones, the rebellion of the *Ejército Zapatista de Liberación Nacional* (EZLN) in Chiapas in southern Mexico, and, of course, the increasing isolation of Cuba in the hemisphere (though not internationally where the United States government's clumsy attempts to impose unilaterally an international trade embargo to strangle the Castro regime have been met by stubborn resistance, albeit a resistance itself waged in the name of free-market capitalism). Given this moment in regional history, and the larger conjuncture of the history of the interna-tional class struggle of which it forms a part, it appears as equally perilous and vital—both intellectually and practically—for leftist academics to continue serious critical engagement with the visions generated by revolu-tionary societies.

Retamar's *Caliban* was one such vision. In some ways, it was the definitive cultural vision emerging from the heady period of hopes and ambitious social enterprises known as the era of the Cuban revolution in

Latin America. Together with the so-called "boom novel" (those famous epics of Mario Vargas Llosa, Carlos Fuentes, Julio Cortázar, and, of course, Gabriel García Márquez), the testimonial narrative that emerged directly from the Cuban revolution, and the substantial body of scholarship in political economy known as "dependency theory," Retamar's essay must stand as one of the crucial documentary links to a recent past that seems, from certain perspectives at any rate, impossibly far removed from our own present.

To critically review such a document today is far from an attempt to restore in flesh and blood a collective enterprise probably ill-suited for our times. Rather, it might be understood as an effort to resuscitate the utopian dimensions of the epoch while soberly forcing the text to admit its errors and ideological slips. We certainly should remember, as Fredric Jameson has recommended, "that Utopian visions are not yet themselves a politics."[29] But we should remember this, especially, because, as he further suggests, it is

> the limits, the systemic restrictions and repressions, or empty places, in the Utopian blueprint that are the most interesting, for these alone testify to the ways a culture or a system marks the most visionary mind and contains its movement toward transcendence. But such limits, which can also be discussed in terms of ideological restriction, are concrete and articulated in the great Utopian visions: they do not become visible except in the desperate attempt to imagine something else; so that a relaxed consent to immanence—a consciousness in advance of the necessary failure of the project that leads us to renounce it—can yield no experimental information as to the shape of the system and its boundaries, the specific social and historical fashion in which an outside is unattainable and we are turned back in on ourselves.[30]

At any rate, as Jameson himself has persuasively argued, disdainful rejections of utopian visions in advance—as fatally flawed by virtue of their totalizing impulses—bear an unsavory historical provenance of their own. I'm talking about the Cold War in which, through a profoundly damaging ideological conjuring trick, any attempt to think the concept of totality or to act in the service of the struggle for total human happiness was transformed into a threatening impulse toward totalitarianism. My critique of Retamar's *Caliban*, and of Calibanism, in general seeks to steer between the Scylla of such facile Cold War denunciations and the Charybdis of uncritical leftist celebrations of all things made in revolutionary Cuba.

And so we hit the punchline, the real historical and material limitations shattering the stirring poetic vision of Calibanism. A revolution that had begun, as James for one knew, not through the spark of a mythologized vanguard *foco*, but through the historical preparedness and spirit of self-sacrifice of the vast majority of the Cuban population; a revolution that unfolded not according to bureaucratic masterplans, but rather—again as James saw—in the dialectical give-and-take between the struggle for happiness of its driving popular force and the essentially planless respect for and responsibility to that struggle of its leaders; this inspiring revolution had, by 1968, begun to freeze over into a sclerotic, minor dependency on the Soviet Union. Its leaders idealistically enchanted themselves with their own fatally contradictory dream of their identification with a people whose real, material role in the revolution they never concretely acknowledged and whose desires they consistently repressed. This is, finally, why Calibanism (and cannibalism)—with all its complex contradictions—provides so apt a metaphor for the fraught desires of intellectuals in this revolutionary situation. What could more painlessly express the historical reality—Cronus, of course, would be too painfully frank—of a revolutionary elite so voracious that it finally devoured what it thought of as its own child: the revolution itself?

NOTES

1. The first reference to human-eating natives in Columbus's *Diary of the First Voyage* comes in the entry for Sunday, November 4, 1492. The first mention of the word *canibales* comes on Friday, November 23. See Cristóbal Colón, *Diario del Primer Viaje in Textos y documentos completos. Relaciones de viajes, cartas, y memoriales*, 2nd ed., ed. Consuelo Varela (Madrid: Alianza Editorial, 1984), 51, 62. For a comprehensive, critical account of the appearance and subsequent force of the term *cannibalism*, up through 1797, see Peter Hulme, *Colonial Encounters: Europe and the Native Caribbean 1492–1797* (London: Routledge, 1992).

2. Oswald de Andrade, *Manifiesto antropófago* [1928], in *Obra Escogida*, ed. Haroldo de Campos, trad. Héctor Olea (Caracas: Biblioteca Ayacucho,1981), 67–72. For a brief summary of the movement and its contemporary Brazilian manifestations, see Randal Johnson, "Tupy or not Tupy: Cannibalism and Nationalism in Contemporary Brazilian Literature and Culture," in *On Modern Latin American Fiction*, ed. John King (New York: Noonday, 1987), 41–59; also Mike Gonzalez and David Treece, *The Gathering of Voices: The Twentieth-Century Poetry of Latin America* (London: Verso, 1992), 96–101. Finally, for a

collection of brilliant contemporary reflections on Brazilian culture, including an assessment of the *anthropofagist* moment, see Roberto Schwarz, *Misplaced Ideas: Essays on Brazilian Culture*, ed. John Gledson (London: Verso, 1992), esp. 1–18 and 108–25. For more recent work, see Sergio Luiz Prado Bellei, "Brazilian Anthropophagy Revisited" and Luís Madureira, "Lapses in Taste: 'Cannibal-Tropicalist' Cinema and the Brazilian Aesthetic of Underdevelopment," both in Peter Hulme, Francis Baker, and Margaret Iverson, eds., *Cannibalism in the Colonial World* (New York: Cambridge UP, 1998), 87–109 and 110–25, respectively.

3. William Shakespeare, *The Tempest*, I.ii.363–64, in *The Riverside Shakespeare*, ed. G. Blakemore Evans, (Boston: Houghton Mifflin, 1974), 1616.

4. In the original Spanish: "le propuso a Ariel, con su propio ejemplo luminoso y aéreo si lo ha habido, que pidiera a Calibán el privilegio de un puesto en sus filas revueltas y gloriosas." Roberto Fernández Retamar, *Calibán: Apuntes sobre la cultura en nestra América*, 2nd ed. (México: Editorial Diógenes, 1974), 95. The English version appears under the title *Caliban: Notes Toward a Discussion of Culture in Our America*, in *Caliban and Other Essays*, trans. Edward Baker, (Minneapolis: University of Minnesota Press, 1989), 45.

5. Karl Marx, "Concerning Feuerbach" [1845], in *Early Writings*, trans. Rodney Livingstone and Gregor Benton (London: Penguin, 1995), 423.

6. Karl Marx and Frederick Engels, *Manifesto of the Communist Party* [1848], in *The Revolutions of 1848, Political Writings: Volume 1*, ed. David Fernbach (London: Penguin, 1993), 77.

7. In Spanish: "La universidad europea ha de ceder a la universidad americana." José Martí, *Nuestra América* [1891], in *Nuestra América*, ed. Hugo Achugar (Caracas: Biblioteca Ayacucho, 1977), 29 [my translation].

8. In the original: "el libro importado ha sido vencido en América por el hombre natural", Martí, *Nuestra América*, p. 28.

9. Retamar, *Caliban and Other Essays*, 21. In Spanish: "rechazo violento a la imposición de Próspero ('la universidad europea . . . el libro europeo . . . el libro yanqui') que '*ha de ceder*' ante la realidad de Calibán ('la universidad hispanoamericana . . . el enigma hispanoamericano')", from Retamar, *Calibán*, 46.

10. "The violent primal father had doubtless been the feared and envied model of each one of the company of brothers: and in the act of devouring him they accomplished their identification with him, and each one of them acquired a portion of his strength." Sigmund Freud, *Totem and Taboo* [1913], in *The Standard Edition of the Complete Psychological Works of Sigmund Freud*, trans. and ed. James Strachey (London: Hogarth, 1955), 13: 142. Freud's stab at anthropology is doubtless of tenuous scientific validity, but Freud makes the same connection between oral ingestion and identification in more precise writings on incorporation and introjection. See, for example, Freud's "Mourning and Melancholia" [1917], in *Standard Edition*, 14; 243–58.

11. Guevara first appears in a long list of cultural figures and artifacts comprising what Retamar calls "our cultural situation" for which, he says, he knows "of no other metaphor more expressive" than that of Caliban. Retamar, *Calibán*, 30–31, or, in the English edition, 14. And then, of course, in the book's final passage, Guevara sets the example for all other Ariels to follow.

12. In this vein, see Retamar's recent essay "Adiós a Calibán" ["Goodbye to Caliban"], in which the author writes "Pues si a él lo despojaron de su ínsula, él casi me despoja de mi magro ser. A punto estuve de no saber cuál de los dos escribiría estas líneas, come en la memorable página 'Borges y yo'. Llegué a confesarles a algunos amigos, sonriendo, que Calibán se me había convertido en mi Próspero." Retamar, "Adios a Calibán," *Revista Casa de las Americas* 191 (April–June, 1993), 116. ["If they dispossessed him (Caliban) of his island, he nearly dispossessed me of my thin being. I was at the point of not knowing which of the two of us was writing these lines, as in the memorable page "Borges and I." I wound up confessing to some friends, smiling, that Caliban had become my Prospero." [my translation]

13. An account of the congress is offered by Andrew Salkey in his *Havana Journal* (Harmondsworth: Penguin, 1971). James's proposals appear on pp. 105 and 117; Retamar's responses on pp. 105 and 112. For a full account of James's very original thinking about the Cuban revolution, see my "Silence and Dialectics: Speculations on C. L. R. James and Latin America," in *Rethinking C. L. R. James*, ed. Grant Farred (Oxford: Blackwell, 1996), 131–63.

14. I have elsewhere developed a more detailed analysis of Cuban revolutionary rhetoric, relating it to the discourses of nineteenth century Latin American independence. See "Of Creole Symptoms, Cuban Fantasies, and Other Latin American Postcolonial Ideologies," *PMLA* 110.3 (May, 1995): 382–96.

15. Fidel Castro, "Words to the Intellectuals" [1961], in *Radical Perspectives in the Arts*, ed. Lee Baxandall (Harmondsworth: Penguin, 1973), 276, 274. In the Spanish original: "las clases oprimidas y explotadas del pueblo . . . para nosotros será buenos lo que sea buenos para ellas; para nosotros será noble, será bello y será útil, todo lo que sea noble, sea útil, y sea bello para ellas." Fidel Castro, "Palabras a los intelectuales," in *La revolución Cubana, 1953-1962*, 5th ed. Adolfo Sánchez Rebolledo (Mexico City: Era, 1983), 360–61.

16. See, for example, Castro, "Words to the Intellectuals", 279 ["Palabras a los intelectuales," 363–64].

17. Karl Marx, *Critique of Hegel's Doctrine of the State* [1843], in *Early Writings*, 145.

18. Fidel Castro, "La historia me absolverá" [1953] in *La revolución Cubana*, 37.

19. See more below. The original manual of *foquismo* is Guevara's, *Guerrilla Warfare*, ed. Brian Loveman and Thomas M. Davies, Jr., trans. J. P. Morray (Lincoln: University of Nebraska Press, 1985), 37–179. The theory was

then generalized by Régis Debray in his *Revolution in the Revolution?*, trans. Bobbye Ortiz (New York: Monthly Review Press, 1967).

20. Guevara, *Guerrilla Warfare*, 79. In the original Spanish: "Al campesino siempre hay que ayudarlo técnica, económica, moral y culturalmente. El guerrillero será una especie de ángel tutelar caído sobre la zona" (Guevara, *La guerra de guerrillas* [1960], in *Obra revolucionaria*, ed. Roberto Fernández Retamar [Mexico City.: Era, 1989], 47).

21. "The mysterious character of the commodity-form consists therefore simply in the fact that the commodity reflects the social characteristics of men's own labour as objective characteristics of the products of labour themselves, as the socio-natural properties of these things. Hence it also reflects the social relation of the producers to the sum total of labour as a social relation between objects, a relation which exists apart from and outside the producers. Through this substitution, the products of labour become commodities, sensuous things which are at the same time suprasensible or social." Karl Marx, *Capital, vol. 1* [1867], trans. Ben Fowkes (London: Penguin, 1990), 164–65.

22. Castro, "La historia me absolverá," 71.

23. Guevara, "Notes on Man and Socialism in Cuba" [1965], in *Che Guevara Speaks*, ed. George Lavan (New York: Pathfinder, 1987), 135. In Spanish: "El partido es una organización de vanguardia. Los mejores trabajadores son propuestos por sus compañeros para integrarlo. Este es minoritario pero de gran autoridad por la calidad de sus cuadros. Nuestra aspiración es que el partido sea de masas, pero cuando las masas hayan alcanzado el nivel de desarrollo de la vanguardia" in ("El socialismo y el hombre en Cuba," *Obra revolucionaria*, 637).

24. Fidel Castro, "Waves of the Future" [1967], in *Latin American Radicalism: A Documentary Report on Left and Nationalist Movements*, ed. Irving Louis Horowitz, Josué de Castro, and John Gerassi (New York: Vintage, 1969), 578–79.

25. For this narrative, I draw variously from *The Cuba Reader: The Making of a Revolutionary Society*, ed. Philip Brenner, William M. LeoGrande, Donna Rich, and Daniel Siegel (New York: Grove Press, 1989); Louis A. Pérez, Jr., *Cuba: Between Reform and Revolution* (New York: Oxford UP, 1988); and *Cuba and the United States: Ties of Singular Intimacy* (Athens: University of Georgia Press, 1990); Nicola Miller, *Soviet Relations with Latin America 1959–1987* (Cambridge: Cambridge UP, 1989); and Janette Habel, *Cuba: The Revolution in Peril*, rev. ed., trans. Jon Barnes (London: Verso, 1991).

26. Guevara, "Mensaje a la Tricontinental" [1967], *Obra revolucionaria*, 650.

27. "Los lugares más agrestes, más intricados" in Guevara, *La guerra de guerrillas*, 70, my translation.

28. George N. Katsiaficas, *The Imagination of the New Left: A Global Analysis of 1968* (Boston, Mass.: South End, 1987).

29. Fredric Jameson, *Postmodernism, or, The Cultural Logic of Late Capitalism* (Durham, N.C.: Duke UP, 1990), 159.

30. Jameson, 209.

8

Cannibals at the Core: Juicy Rumors and the Hollow Earth Chronotope in Ian Wedde's *Symmes Hole*

BRIAN GREENSPAN

The aviator who will be the first to reach this New Territory, unknown until Admiral Byrd first discovered it, will go down in history as a New Columbus and greater than Columbus, for while Columbus discovered a new continent, he will discover a New World.

—Dr. Raymond Bernard, *The Hollow Earth: The Greatest Geographical Discovery in History, Made by Admiral Richard E. Byrd in the Mysterious Land Beyond the Poles—The True Origin of the Flying Saucers.* (New York: Bell, 1979), unpaginated epigraph.

Hamburgers . . . have been aestheticized to such a point of frenzy and hysteria that the McDonald's hamburger has actually vanished into its own sign. . . . McDonald's is a perfect technological hologram of suburban America, and of its extension by the capillaries of highways across the nation.

—*The Panic Encyclopedia.* Arthur Kroker (Montreal: New World Perspectives, 1989), 119.

None of us was born solid.

—Petronius, *The Satyricon and the Apocolocyntosis.* Trans. J. P. Sullivan (New York: Viking Penguin, 1986), 66.

As the limiting case of intercultural conflict, cannibalism poses a special threat to postcolonial literary studies. Fictional texts find in cannibalism a convenient trope for intertextuality and intercultural negotiation, a metaphor that enables the synthesis of widely different literary and cultural traditions. Yet postcolonial theorists have rightfully stressed the discursive specificity of intertextuality. As Stephen Slemon puts it, textuality (and intertextuality) in colonial centers should not be assumed to be "coterminous with the circulation of textual images in other cultural locations, which are of course in their own ways produced and consumed ideologically."[1] Theories of intertextuality as developed in reference to the western canon and its transmission need to be reconsidered within nonwestern signifying contexts in ways that emphasize rather than eclipse the history of discursive struggle. Indeed, a contextualized study of cannibalism can actually enable a culturally specific analysis of intertextuality.

One fictional text which does just that is Ian Wedde's *Symmes Hole*, a paranoid historiographic satire that explores the continuing legacies of British and American cultural and economic imperialism in the Pacific. The most extended work in prose or verse to date by this New Zealand writer who is better known for his poetry and curatorial work in the visual arts, *Symmes Hole* tackles many themes, not least among them the history of cannibalism as practiced by both the Maori people and their conquerors. Part narrative, part historical essay, Wedde's very method is cannibalistic, mixing historical periods, literary traditions, and high modes of official discourse with sailors' slang, nineteenth-century folk rumors, and modern-day advertising jingles. Through this discursive saturnalia, Wedde connects the cannibal theme and method to an identifiably western strain of satire, all the while retaining the specific history of power relations for which cannibal acts stand in as a cryptic code. Appropriately, the topographical image which binds his text—and, I will argue, the history of cannibalistic satire generally—is an image capable of swallowing the whole world.

CANNIBALS IN PARADISE: MAPPING THE TERRITORY

The colonial ideology that determines historical reports of cannibalism is nowhere more clearly inscribed than upon the maps of empire. Civilization abhors a void and rushes to fill in the blank spaces that represent the limits of imperial rule. As late as 1759, western cartographers were still rushing to plug the fearful absences that ate up their drawings of the world. Blank spots were filled in with the biblical images of Eden and Magog, of paradise and cannibal lands.[2] These empty spaces did eventually vanish beneath coastlines that were perhaps more realistic, if no less ideological. But the paradigm of the cannibal in paradise lasted well into the nineteenth century, sublimated in the ideology of empire. The quest for an earthly paradise allowed colonizers to allegorize their enterprise as a return to an unmarked, prelapsarian land, while rumors of cannibal natives confirmed the doctrine of Manifest Destiny.[3] The paired motifs of the cannibal in paradise coexisted uneasily, each constantly threatening to swallow up the other. Reports of cannibal tribes from the antipodes suggested to many that the Pacific paradise could yet turn out to be a fallen underworld, that the void could reassert itself.

Wedde explores how the colonial myth of the cannibal in paradise survives in the postmodern mode of information through the narrative perspective of James "Worser" Heberley, a nineteenth-century settler who lived among Maori and whose *Journal* rests in Wellington's Alexander Turnbull Library. Worser was one of the so-called new people, a group of New Zealand settlers whose "unofficial" methods were radically different from those of the British imperialists. Wedde rewrites Melville's *Typee* through vignettes that depict Worser among his Maori wife and children, contrasting these realistic slices of life with the American author's chivalrous vision of his Fayaway. Wedde reminds his reader that before Melville was canonized, he too stood for a new class of writer-adventurer, a "new people" who ingested stories like a rare and radical delicacy. "[T]o love Melville," one early reviewer said, "was to join a very small circle. It was like eating hasheesh."[4] Worser's dense, fragmented story is partially reconstructed by an authorial surrogate, an unnamed researcher living in modernday Wellington, who suffers a crisis of rationality as he tries to awaken from the nightmares of New Zealand's colonial history and commercialized present. His research uncovers a grand and bizarre philosophical notion behind Melville's writings, as well as British colonialism and American late capitalism: that the earth itself is hollow, and habitable within.

Wedde is not by far the first writer to explore the hollow earth motif. Around 1880 the Canadian author James de Mille wrote *A Strange Manuscript Found in a Copper Cylinder*, the dystopian narrative of a hapless explorer who discovers two cannibal tribes, one living at the South Pole and one dwelling beneath it. As his craft is swept into the abyss, de Mille's narrator recalls

that old theory . . . the notion that at each pole there is a vast opening; that into one of them all the waters of the ocean pour themselves, and, after passing through the earth, come out the other pole.[5]

Although the original referent of this very "old theory" remains unknown,
de Mille may have heard of John Cleves Symmes of Ohio, an American
soldier in the early nineteenth century who firmly believed the earth to be
"hollow, and habitable within."[6] No one knows where Symmes heard of
the venerable, though esoteric, notion of a hollow earth, but one can imagine what a fertile new New World inside the earth's crust must have meant
to a young frontier soldier fighting for elbow room.

Symmes's theory was widely disseminated in the early 1800s—and
broadly ridiculed in the popular press. The idea of a hollow earth might
eventually have passed the way of mesmerism and phrenology were it not
for the publicity campaign of one Jeremiah Reynolds, Symmes's greatest
disciple and arguably the most influential rumormonger of the American
Renaissance. After all, it was Reynolds who first spread the sailor's legend
of a Pacific leviathan called Mocha Dick.[7] He also exerted a profound
influence on the writings of Edgar Allan Poe, especially visible in *The
Narrative of Arthur Gordon Pym of Nantucket*.[8] In 1836, after twelve years
of lobbying, Reynolds convinced Congress to send six naval vessels in
search of the South Polar void.[9] The United States Naval Exploring
Expedition never reached the mythic chasm; it did, however, stake an
American claim in Antarctica and produced endless maps and soundings
that fueled an already thriving domestic whaling industry. The search for
Symmes Hole thus marks the beginning of America's global economic
ascendancy. How mysterious, then, that the White Whale should persist as
a founding American myth, while the corresponding rumors of a hollow
earth have been all but forgotten, sunk in the subcultural denizens of pulp
sci-fi, Florida communes, and Melville scholarship.

This secret history of the intertextual "gam" between Melville, Poe,
and Reynolds, that mysterious "third term," is the subject of Wedde's
strange literary cartography, which presents a fictionalized Herman
Melville. Michael Hollister has shown how Melville recruits one of his
characters from the *Grampus*, the ship in *Arthur Gordon Pym*, thereby setting his characters afloat upon the same fictional waters as Poe.[10] Similarly,
by alluding to both Pym and Moby-Dick within a single narrative, *Symmes
Hole* transforms all three works into intertexts. *Symmes Hole* "unfinalizes"
Melville's *Typee*, his book of life among the cannibals, through vignettes

that depict Worser among his Maori wife and children in Tommolike fashion. Melville was also one of the "new people," and occupied the dissident settler's dialogic relation to colonizer and colonized. Wedde reminds his reader that before Melville was canonized, he stood for a new class of writer-adventurer, as one who ingested stories like a rare and radical delicacy, similar to the frozen fish bait Wedde's narrator swallows, the "mystery history drug" that allows him to commune with the past. Melville is thus reclaimed from the canon of American letters and returned to the realm of popular adventure, unofficial history, and maritime gossip.

RUMORS AND RUMBLINGS

Symmes Hole refuses any stable historical referents, choosing instead to recede into interminably and undecidably nested frames of reported speech, parody, and allusion. Wedde leaves the realm of official literary history in order to engage the colonial legacy of 150 years of rumors—rumors of white whales, cannibals, and secret societies living inside the hollow earth. One's certainties about literature and the world must be temporarily relaxed to figure out this chronotope—this textual and historical timespace—called *Symmes Hole*.[11] In response to Wells and the tradition he represents, Wedde uses the fanciful hollow earth chronotope to debunk that other, closely connected colonial myth of cannibalism. He takes his reader back through the paranoid history of colonial appropriation, in an attempt to understand reports of Pacific cannibalism past and present, both literal and metaphorical, through the better-kept secret of the earth's inner void.

Maggie Kilgour has shown that cannibalism frequently operates as a satiric trope,[12] but the narratives which link cannibalism to the hollow earth chronotope constitute a special satiric subgenre. The most closely related genre is the *nekyia*, or satiric dialogue of the dead. As Bakhtin explains, in the classical *nekyia*, the living confront dead figures of myth and legend in order to interrogate through dialogue the received authority they embody.[13] In the Renaissance the *nekyia* genre was revived largely by Erasmus but took a different turn in the hand of later writers like Thomas Nashe and Thomas Dekker, who wedded the classical fantasy of communicating with the underworld to the new spirit of territorial expansion. Suddenly, there emerged a new kind of dialogue that imagined impossible communication not across the metaphysical threshold of death but across geographic and cultural barriers instead. The idea of a hollow earth emerged in this period as a legendary shortcut to new worlds, a communicating passage that would permit discourse, and commerce, with new worlds across—and ultimately within—the globe.

Perhaps it was ecclesiastical images of hell as a place of anthropophagy which first suggested the cannibalistic element of infernal dialogues. On the other hand, at least since Rabelais, the subterranean dialogue has suggested another, closely related carnival motif: that of the underworld banquet. Bakhtin shows through the example of Epistemon's voyage in book 2 of Rabelais's *Pantagruel* that the underworld chronotope is closely connected to excremental and gastronomic satire.[14] But it was in the nineteenth century, with the ascendency of the scientific discourses of exploration and evolution, that the cannibal banquet within the hollow earth took on colonial dimensions. Owing perhaps to the Franklin expedition of 1845, which certainly helped to transplant the fear of degeneration to the polar void, both the popular and literary imagination in this period figured the hollow earth motif as an avatar affording access to an imagined, originary state of humanity—one which included cannibalism. For authors like Wells and Edgar Bulwer-Lytton, a terrestrial avatar offering access to so-called "bygone" and "primitive" societies could be used to "confirm" dominant scientific theories of the biological and cultural superiority of Europeans. Accordingly, the subterraneum was imagined as the repository of our cannibal descendents, with their unspeakable feeding habits drawn from the dark vestiges of racial memory.[15] The hollow earth chronotope thus permitted a metaphorical mapping of evolutionary time onto geographical space. Even today, it still seems that the most sober and "scientifical" discussions of the earth's interior as a window to past times and prehuman societies somehow give rise to the issue of cannibalism.[16]

By invoking this venerable literary association of cannibal narratives with the fantastic hollow earth chronotope, Wedde engages a vast tradition of dialogic romance that links these two themes, a tradition which includes the classical nekyia of Homer, Virgil, and Dante and the long tradition of satiric dialogues they spawned, as well as the romances of Poe and de Mille, Edgar Rice Burroughs's *Tarzan at the Earth's Core* (1930), and the Lemurian stories of carnivorous subterranean "deros" and the "vampiras" which ran in *Amazing Stories* in the 1940s.[17] More recently, a barage of sci-fi and B-horror movies have explored the themes, including *Beneath the Planet of the Apes* (1969), which features an underground tribe of postapocalyptic mutant cannibals, and the *C.H.U.D.* (1984), which posits a species of "cannibalistic humanoid underground dwellers" in the New

York sewer system.[18] However varied in style and purpose these various hollow-earth texts may be, it is intriguing that they all have one aspect in common: they all depict the earth's center as home to a troglodyte race of cannibals.

This strong chronotopic connection between cannibalism and subterranean dwelling can, I believe, be explained through the chief interest of the satiric *nekyia* genre—namely, the fear and fascination raised by the trope of the speaking dead. Rabelais extended the dialogue of the dead to include swallowed characters, but Epistemon only tells the story of his alimentary voyage after he is disgorged. And Dostoevsky's pedantic Ivan Matveich from "The Crocodile" continues to profess from within the very belly of his reptilian captor. Nevertheless, it seems to be a satiric law that no one ever speaks from inside the anthropophagite's belly. Cannibalism is a subject that at once occasions and swallows up utterance, like the maelstrom that both engenders and engulfs Arthur Gordon Pym's narrative. European notions of cannibalism were born of silence, in the gaps between languages and cultures. Gananath Obeyesekere shows that the discourse of Maori cannibalism specifically was forged in taciturn interactions between Europeans and Polynesians, a "conversation" of sorts that developed only through third-party translations and elaborate pantomimes.[19]

Wedde likewise represents alleged incidents of cannibalism only through fragmentary, secondhand reports. Significantly, he never represents cannibalistic acts through any omniscient narrative perspective. The story of the murdered slave-girl whose blood was drunk by the Maori chief (105), the case of Betty Guard who was offered her own brother to eat (224)—all such incidents are represented as reports by secondhand witnesses:

> but then about eight on a cold foggy morning the Maori rushed across the river and cut down two of the seamen . . . Guard had told how they whacked one of them up into joints 'for their cannibal repast, tell the Colonel here if I'm not speaking the Lord's . . .'
> 'It's true, so I . . .' (224; ellipses in original)

This indirect narrative perspective expresses the necessarily vague understanding of cannibalism, an all-consuming act of violence which leaves little in the way of material evidence behind. More importantly, however, the fact that these incidents are reported as the yarns of sailors renders their validity ambivalent in the eyes of the novel's chief agent of empire, Colonel Wakefield. Whether these reports of cannibals were factually true, or merely rumors incited by colonial myth, is left unanswered in Wedde's text. The authenticity of the reports of cannibals must remain lost, like Wedde's researcher, "between the shifting faces of history, reality and 'reality'" (10–11). Ellipses dot his text like seismic rifts, giving vent to ominous, sybilline gossip from sailors and squatters long since dead.

If hollow earth theories are implicitly totalizing, then discussions of cannibalism are by contrast habitually underdetermined. As a crime *non habeus corpus*, cannibalism has since Cook's first voyages been the occasion of more nautical rumor than narrative. Even Melville perpetuates this conspiracy of silence. Writing in his public role of Tommo, the Man who Lived among Cannibals, Melville introduces the topic in *Typee* by alluding to "vague accounts of such things [that] reach our firesides."[20] His reticence is typical, for anthropophagy was in the nineteenth century, and remains today, inscribed within what Caleb Crain calls a "discourse of preterition."[21] By this, Crain means to indicate how the cannibal act was used by writers and artists to "stand in" for other subjects that were considered unrepresentable, such as homosexuality among British sailors. Crain's choice of phrase, the "discourse of preterition," is more apt than even he acknowledges. In legal vocabulary, "preterition" signifies the deliberate omission of a name from the list of beneficiaries to a willed estate. The discourse of cannibalism is preterite in this specific sense, for it is generally invoked for the purpose of divesting indigenous peoples of their rightful inheritance. A culture labeled as cannibal belongs to a precivilized past and, therefore, cannot hold title over property.

As Harold Skulsky speculates in a study of Jonson's drama, the taboo prohibiting anthropophagy does not arise from our fear of being consumed; on the contrary, it is the projected fear of consuming another from which we cringe, the apprehension of *possessing* another willful and cognizant being within us.[22] Our fear of hosting a malignant, thinking being within one's belly makes the cannibal act disgusting. The preterite discourse of cannibalism is thus hollow at the core: it reveals nothing but the fear of the colonizer when confronted with the emptiness of his own identity. Herein, I suggest, lies the connection between cannibalism and the hollow earth: both notions reduce the western subject to a shell subject to possession by another. Images of cannibals and the hollow center both compel us to regain our self-possession assertively, through appropriative acts of consumption.

Wedde lays bare this fundamental connection between colonial myths of cannibal attacks, and the colonizer's repressed revulsion at his own invasive actions. The fear of cannibalism is actually the predator's projected fear of ingesting an entity which, in turn, consumes his identity.

In *Symmes Hole*, this fear is modeled as a projection of the capitalist drive, the parasite of conspicuous consumption which would invade all of our bodies and infect us with its malevolent will. Thus, in the perforated but telling synthesis of Wedde's researcher, the need to invade every human being in the form of cheeseburgers and McFries is, like Captain Wilke's need to penetrate to the center of the earth, the final act of appropriation:

> The Renaissance wanted to 'civilise' Caliban. . . . [T]he Enlightenment wanted to appropriate 'natural innocence' . . . and Jeremiah Reynolds wanted to get inside [the earth]—and his descendants did: nuclear submarines and fast food. It may be that Wilkes and Reynolds had a metaphorical understanding (154).

Here, the colonial desire to "civilize" an indigenous people is revealed as a systematic, parasitic invasion of their bodies. Once and for all, the colonizer's horror of cannibals is laid open as the fear of consuming something that cannot be digested.

McTHEORY FOR A HOLLOW EARTH

Cannibalism is literally disgusting only when one imagines oneself as the consumer of an unsavory meal, as unwitting host to a bodily parasite, perhaps "something malignant, intelligent, and alive"[23]—or worse yet, something still talking. If few dare to talk about cannibalism, then, it is because utterance only intensifies the horror of the act. Given this general lack of dialogue, early descriptions of Maori cannibalism were perforce elaborated from British explorers' own culinary experiences. It's probably safe to say that more is known about British cannibalism than any other variety. Whenever the crews of stranded navy or merchant vessels began to crave their bangers, it was typically that passenger marked as Other who furnished forth the funeral sweetmeats. It was easier to eat the Spaniard, slave, or cabin boy because he was marked as different—not only physically, as Obeyesekere argues,[24] but also linguistically—and thus posed less of a threat of talking back, as it were, from beyond the intestinal grave.

Oddly enough, contemporary postindustrial culture has thoroughly fetishized this taboo of ingesting a living, speaking being through marketing campaigns that resemble cannibal feasts. From articulate, bipedal cheeseburgers, to giggling doughboys, to socialite tunas that beg to be caught, mass-mediated commodity culture regularly appeals to fantasies of ingesting speaking entities. Furthermore, with so-called "smart" products like talking beer caps and milk cartons that low upon being opened, technology has created a consumer's wonderland in which we are constantly hailed by potions that say, "Drink Me," and cakes that say, "Eat Me." Here Montaigne's familiar thesis can be updated for the fin de millenium: not only are "civilized" peoples at least as "barbarous" as cannibals, in postindustrial society, they actually aspire to become cannibals. It is in such a climate that a recent ad in the Toronto subway could feature a postcard from a young woman traveling to Borneo, who claims to have met a tribe of cannibals that enjoy her Juicy Fruit chewing gum, an offering which presumably sates the dangerous indigenous appetite. Perhaps this development is to be expected in a culture that increasingly fetishizes information, for commodity cannibalism offers to fulfill the Swiftian fantasy of learning through eating—food for information, if not for thought. Consume a product and you consume a lifestyle; incorporate an ideology, and you likewise become incorporated. Contemporary marketing strategies are at heart based in a magicoreligious repast that promises to transfer the spiritual qualities of the product to the consumer.

But Jhally discusses advertising's role today as a ritual that transforms quotidian, mass-produced objects into magically healing totems:

> Production empties. Advertising fills. . . . The hollow husk of the commodity-form needs to be filled by some kind of meaning, however superficial. . . . People need meaning for the world of goods.[25]

It is this belief system which an iconoclastic Wedde would empty out by filling the multinational market's most visible and most empty commodity form with meanings that it can neither contain nor readily purge. In Wedde's seriocomic conspiracy theory of commerce, it is, hilariously, the McDonald's hamburger that links the predatory act not to the Maori but rather to the consumption of traditional indigenous lifestyles by multinational corporations. Wedde critiques the totalizing grid of corporate power by connecting the insatiable appetite of the western fast-food financier, Ray "Big Mac" Kroc, to a cannibalistic impulse.

Ross Bowden shows that Maori cannibalism, far from any random expression of violence, in fact was practiced as a form of political revenge within an intricate sociocultural system in which people, things, and events are contrasted as either *tapu* (sacred) or *noa* (profane). In traditional Maori culture, the head is *tapu*, the lower body *noa*; warfare is *tapu*, foodstuff and eating are emphatically *noa*. To transubstantiate one's enemy into a foodstuff, either literally by eating them or figuratively through a culinary billingsgate, was traditionally the greatest possible insult among the Maori. One of the worst traditional slanders was "*kai upoko*, an expression which literally means to eat or make food (*kai*) of a person's head (*upoko*)."[26] Perhaps the greatest difference between traditional Maori and contemporary western culture lies in the fact that the Maori apparently ate only their vanquished foes, while the West vanquishes its foes by eating them.

Wedde shows that, as far as enemies go on the national scale, McDonald's Restaurants is inherently *noa*. As Mark Williams remarks,

> The Pacific world in Moby Dick [*sic*] is represented as a map of conquest and the expansion of American global economic, technological, and military power. In *Symmes Hole* the process of American expansion across the Pacific is complete, but the vehicle of that power is not the whaling ships, . . . but Ray Kroc's McDonald's hamburger empire. Behind both the whaling and fast food industries lie the same ideas that encourage the human subjugation of matter.[27]

Indeed, Wedde's researcher launches an ecological critique of McDonald's in no uncertain terms, citing the incredible stretches of forest which cardboard packaging alone has consumed in the history of the company (265). However, Williams neglects to mention the parallel between the fast-food enterprise and the colonial myth of Maori cannibalism. If cannibalism represented for Victorian society the threat of regression from a state of civilization into one of barbarism, then Wedde reverses the threat to suggest that *homo oeconomicus* has been steadily devolving since the onset of late capitalism: "Victors, 'doers of deeds,' Hamburger Rings, Clown Princes, Ronald McDonald, The Descent of Man (his finger that had poked through the clammy burger smelled faintly of onion and arsehole)" (246).

The anonymous modern-day researcher whose research into Reynolds and Kroc counterpoints the historical chapters of Wedde's text arrives at this Wellsian inversion of Darwin's theory while playing with a McDonalds hamburger, to the amazement and delight of onlooking Maori children. By poking a hole through the center of the burger, Wedde turns his Big Mac into a model of the world as Symmes perceived it—hollow at the core. Ultimately, it is the logic of digestion, not the logic of analysis, which holds his fragmented fictional world together:

that flow pattern's the ali', the elementary one, that's the surface movement, . . . but then there's the deeper drifts and flows, there's the weft that complicates your prevailing persistence warp, there's the Menu on which is recorded another consumption altogether, and that's the one where the Pacific is served up, to McDonald's. . . . (254)

For Wedde, Symmes Hole represents "the hole in the bottom of your body," the crowning reminder of the biological necessity which chains humanity to a logic of consumption and waste (77). At the same time, it is the "Hollow Mountain" upon which Wellington is built, reconfigured to resemble McDonald's trademark golden arches (165–66). Symmes Hole provides a paradoxical globalizing image that self-consciously foregrounds the aporia in the coordinate-grid model of corporate takeover. Just as the sausage figures in Renaissance farce as a grotesque reminder of the indeterminate boundary between inner and outer, between animal and human flesh, between consumer and consumed,[28] so Wedde shows that, for a postindustrial world, the doubly invaginated hamburger is the carnivalesque foodstuff par excellence. Through this postmodern kitchen war, Wedde demonstrates how Moby-Dick can serve New Zealand, without serving her up to America, the great devourer. Above all, Wedde's comestible macrocosm is a *reductio ad absurdum* of the entrepreneurial schemes of historical alazons like Reynolds and Kroc. By operating from within the superficial realm of rumor, Wedde counters their drive to "get inside" the bowels of the earth, or of billions served; in his postmodern *nekyia*, the deep truth must remain unsounded.

Wedde thus returns to the dispossessed and devoured the communicating passage that colonial discourse has denied them. Admittedly, I have found nothing to verify Wedde's suggestion that Reynolds also manufactures the aluminum for the nuclear submarines with which the American government still searches for the inner earth's polar access. The truth behind his story must remain submerged, "a constant nuisance, like a lone whale in the vast Pacific whose rumor haunts and infects those plying the marketing grids that whaling bequeathed to the fast food industry" (9). Drawing on the power of marketplace gossip, Wedde neither fictionalizes history, nor claims to set the record straight; he simply instills doubt by spreading rumor, that juiciest of polyglot genres. If the paranoid connections he draws between cannibalism and the historical search for a New (interior) World are, in the final estimate, hard to swallow, that is precisely what distinguishes them from the readily comestible and eagerly devoured products of Kroc's fast-food, "Fast History," empire.

In a paper delivered to the Humanities Society of New Zealand in 1996, Wedde pointed out how digital mediation is helping to conflate history with mere entertainment: "Rock concerts will soon be on-line in formats into which archival footage is inserted, thereby collapsing the space between performance present and documentary history."[29] Of course, the chronotopes of history are already collapsing in *Symmes Hole*. And yet there is some debate as to whether any imported theories of transnational media can ever speak for a postcolonial nation. Leonard Wilcox, for one, claims that New Zealand's isolation from media culture (i.e., television, films, advertising, and pop music) prevents the country from even considering the darker possibilities of the postmodern world.[30] He dismisses Alan Curnow's "pastoral" vision of the nation, labeling it an "anti-modern" and conservative attempt to depict New Zealand as a "transparent space, free of ideological distortion and class conflict."[31] Too often, Wilcox claims, New Zealand is represented as "a pure and transparent space" of information exchange, in which culture and nature, the indigenous and the imported, mingle freely and directly, without need for mediation.

Into this pastoral paradise, Wedde reintroduces the fear of the cannibal. His very narrative incorporates various channels of represented information—biological, musical, electronic, historical—without, however, naively erasing the interference between them. Maori versions of antipodean sea shanties ("New-come buckra/He get sick/He tak fever/He be die . . . ," 33) must take their place next to Calvin Coolidge's political slogans ("PERSISTENCE AND DETERMINATION ALONE ARE OMNIPOTENT," 253) and pop songs:

> 'All that stuff about, what's *Dionysus* got to do. . . ?'—and then a young grinning Maori man standing next to her turns his transistor radio up, it's Ray Davies singing with The Kinks . . .

Far from any provincial scenes, the landscape Wedde presents is a noisy vista of commodified images and superficial signifiers—as though "paradise *did* have musak in it" (48). As his protagonist strolls through modern-day Wellington, contemplating "the exhausting artificiality of the consumer process" (47), he observes an urban landscape that is buzzing, threatening, synthetic, and above all, alive: "Ahead of him the big digital clock with the illuminated weather-forecast flicked its numbers over. . . . [L]ights shone reflected in the water of the artificial lagoon. . . . The container wharf emitted a cybernetic hum" (49). No longer Colonel Wakefield's safe British garden, Wedde's postpastoral New Zealand more closely resembles the omnivorous cosmos of *Moby-Dick*, which, as Randall Bohrer writes, swallows up everything without for a moment believing that this grotesque "whole is synonymous with the good."[32]

Oswald de Andrade bloated reports of Tupi cannibalism into a howling predatory movement with the cry, "Down with the vegetable elites. In with communication with the soil."[33] By contrast, Wedde's postmodern, postprovincial text speaks with the submerged voice of the prey, like a subterranean rumble from a bit of undigested rarebit. He writes, "this rumor of another history—something with the quality of the invisible, the unofficial, the disquieting, the subversive—must not become official or successful: must remain a 'failure' as . . . Melville used the term of *Moby-Dick*, because in that 'failed' role it can be useful" (8). *Symmes Hole* shows that if *Moby-Dick* still speaks to a contemporary audience, it does so through unfixable, diabolical rumors. And if Melville's postmodern readers can at all identify with Tommo, then that is because in today's globalized McDonaldland, we all live among cannibals.

NOTES

1. Stephen Slemon, "Post-Colonial Allegory and the Transformation of History," *Journal of Commonwealth Literature* 23.1 (1988): 158.

2. Muriel Barnett discusses the colorful portrayal of cannibals and paradises on early world maps. Gog and Magog "appeared in early maps in Northern Siberia, confined behind an Iron Wall. They were cannibals. In a world map of 1235, they are shown eating legs and arms amputated from victims whose severed stumps spout blood all over the snow"; "Here Be Monsters." *Contemporary Review* 255 (October 1989): 208.

3. As John R. Clark and Anna Lydia Motto point out, "benign Europeans were, it was claimed, 'rescuing' natives and transporting them to the New World of Christianity and civilized capitivity where they would be forced to adhere to more sanitary diets"; "The Progress of Cannibalism in Satire," *The Midwest Quarterly* 25 (winter 1984): 174.

4. Quoted in Paul Lauter, "Melville Climbs the Canon," *American Literature* 66 .1 (March 1994): 15 .

5. James de Mille, *A Strange Manuscript Found in a Copper Cylinder*, New Canadian Library 68 (Toronto: McClelland and Stewart, 1969 [1888]), 54.

6. Quoted in Walter Rafton-Minkel, *Subterranean Worlds: 100,000 Years of Dragons, Dwarfs, the Dead, Lost Races and UFOS from Inside the Earth* (Port Townsend, Wash.: Loompanics, 1989), 61. I must thank Peter Fitting for

bringing to my attention Kafton-Minkel's study, which provides the most comprehensive survey to date of the various popular and literary manifestations of hollow earth theory. See also Fitting's own article, "Buried Treasures: Reconsidering Holberg's *Niels Klim in the World Underground, Utopian Studies* 7.2 (1996): 93–112.

7. "Mocha Dick: or The White Whale of The Pacific; A Leaf From a Manuscript Journal", by J. N. Reynolds, Esq., appeared in *The Knicker-bocker* 9 in May 1839: 705–15. Melville could easily have seen it, and doubtless did; for internal evidence to this effect, see Henry A. Murray and Eugene Taylor, "From Mocha to Moby," *Melville Society Extracts* 64 (November 1985): 6–7.

8. For convincing proof of Reynolds's direct influence on Poe, see Robert Lee Rhea, "Some Observations on Poe's Origins," *Texas Studies in English* 10 (July 1930): 135–46; J. O. Bailey, "The Geography of Poe's 'Dreamland' and 'Ulalume,'" *Studies in Philology* 45 (1950): 512–23; Aubrey Starke, "Poe's Friend Reynolds," *American Literature* 2 (May 1930): 152–59. For convincing proof that Jeremiah Reynolds was *not* the Reynolds for whom Poe purportedly cried out on his deathbed, see W. T. Bandy, "Dr. Moran and the Poe-Reynolds Myth," in *Myths and Reality: The Mysterious Mr. Poe*, ed. Benjamin Franklin Fisher IV (Baltimore: Edgar Allan Poe Society, 1987), 26–36.

9. It has been rumored that Wilkes, a fiery personality who was twice court-martialed, was Melville's model for Ahab.

10. Michael Hollister, "Melville's Gam with Poe in *Moby-Dick*: Bulkington and Pym," *Studies in the Novel* 9 (fall 1989): 279.

11. I use the term *chronotope* here in Bakhtin's sense of the recurring literary figures that configure particular time-spaces into generic forms.

12. "The Function of Cannibalism at the Present Time," in *Cannibalism and the Colonial World*, ed. Francis Barker, Peter Hulme, and Margaret Iversen (Cambridge: Cambridge UP, 1998).

13. For his discussion of the *nekyia* as a Menippean subgenre, see *Problems of Dostoevsky's Poetics*, trans. Caryl Emerson (Minneapolis: University of Minnesota Press, 1984).

14. See *Rabelais and His World*, trans. Hélène Iswolsky (Bloomington: Indiana UP,1984), 381–86. For an opposing view of Rabelais's banquet imagery, cf. Frank Lestringant, *Cannibals*, trans. Rosemary Morris (Berkeley: University of California Press, 1997), 36–37.

15. James E. Marlow, "English Cannibalism: Dickens After 1859." *Studies in English Literature 1500–1900* 23 (autumn 1983): 650ff.

16. Most recently, these dual motifs appear in the January 1996 edition of *National Geographic*, which features articles on the composition of the earth (mentioning Athenasius Kircher, who influenced early authors of hollow earth romances like Ludwig Holberg), Neanderthal cannibalism, and polar ice crossings—not to mention John Mormon, founder of the Church of Mormon and

cousin to John Reed Tead, "the man who lived inside the earth" (see Kafton-Minkel, 90–107).

17. Outlined in "The Shaver Mystery," chap. 8 of Kafton-Minkel.

18. A more recent instance of the intratellurian anthropophagic tale is Paul Metcalf's *Both* (1982), a textual collage that combines details from Poe's biography and the history of *Pym*'s composition, with the fictionalized diary of the actual nineteenth-century cannibalization of a Portugese girl by Australian sailors.

19. "'British Cannibals': Contemplation of an Event in the Death and Resurrection of James Cook, Explorer," *Critical Inquiry* 18 (summer 1992): 637ff.

20. Herman Melville, *Typee: A Peep at Polynesian Life During a Four Months' Residence in a Valley of the Marquesas, With Notices of the French Occupation of Tahiti and the Provisional Cession of the Sandwich Islands to Lord Paulet, and a Sequel, The Story of Toby* (London: Constable and Company, 1922 [1846]), 63.

21. Caleb Crain, "Lovers of Human Flesh: Homosexuality and Cannibalism in Melville's Novels," *American Literature* 66.1 (March 1994): 25–53.

22. Harold Skulsky, "Cannibals vs. Demons in *Volpone*," *Studies in English Literature 1500–1900* 29.2 (spring 1989): 303.

23. Skulsky, 303.

24. Gananeth Obeyesekere, "'British Cannibals': Contemplation of an Event in the Death and Resurrection of James Cook, Explorer," *Critical Inquiry* 18 (summer 1992): 640.

25. Sut Jhally, "Advertising as Religion: The Dialectic of Technology and Magic," in *Cultural Politics in Contemporary America*, ed. Ian Angus and Sut Jhally (New York: Routledge, 1989), 222.

26. Ross Bowden, "Maori Cannibalism: An Interpretation," *Oceania* 55.2 (December 1984): 94.

27. Mark Williams, "Ian Wedde's Relocations," *Leaving the Highway: Six Contemporary New Zealand Novelists* (Auckland, N.Z.: Auckland UP, 1990), 160.

28. Bakhtin, *Rabelais*, 221–31.

29. Ian Wedde, "Information and Entertainment Information and Entertainment: A paper given by Ian Wedde, Museum Projects Museum of New Zealand, 16 May 1996, at the third seminar in the series Communications Technologies—What are their Social and Cultural Implications for New Zealand?", 1996, *http://www.vuw.ac.nz/humanz/ seminar/seminarwedde.html* (8 May 2000).

30. Leonard Wilcox, "Postmodernism or Anti-modernism?" *Landfall* 39 (spring 1985): 347–48.

31. Wilcox, 352.

32. Randall Bohrer, "Melville's New Witness: Cannibalism and the Microcosm-Macrocosm Cosmology of *Moby-Dick*," *Studies in Romanticism* 22 (spring 1983): 89.

33. Quoted in Leslie Bary, "Oswald de Andrade's 'Cannibalist Manifesto,'" *Latin American Literary Review* 19 (1991): 40.

9

Margaret Atwood's *Wilderness Tips:* Apocalyptic Cannibal Fiction

MARLENE GOLDMAN

In *Culture and Imperialism*, Edward Said argues against taking up a settled, established, and centered interpretive position, in favor of a perspective located "between domains, between forms . . . and between languages."[1] According to Said, this liminal perspective allows critics to read "contrapuntally" and exposes important connections among literary traditions; as a result, we become aware of our cultural hybridity. In keeping with Said's injunction to read contrapuntally, this study begins by exploring the hybrid status of native Wendigo stories, tales of flesh-eating monsters that, historically, have been interpreted as the distinct products of native culture. Yet, as we will see, evidence suggests that Wendigo stories emerge from and offer a response to the disastrous clash between native and European cultures. Rather than view these tales as exotic artifacts of a primitive culture, Wendigo stories should more properly be understood as disaster narratives that register the impact of imperialism and colonization.

Read as disaster narratives, Wendigo stories have a great deal in common with Atwood's fiction. Her short-story collection *Wilderness Tips* draws on elements of Wendigo tales to reflect on the legacy of imperialism and colonization in contemporary Canadian society. More precisely, Atwood's stories invoke the European and western counterparts of the

Wendigo tales—western culture's very own disaster narratives, including Mary Shelley's *Frankenstein*, accounts of the ill-fated Franklin expedition, the Titanic, and Revelation. These intertexts—all western cannibal narratives—mirror the native Wendigo tales in that they too register the ongoing impact of imperialism.

By alluding to Wendigo stories and invoking their western counterparts, Atwood's stories also highlight important parallels between the settler-invader society's treatment of natives and its treatment of women. As we will see, *Wilderness Tips* demonstrates how women, like natives, are transformed into the demonic cannibal to justify their subordinate position within the male-dominated, European social order.

In what the magazine *Saturday Night* playfully describes as her "Cannibal Lecture," Atwood professes her ongoing fascination with cannibalism and ponders how a "culture so boring as ours" has come to embrace the notion of the flesh-devouring Wendigo.[2] In her lecture, given as part of the Clarendon Lecture Series at Oxford in 1991, she outlines the features of the Wendigo, the cannibal monster who stalks the northern Canadian wilderness and haunts the legends and stories of the Woodland Cree and the Ojibway. As Atwood explains, all accounts confirm that the Wendigo is "a giant spirit-creature with a heart and sometimes an entire body of ice." Endowed with "prodigious strength," it can travel "as fast as the wind."[3] She goes on to point out that, in stories featuring this creature, the fear generated by the Wendigo is twofold: "fear of being eaten by one, and fear of becoming one."[4] Ultimately, becoming one is the real horror, because, as she explains, "if you go Wendigo, you may end by losing your human mind and personality and destroying your own family members, or those you love most."[5]

In a discussion of the portrait of the Wendigo found in longer literary narratives, Atwood offers a psychological explanation for its appearance and suggests that, in some cases, this otherworldly creature represents "a fragment of the protagonist's psyche, a sliver of his repressed inner life made visible."[6] In these narratives, the creature that the characters fear or dream about "splits off from the rest of the personality, destroys it, and becomes manifest through the victim's body."[7] In her subsequent analysis of Wayland Drew's novel *The Wabeno Feast* (1973), she argues that the monster offers a tangible illustration of your fate if you succumb to the desire to be superhuman—a desire that results in "the loss of whatever small amount of humanity you may still retain."[8] At the conclusion of her lecture series, which repeatedly returns to the theme of cannibalism and the Wendigo, Atwood states: "A number of you have asked me . . . whether any of this stuff is connected at all with my own work. The answer, in a word, is Yes."[9]

Although she is not known for penning folktales featuring monsters as swift as the wind, who gobble up unsuspecting victims in the Canadian north, I would argue that the stories in her most recent collection *Wilderness Tips* introduce themes of predation, orality, and the translation of human flesh into economic gain—all metaphoric cannibalism—by adopting and strategically adapting many of the attributes associated with the Wendigo. Whereas non-native readings of the Wendigo tend to categorize this figure as the fanciful product of an alien culture, Atwood must be credited for rejecting this approach. Instead, she takes the features of the cannibal monster and maps them onto her characters. In doing so, she emphasizes that the forms of hunger and aggression associated with the cannibal monster are not restricted to native culture, but arise, more generally, in social systems in crisis. In her stories, this crisis is specifically tied to the legacy of imperialism and colonialism which shapes both the condition of the characters' conflicts and their mode of resolving them.

While a much longer study would engage in a story-by-story analysis, in what follows, I rely on one story in particular—"Hairball"—to draw out the central Wendigo characteristics that Atwood uses to delimit a conception of "contemporary cannibalism." Although I concentrate intensively (although not exclusively) on "Hairball," evidence of the relationship between the Wendigo tales and Atwood's stories, the use of cannibal imagery, and finally, Atwood's view of how contemporary cannibalism affects lives and relationships is available in all of the stories. Where appropriate, I will discuss the more overt connections among the stories in the collection.

In her description of the Wendigo, Atwood offers the standard account of the evil cannibal giant.[10] But this account omits crucial information concerning the meaning of the term and the evolution of Wendigo stories. Without this information, readers cannot fully appreciate how the stories in *Wilderness Tips* engage with the traditional Wendigo tales. Before looking at how the concept of the cannibal monster informs her writing, it is important to take the time to gain a broader understanding of this widely misunderstood figure.[11]

Basic misunderstandings concerning the term *wendigo* arise from errors in translation. One well-known mistake was traced to a compiler of a dictionary, who entered the information regarding the word *wendigo* and substituted the word *ghoul* for the appropriate word *fool* because he thought that the natives meant *ghoul*. But the correct translation was, indeed, *fool*. Among the Northern Algonkians, the word *wendigo* was frequently used to "denote something like 'a fool,'" namely, "an individual who had lost his or her wits, but never in the sense of 'a ghoul.'"[12]

Confusion also occurs because the words of Algonkian-speaking peoples are "too often taken as literal (rather than imaginative or symbolic) representations of events."[13] Native author and ethnographer Basil Johnston has repeatedly observed that nonnatives very often reduce the metaphorical aspects of words and seize on their literal interpretations.[14] In the case of the word *wendigo*, Johnston states that, whereas white people typically translate it as a cannibal monster, the word also functions symbolically to connote gluttony and "the image of excess."[15] According to Johnston, "turning Wendigo" is a real possibility because the word refers to the more abstract capacity for self-destruction.[16]

By far the greatest misunderstanding concerning the Wendigo (which directly relates to Atwood's depictions of cannibalism), involves the belief that the image of the blood-thirsty cannibal monster sprang fully formed from within native culture. As Raymond Fogelson notes, however, early references to the Wendigo relate to an evil god who posed a threat to humans and had to be propitiated. In these accounts, "characteristics which were later associated with the Windigo being *are absent*, including his gigantic stature, his anthropophagous or cannibal propensities, and his symbolic connection with the north, winter, and starvation."[17] The shift from evil deity to flesh-eating monster has led a number of anthropologists to speculate that "the attribute of cannibalism or the concept of wendigo as a category or race of non-human entities developed after European contact."[18] Anthropologist Lou Marano confirms that the native category "carried no semantic connotation of cannibalism, but took on this ancillary meaning for 150 years or more during crisis conditions of a particular kind."[19] He concludes that the Europeans played a significant role in creating the cannibal monster that they looked on with such revulsion and fascination.

In keeping with Marano's findings, Charles Bishop argues that the incidence of Wendigo accusations, like the extensive witch trials in America, are tied to stress within the community. In the case of natives in North America, this stress was largely brought about by dwindling resources and increased dependence on trading posts. Europeans, who made contact with native communities, introduced deadly diseases, including small pox, sexually transmitted diseases, and tuberculosis. As a result of the spread of these illnesses, kinship groups faced huge losses;

hunters died, and without them, starvation was inevitable. Unwittingly, the explorers and fur traders who reported the savagery of the natives—a savagery epitomized by anthropophagy—were themselves responsible for creating starvation conditions. According to Bishop, the extermination of game aroused legitimate fears of starvation, which, in turn, led to increased reports of wendigo behavior.[20]

Wendigo tales, passed down from generation to generation, attest to the native people's awareness that the Europeans posed a threat to the health and well-being of their society. A short fable, told by the Northern Algonkians, illustrates their understanding of the connection between the arrival of the Europeans and the Wendigo:

> [Wahpun, the East Wind] saw that the living on this earth, they would require light to guide them through life. . . . Wahpun would [also] introduce many foreign wares from abroad to support life: food, tools, and raiment. "Oh!" called out the Rabbit [Wahpus], yes you will introduce many useful things such as you mention, but you will also introduce the Wendigo who will cross the Atlantic and consume human flesh.[21]

Told by an old man at an Indian feast at York Factory in the fall of 1823, this story clarifies that the Wendigo is not indigenous, but crosses the Atlantic, arriving in conjunction with the Europeans.

I offer this detailed contextual information because Atwood's adaptation of the figure of the cannibal will not make sense if Wendigo tales are dismissed as the fanciful product of an exotic culture. Nor will they make sense if they are treated as so-called empirical facts about native civilization. Instead, they must be read as disaster narratives that register the impact of imperialism and colonization. The links between the evolution of the flesh-eating Wendigo and the arrival of the Europeans help to explain why Atwood can state emphatically that her stories are informed by Wendigo tales, even though they do not feature flesh-eating monsters from the Canadian north. This seeming inconsistency is resolved only if one recognizes that the stories in *Wilderness Tips*, which span in narrative time from the 1940s to the 1980s, show us the face of the "white cannibal." By recounting parallel disasters and alluding to canonical disaster narratives of the settler-invader society, including *Frankenstein*, the Franklin expedition, the Titanic, and Revelation, the stories in *Wilderness Tips* trace the postcontact Wendigo's mirror image and expose the consumptive mentality and violence that underpins the ongoing legacy of imperialism.

The unchecked will to consume at the heart of the western and European model of society reaches pathological proportions in "Hairball," a story that explores the life of Kat, a young Canadian woman, who claws her way to a senior position at an avant-garde magazine in London, England. Her success at the heart of the empire rests on her predatory skills. As the narrator explains, when "knives were slated for backs, she'd always done the stabbing."[22] But Kat's achievement is also owing to her ability to infect others with the Wendigo spirit, by reinforcing the belief that consumption equals power. Contemplating the basis of her success, she explains:

> What you had to make them believe was that you knew something they didn't know yet. What you also had to make them believe was that they too could know this thing, this thing that would give them eminence and power and sexual allure, that would attract envy to them—but for a price. The price of the magazine.[23]

The story makes it clear, however, that like the Wendigo who eats and eats but is never sated, consumer culture leaves everyone famished. The people who buy the magazine are never satisfied because, as Kat admits, "it was all photography, it was all iconography. . . . This was the thing that could never be bought, no matter how much of your pitiful monthly wage you blew on snakeskin."[24] And even though Kat appears to be at the top of the food chain, she too remains hungry. As the narrator explains, unable to "afford many of the things she contextualized so well,"[25] she gorges on "the canapes at literary launches in order to scrimp on groceries."[26]

Unsatisfied, Kat becomes disillusioned with her exhausting life in England. We are told that she "got tired of the grottiness and expense of London,"[27] its class divisions, competition, conspicuous consumption, and the English men, who were, according to Kat, "very competitive" and "liked to win."[28] Although she revels in her power, boasting that "it was like being God,"[29] as a colonial in Britain, she admits that she was "of no class. She had no class," and is deemed to be of "no consequence."[30] When Gerald, a scout from a new fashion magazine in Toronto recruits her, Kat, weary of life as an exile, is secretly grateful for the opportunity to escape.

Returning to Toronto with apparent cultural caché, street smarts, and a heavy dose of imperialist pride, Kat views Canada as an antiquated colonial outpost. Even Gerald, who becomes her boss and lover, strikes her as uniformly harmless and bland. Initially, Kat does not recognize that her Canadian wilderness has tipped and that, in the consumer culture of the 1980s, the relationship between center and margin, predator and prey has become ambiguous. The narrative foreshadows the implication of this ambiguity early on, when Kat compares herself to Victor Frankenstein and brags that Gerald is "her creation."[31] But readers familiar with Mary Shelley's gothic tale know that Victor's belief that he is a father-figure or creator of a new race is similarly hubristic. Later, after Gerald steals her job at the magazine, Kat identifies once again with Victor Frankenstein. She reads Gerald's betrayal as a predictable outcome. As she says, the "monster has turned on its own mad scientist. 'I gave you life!' she wants to scream at him."[32] Not only does the *Frankenstein* intertext underscore the basic confusion concerning who is in power, more importantly, it also reinforces Atwood's reliance on the Wendigo theme.

With its Arctic setting and emphasis on the doubled relationship between creature and creator, *Frankenstein* shares basic features of Wendigo stories. In keeping with Atwood's description of the Wendigo, Frankenstein's monster represents a "fragment of the protagonist's psyche, a sliver of his repressed inner life made visible."[33] At one point, Victor Frankenstein admits that he considers his creature, the "being whom I had cast among mankind, and endowed with the will and power to effect purposes of horror, nearly in the light of my own vampire, my own spirit let loose from the grave and forced to destroy all that was dear to me."[34] Also in keeping with Wendigo tales is *Frankenstein*'s concern for those whom the dominant society marginalizes and consumes. Initially, the monster, akin to Rousseau's noble savage, is innately good, and he condemns unjust European practices. In a memorable episode, the monster weeps when he learns about the colonization of the American hemisphere and the Europeans' brutal treatment of its original inhabitants.[35] Western society's lust for power is seemingly embodied in Victor. Not surprisingly, his fate also mirrors that of the Wendigo's victims. He ends up losing his mind and personality and destroying his family members and those he loves most. Taken together, the parallels between *Frankenstein* and the Wendigo tales signal a related desire to explore the pathological will to consume that characterizes western culture. What I mean by the notion of consumption in the case of *Frankenstein* is Victor's commodification of human flesh in order to create a product, a being that would transcend death.

In her book *Cannibal Culture*, Deborah Root argues that the figure of the cannibal constitutes a powerful, albeit largely "elided and disavowed" metaphor for western society:

> The cannibal seeks human bodies to eat, and the desire for flesh generates escalating desire. This hunger for flesh is generalized into society as a whole when consumption is treated as a virtue and seen as a source of pleasure and excitement in itself. Consumption is power, and the ability to consume excessively and willfully becomes the most desirable aspect of power.[36]

Her comments shed light on Kat's skill in making the public think that consumption equals power. But Root argues further that the figure of the Wendigo offers an accurate picture of the West because it is, paradoxically, both a hungry predator and something horribly confused and ill.[37] According to Root, this predatory mindset and sickness persist because of western culture's inability to come to terms with the centrality of its consumptive impulse. This inability springs from two sources: a failure of reflexivity and a tendency to aestheticize and consume difference.[38]

As noted earlier, Atwood avoids the trap of consuming difference and reifying native Wendigo stories because her fiction focuses on the presence of the Wendigo in its European and western narrative counterparts. More specifically, the repeated allusions to *Frankenstein*, accounts of the ill-fated Franklin expedition, the Titanic, and Revelation facilitate the type of reflexivity that Root argues is missing from western discourse because these intertexts remind readers that a penchant for violence, greed, and in some cases, an appetite for flesh are inextricable elements of our own cannibal culture. Relying on western culture's own canonical Wendigo tales, Atwood's stories underscore the dangers inherent in an imperialist agenda that rests on the misguided belief that we are superhuman beings destined to master our environment. In "Hairball," as we have seen, allusions to *Frankenstein* convey the dangers associated with the desire to seize power in order to transcend the human—dangers that are predicated on the commodification of human flesh.

To further illustrate the pervasive use of the Wendigo theme throughout Atwood's collection, this study will digress from the analysis of "Hairball" briefly to discuss several other stories that also allude to canonical western cannibal fictions. For example, in "The Age of Lead," references to the story of the Franklin expedition reinforce the dangers associated with imperialist consumption. Similarly, in the story "Weight," and in the title story, "Wilderness Tips," the image of the Titanic symbolizes the disaster that attends the West's voracious pursuit of pleasure, material gain, and mastery over nature. As the story of the Franklin expedition is central to Atwood's fiction but may not be widely known, I will outline the details.

In May of 1845, Sir John Franklin and 135 men sailed from England in search of the Northwest Passage. Europeans had been attempting to find a way across North America for 300 years. The voyage's primary motive was economic, but as Sherrill Grace notes, "economic motives included, of course, imperialist pride, power, and domination."[39] However, something went terribly wrong with Franklin's voyage of discovery. Predator ended up becoming prey when the men were swallowed by the Arctic, virtually without a trace.

The expedition was last sighted in Baffin Bay, in July of 1845. After that, the ships simply vanished. Almost ten years later, the surveyor John Rae learned from some Inuit hunters that the ships had been crushed in the ice and the expedition's men had starved to death while trying to make their way south. The story of the Franklin expedition is also a cannibal fiction. As Atwood cheerfully explains, the men indulged "in a little cannibalism along the way. (Mention "has been made, for instance, of a bootful of human flesh)."[40] Relishing every opportunity to reveal the hypocrisy of western culture, Atwood recalls that the Inuit who relayed this information were "indignantly denounced as barbaric liars, because a Briton could not possibly have behaved so hungrily; though later research has proved them true."[41]

Eventually, bodies and remnants of the expedition were discovered, and, from samples of hair and fingernails, the scientists concluded that the men had been suffering from high levels of lead poisoning. Ironically, the seemingly god-like technological advancements on which their confidence was based betrayed them. The up-to-date tin cans they took with them, packed full of meat and soup, were soldered together with lead. The food and the landscape they expected to consume ended up consuming them.

In the story "The Age of Lead," Atwood draws a parallel between lead poisoning in the Arctic over a hundred years ago and conditions in the contemporary urban wasteland. Just as Franklin's sailors perished at an early age, in the 1980s disaster strikes again; as the narrator explains, people began dying "too early": "It was as if they had been weakened by some mysterious agent, a thing like a colorless gas, scentless and invisible, so that any germ that happened along could invade their bodies, take them over."[42]

The final story, "Hack Wednesday," continues to highlight the related motifs of disaster and consumption. The moment she wakes up, the protagonist, Marcia, hears the radio announcer's voice filled with heightened energy because, as she notes, he is describing "a disaster of some kind."[43] Every catastrophe, from the Panama invasion to global warming, makes an appearance. On her way to work, Marcia sees two homeless natives and imagines that they've "had it with this city, they've had it with suicide as an option, they've had it with the twentieth century."[44] In an episode that reinforces the connections among disaster, imperialism, and consumption, Marcia's husband, Eric, battles against the destructive forces of neoimperialism by restricting his family's consumption. As Marcia explains, he won't eat Cheerios "because they're American." She recounts that "ever since the Free Trade deal with the States went through he has refused to purchase anything from south of the border."[45] However noble, his efforts prove futile and despair is pervasive. Ultimately, "The Age of Lead," "Hack Wednesday," and their intertexts reveal that the Wendigo constitutes a prominent feature of contemporary Canadian society.

Turning back to "Hairball," we can see the theme of consumption surfacing with a vengeance. To a great extent, the story invokes elements from Wendigo tales to highlight parallels between the settler-invader society's treatment of natives and its treatment of women. As I suggested in the introduction, Atwood's stories underscore the connections between the legacy of imperialism and colonization, and the predatory and consumptive nature of gender politics.

The story "Hairball" highlights the theme of consumption early on. When Gerald first meets Kat, he takes her to an expensive restaurant. After he entreats her to consider working in Toronto, she coolly surveys the posh establishment and asks, "Where would I eat?" He assures her that Toronto is now the restaurant capital of the world and goes on to inquire about her unusual name. Although the ostensible subject has changed, they are still talking about food. "Is that Kat as in Krazy?" he asks. She replies, "No . . . It's Kat as in KitKat. That's a chocolate bar. Melts in your mouth."[46] In this brief exchange, Kat aligns herself with food.

An interesting parallel can be drawn between Kat's remark (which ties in with the preoccupation with chocolate throughout the story) and the Lakota term used for white people, "Wasi'chu," which means "fat-eater," or "greedy one who takes the fat." There are also strong similarities between "Wasi'chu" and the notion of the Wendigo. As Deborah Root explains, the Lakota term delineates "a particular mentality, a bizarre obsession that is organized almost entirely around consumption and excess."[47]

As their relationship unfolds, orality and food, specifically chocolate, continues to play a central role. At the first opportunity, Kat seduces Gerald in his office. Kneeling on the broadloom, she unzips his pants and, although it is not made explicit, presumably engages in oral sex.[48] The next day, Gerald expresses his gratitude by presenting her with an expensive box of chocolate truffles.[49] Secure in the belief that she has utterly conquered and consumed him, Kat remarks that she finds this gesture "banal, but also sweet."[50] In hindsight, the reader understands that, in offering her this gift, Gerald has taken her at her word: he equates her with chocolate—a luxury to be consumed. In the end, it comes as no surprise when he swallows her whole; while she recovers from an operation to remove an ovarian cyst, Gerald fires her and takes over her job at the magazine. Wendigo legends confirm that it is better to be consumed outright than caught by the creature because the victim who walks out alive becomes a cannibal, totally devoid of individuality.[51] After his encounter with Kat, Gerald emerges as a Wendigo.

Ultimately, it is Kat who epitomizes the sickness at the core of Western culture—a culture that, as Deborah Root suggests, is, paradoxically, both a hungry predator and something terribly confused and ill.[52] Much to Gerald's horror, Kat decides to save the cyst she dubs Hairball in a jar of formaldehyde and display it on her mantlepiece. As she says, it is no different "than having a stuffed bear's head or anything else with fur and teeth looming over your fireplace."[53] Her comment forges a connection between Hairball and other uncanny creatures that haunt the wilderness. Its mysterious nature is also emphasized when Kat's doctor states that, while some people thought "it was present in seedling form from birth, it might also 'be the woman's undeveloped twin'; but, ultimately, what they really were was unknown."[54] His eerie pronouncement highlights the parallels between Kat's relationship to her cyst and the Wendigo's relationship to its victims. When Kat begins to converse with Hairball, it becomes apparent that, like the Wendigo, her cyst represents "a fragment of [her] . . . psyche, a sliver of [her] . . . repressed inner life made visible."[55] In accordance with Atwood's description of the flesh-eating monster, Hairball manifests itself "through the victim's body," splits "off from the rest of the personality, and destroys it."[56]

As suggested earlier, Atwood's stories avoid the failure of nonreflexivity by forcing readers to come to terms with the Wendigo within western culture rather than project the image of barbaric cannibal onto native culture. In "Hairball," these reflexive moments are embedded within the narrative itself. In one scene, Kat looks at herself in the mirror and ponders her violent, predatory behavior—the smash-and-grab imperialist mentality that guided her every move. As she observes:

> She's only thirty-five, and she's already losing track of what people ten years younger are thinking. That could be fatal. As time goes by she'll have to race faster and faster to keep up, and for what? Part of the life she should have had is just a gap, it isn't there, it's nothing.[57]

Her musings on the rat race, in conjunction with the description of her illness and subsequent infection as a "running sore, a sore from running so hard," suggest that she has succumbed not to an isolated medical problem but to the diseased, obsessive lifestyle that characterizes consumer culture. Like the Wendigo, she is both "sick *and* predatory."[58] Toward the conclusion of "Hairball," Kat seethes with resentment because she has been consumed and rejected: Gerald fires her. To add insult to injury, after she is fired, she receives an invitation to a party hosted by Gerald and his wife, Cheryl. Perhaps it is only fitting that Kat, whom the Lakota would view as a greedy "fat-eater," should find herself "crackling inside, like hot fat under the broiler."[59] But the story prevents the reader from deriving any satisfaction from her downfall, by making it abundantly clear that there is something horrifically familiar about the way in which this game of consumption played by men and women draws to a close. Parallels between this episode and the biblical story Revelation show how women, like natives, are viewed as figures of abjection to legitimate their marginalization and ultimate consumption.

Imagining Gerald and his wife preparing for the party, Kat reels from the unfairness of it all. As she remarks, it is a "connubial scene. His conscience is nicely washed. The witch is dead, his foot is on the body, the trophy; he's had his dirty fling, he's ready now for the rest of his life."[60] The stark opposition between the death of the witch/whore and the marriage feast specifically recalls the notorious cannibal narrative, Revelation. In the biblical narrative, the whore/goddess of Babylon is also murdered and eaten. As the angel explains to John: "And the ten horns that you saw, they and the beast will eat the whore; they will make her desolate and naked; they will devour her flesh and burn her up with fire";[61] meanwhile, the Bride dines at the Eucharistic wedding feast. In this instance, Atwood's use of the Wendigo story, with its themes of consumption and excess, intimates that, in contemporary western society, it is typically women who are demonized and consumed. The link between consumption and women is evident throughout Atwood's corpus, beginning with her first novel, *The Edible Woman* (1969) .

In *Death and Desire*, Tina Pippin points out that the story of Revelation figures the "ultimate release of a colonized people," but this release is figured by the murder and consumption of a powerful female.[62] Revelation focuses on the "desire for and death of the female."[63] In the apocalyptic story, the body of woman "is marginalized . . . or violently destroyed. . . . What is considered unclean and dangerous by the male hierarchy has to be placed outside the camp. Those on the inside .. . in this cultural system are all male."[64] Only the 144,000 men "who have not defiled themselves with women" can enter the New Jerusalem.[65] Kat's position as the lone female entrepreneur forced to work with an all-male board of Canadian businessmen ironically recalls the fate of the goddess of Babylon. Kat likewise offends the male hierarchy. They "think she's too bizarre, they think she goes way too far."[66] At bottom, she threatens them and they place her outside the camp. Only domesticated women—women willing to serve the dominant order's agenda are allowed through the gates.

Pippin comments on the famous mid-sixteenth-century Brussels Tapestry of the apocalyptic marriage that shows the marriage supper, "with a beautiful, smiling Bride with her arm around the Lamb . . . [and] directly above the Bride's head lies the burning Whore, surrounded by flames with a look of horror on her face."[67] In the light of its treatment of women, Pippin concludes that Revelation is "the 'writing of the disaster' of the history of women in male-dominated societies."[68]

By harkening to the cannibalism and marriage feast in Revelation, "Hairball" and the collection as a whole force readers to grapple with the fact that, in the cannibal narratives of western culture, women, like savages, are demonized and consumed. In Atwood's stories, it is primarily women who are vilified and dismembered for consumption. For example, in the opening story "True Trash," repeated parallels are drawn between women and butchered meat.[69] Similarly, in the story "Weight," the narrator's best friend, Molly, is literally dismembered by her psychotic husband.

As mentioned earlier, "Weight" alludes to yet another of western culture's disaster narratives. The narrator, who raises funds for Molly's Place, a shelter for battered women, meets with a prospective donor at a restaurant. Thinking of her friend's tragic death, she surveys the crowd and imagines that "[i]t's like the Titanic just before the iceberg; power and influence disporting themselves, not a care in the world. What do they know about the serfs down in steerage? Piss all, and pass the port."[70] Images of consumption and the Titanic also appear in the title story, "Wilderness Tips," and here, too, they signal the disaster associated with the consumption of women.

In "Wilderness Tips," a predatory man named George, a refugee from Hungary, marries into a wealthy, established Canadian family. Early on, George describes his innocent and youthful future wife, Portia, as his "host." The girl's sister, Pamela, attempts to correct him, explaining that he should have said "hostess" because a "'host' is male, like 'mine host' in an inn, or else it's the wafer you eat at Communion. Or the caterpillar that all the parasites lay their eggs on."[71] Her comments, with their references to the Eucharist and to caterpillars devoured by parasites, bring together the sacred and profane facets of cannibalism associated with the Christian vision of the apocalypse.

The story concludes with an image of the Titanic. Portia, who discovers that George has slept with Pamela, the sister she most trusted, equates the betrayal with the sinking of the Titanic:

> She sees herself running naked through the ballroom—an absurd, disturbing figure, with dripping hair and flailing arms, screaming at them, "don't you see? It's coming apart, everything's coming apart, you're sinking. You're finished, you're over, you're dead!"[72]

Taken together, the references both to Revelation and the Titanic in Atwood's collection support Tina Pippin's belief that misogyny at the end of the twentieth century may be "more technologically advanced, but the roots and results of woman-hatred are the same."[73]

To my mind, of all the stories, "Hairball" is most intriguing because Kat attempts to challenge the misogynist ideology that informs the biblical cannibal narrative, although the outcome of her challenge remains unclear. In a gesture of defiance (and a most disquieting culinary endeavor), Kat buys two dozen chocolate truffles, nestles her cyst in the box of goodies, and sends the package to Gerald's wife. All along, the text has hinted at the consumptive basis of their relationship, but with this act, Kat foregrounds a distinctly cannibalistic element. Afterward, feverish and weak, Kat "foolishly" walks out into the snowfall. As the narrator explains:

> She intends to walk just to the corner, but when she reaches the corner she goes on. . . . She has done an outrageous thing, but she doesn't feel guilty. She feels light and peaceful and filled with charity, and temporarily without a name.[74]

On the one hand, her gruesome gift, coupled with her "foolish" disappearance into the snow, and the erasure of her name (a sign of her humanity) suggest that she has "gone Wendigo."[75] Like the poor souls caught by the cannibal monster, Kat ends up losing her human mind and destroying those she loves. Interpreted in this way, this episode suggests that she remains a victim of a contemporary western Wendigo tale.

On the other hand, the allusions to the consumption of human flesh in this episode specifically can be read in the light of Northrop Frye's analysis of the dialectical relationship between the Eucharist symbolism of the apocalyptic world and its demonic parody.[76] According to Frye, in the apocalyptic world we often "find the cannibal feast, the serving up of a child or lover as food."[77] One could argue that, by self-consciously viewing a fragment of her body as food for her lover's consumption, Kat manages to transform western culture's brutal acts of cannibalism into a conscious, Christ-like act of communion.[78] Atwood's fictions repeatedly allude to the degradation of the human community and the rituals that sustain it, specifically, the Eucharist. For example, in *Surfacing*, the narrator chastises people for their profane attitude toward consumption, a practice that she believes should be viewed as sacred. As she says:

> The animals die that we may live, they are substitute people, hunters in the fall killing the deer, that is Christ also. And we eat them, out of cans or otherwise; we are eaters of death, dead Christ-flesh resurrecting inside us, granting us life. Canned Spam, canned Jesus, even the plants must be Christ. But we refuse to worship; the body worships with blood and muscle but the thing in the knob of our head will not, wills not to, the head is greedy, it consumes but does not give thanks.[79]

In offering her cyst to her lover, Kat forcibly reminds Gerald and, presumably, his guests that their lives are predicated on sacrifice. More important, Hairball will remind them that the bodies which they degrade, consume, and forget are, in fact, sacred because they ensure the continued existence of the human community. At bottom, with this gesture, Kat invites everyone to do what she has done, and what Atwood has been doing throughout *Wilderness Tips*, namely, to look in the mirror, reflect on our own greedy behavior—the legacy of imperialism at the heart of our disaster narratives—and acknowledge the face of the white cannibal.

NOTES

1. Edward Said, *Culture and Imperialism* (New York: Vintage, 1994), 332.

2. Margaret Atwood, "Cannibal Lecture," *Saturday Night*, Nov. 1995, 81–90.

3. Margaret Atwood, *Strange Things: The Malevolent North in Canadian Literature* (Toronto: Oxford, 1995), 66.

4. Atwood, *Strange*, 67.

5. Atwood, *Strange*, 67.

6. Atwood, *Strange*, 74.

7. Atwood, *Strange*, 74.

8. Atwood, *Strange*, 84.

9. Atwood, *Strange*, 114.

10. In his introduction to *Windigo: an Anthology of Fact and Fantastic Fiction* (Sasktoon, Sask.: Western Producer Prairie Books, 1982), John Robert Columbo provides the same, although more detailed, nonnative account.

11. The information concerning the Wendigo is drawn from my more detailed study "A Taste of the Wild: A Critique of Representations of Natives as Cannibals in Late-Eighteenth-Century and Nineteenth-Century Canadian Exploration Literature," *Literary Studies East and West* 10 (1996): 43-64.

12. Lou Marano, "On Windigo," *Current Anthropology* 24.1 (1983): 124.

13. Richard Preston, *Cree Narrative: Expressing the Personal Meanings of Events* (National Museum of Man, Mercury Series, Canadian Ethnology Service Paper 30, 1975), 112.

14. See his essays "One Generation from Extinction" and "Is That All There Is?" In *An Anthology of Canadian Native Literature in English*. Eds. Daniel David Moses and Terry Goldie. (Toronto: Oxford UP, 1982).

15. Basil Johnson, *Ojibway Heritage* (Toronto: McClelland and Stewart, 1976), 66.

16. Telephone interview, 11 May 1995.

17. Raymond Fogelson, "Psychological Theories of Windigo Psychosis and a Preliminary Application of a Models Approach," *Context and Meaning in Cultural Anthropology: Essays in Honour of A. Irving Hallowell*, ed. Melford E. Spiro (New York: Free Press, 1965), 77.

18. See J. Brown and R. Brighton, *The Orders of the Dreamed: George Nelson on Cree and Northern Ojibwa Religion and Legend* (Winnipeg: University of Manitoba Press), 161.

19. Marano, 124.

20. See Bishop's two studies "Northern Algonkian Cannibalism and the Windigo Psychosis" *Psychological Anthropology*, ed. T. R. Williams (The Hague: Mouton, 1975), 245; and *The Northern Ojibwa and the Fur Trade* (Toronto: Holt, Rinehart and Winston, 1974), 12.

21. Quoted in Bruce Morrison and C. Roderick Wilson, *Native Peoples and the Canadian Experience* (Toronto: McClelland and Stewart, 1986), 225.

22. Atwood, *Wilderness Tips* (Toronto: McClelland-Bantam, 1991), 46.

23. Atwood, *Wilderness Tips*, 37.

24. Atwood, *Wilderness Tips*, 37.

25. Atwood, *Wilderness Tips*, 38.

26. Atwood, *Wilderness Tips*, 38.

27. Atwood, *Wilderness Tips*, 38.

28. Atwood, *Wilderness Tips*, 39.

29. Atwood, *Wilderness Tips*, 37.

30. Atwood, *Wilderness Tips*, 38-9.

31. Atwood, *Wilderness Tips*, 36.

32. Atwood, *Wilderness Tips*, 45.

33. Atwood, *Strange*, 74.

34. Mary Shelley, *Frankenstein*, ed. D. L. Macdonald and Kathleen Scherf (Peterborough, Ont.: Broadview Press, 1994), 105.

35. Shelley, 147.

36. Deborah Root, *Cannibal Culture* (Boulder, Colo.: Westview, 1996), 9.

37. Root, 201.

38. Root, xii.

39. Sherrill Grace, "'Franklin Lives': Atwood's Northern Ghosts," *Various Atwoods*, ed. Lorraine York (Concord, Ont.: Anansi, 1995), 148.

40. Atwood, *Strange*, 13.

41. Atwood, *Strange*, 13.

42. Atwood, *Wilderness Tips*, 166.

43. Atwood, *Wilderness Tips*, 219.

44. Atwood, *Wilderness Tips*, 225.

45. Atwood, *Wilderness Tips*, 222.

46. Atwood, *Wilderness Tips*, 40.

47. Root, 10.

48. Atwood, *Wilderness Tips*, 40-41.

49. Atwood, *Wilderness Tips*, 41.

50. Atwood, *Wilderness Tips*, 41.

51. See Columbo, 3–4.

52. Root, 201.

53. Atwood, *Wilderness Tips*, 34.

54. Atwood, *Wilderness Tips*, 46.

55. Atwood, *Strange*, 74

56. Atwood, *Strange*, 74.

57. Atwood, *Wilderness Tips*, 46.

58. Root, 202.

59. Atwood, *Wilderness Tips*, 47.

60. Atwood, *Wilderness Tips*, 47-48.

61. Rev. 17.16, Revised Standard Edition.

62. Tina Pippin, *Death and Desire: The Rhetoric of Gender in the Apocalypse of John* (Louisville, Ky.: Westminister/John Knox, 1992), 28.

63. Pippin, 16.

64. Pippin, 50.

65. Rev. 14.4, Revised Standard Edition.

66. Atwood, *Wilderness Tips*, 44–45.

67. Pippin, 107.

68. Pippin, 79.

69. As outlined in "True Trash," this process involves teaching boys to objectify women (the campers' use of binoculars is a familiar Atwoodian motif) and to align them with meat. For example, we are told that, in the eyes of the boys, the waitresses basking in the sun resemble a "herd of skinned seals" (1). When he meets Joanne, one of the waitresses, eleven years after his camp experience, Donny, now a connoisseur of women's bodies, happily scrutinizes her legs and thinks of inferior legs as "hams in cloth" (25). In this way, "True Trash" suggests that views of the body can tip or, perhaps more accurately, fall. As a boy, Donny had a crush on Ronette, his favorite waitress, and fought for her honor against his counsellor, Darce, who labeled her "summer sausage."

The commodification of women, which turns them into food/meat, remains a long-standing concern in Atwood's writing. As mentioned earlier, this issue is central to *The Edible Woman*. It returns with a vengeance in *Cat's Eye*, when, as Barbara DeConcini notes, the narrator notices in her art history course "how naked women are presented in the same painterly manner as plates of meat" (see her essay "Narrative Hunger" in *The Daemonic Imagination: Biblical Text and Secular Story*. Eds. Robert Detweiler and William G. Doty (Atlanta: Scholars P, 1990).

70. Atwood, *Wilderness Tips*, 186.

71. Atwood, *Wilderness Tips*, 211.

72. Atwood, *Wilderness Tips*, 216.

73. Pippin, 53.

74. Atwood, *Wilderness Tips*, 48.

75. As John Robert Columbo explains, "the creature has no name. No one may know it and live to tell about it, so the Windigo must remain nameless" (2).

76. See Northrop Frye's *Anatomy of Criticism: Four Essays* (Princeton: Princeton, N.J.: UP, 1957), 147–50.

77. Northrop Frye, *The Secular Scripture: A Study of the Structure of Romance* (Cambridge, Mass.: Harvard UP, 1976), 118.

78. References to the Eucharist can also be understood to express a desire to return to the premodern relationship between the real and the image. In his essay, "The Hazard of Modern Poetry," Erich Heller traces the origin of the modern predicament, the separation of the real from the symbolic, back to sixteenth-cen-

tury Marburg, to the theological dispute between Luther and Zwingli about the nature of the Eucharist. For Luther, the bread and the wine were "the thing itself," the blood and the body of Christ; for Zwingli, they were "mere symbols." According to the postmodern theorist Jean Baudrillard, we have now reached a stage of simulation where "it is no longer a question of imitation, nor of reduplication, nor even of parody. It is rather a question of substituting signs of the real for the real itself" (4). Jean Baudrillard, *Simulations*; trans. Paul Foss, Paul Patton and Philip Beitchman (New York: Columbia, 1983). Viewed in this context, Kat's transformation from a producer of images, who glories in playing with "frozen light" and "frozen time," to a person who offers her tumor as food and insists that it "has the texture of reality, it is not an image" (*Wilderness Tips* 47) represents a return to "the thing itself" and a healing of the rift between the real and the symbolic. Of course, a critic like Baudrillard would read this image of communion both as an indicator of Kat's nostalgia for the real and as further proof of the irrevocable loss of the real. As Baudrillard explains:

> When the real is no longer what it used to be, nostalgia assumes its full meaning. There is a proliferation of myths of origin and *signs of reality*. There is an escalation of the true, of the lived experience. . . . And there is a panic-stricken production of the real and the referential, above and parallel to the panic of material production. (12–13; my emphasis)

79. Atwood, *Surfacing* (Toronto, Ont.: General, 1972), 150.

10

The Missed Encounter: Cannibalism and the Literary Critic

It is the cause, it is the cause, my soul;
Let me not name it to you, you chaste stars,
It is the cause.

—*Othello* v:2, 1–3

GEOFFREY SANBORN

Eight white men are gathered on a beach; their ship is anchored in the harbor behind them (figure, pg.188). The leader of the group, taller and better dressed than the others, is holding up a human hand that he has apparently just taken from a basket held by the man beside him. The hand is oddly over-sized, sharply defined against a background of sky, and its palm, inscribed with the letters "T" and "H," faces the viewer. The eyes of the leader and the man directly across from him in the foreground of the picture are riveted on this object, but the men surrounding them have turned their faces away; several of them appear to be staring into space. In the middle distance, we see three shadowy figures on the shore, one of whom is running from a canoe with his arm outstretched. In the lower left corner, a dog has found some shapeless object and has it in its teeth.

The source of the picture is the *Journal of the Resolution's Voyage*, published anonymously in 1775. The text that accompanies the picture tells of

Lt. James Burney with the hand of Thomas Hill. *Journal of the Resolution's Voyage.* 1775. Reprint, New York: Da Capo Press, 1967.

a search party from the *Resolution*'s sister ship, the *Adventure*, discovering in a New Zealand cove the dismembered bodies of some sailors who had gone among the Maoris the day before. The party, led by Lieutenant James Burney, found in a Maori canoe

> a pair of shoes tied up together. On advancing farther up the beach, they found several of their people's baskets, and saw one of their dogs eating a piece of broiled flesh, which upon examining they suspected to be human, and having found in one of the baskets a hand, which they knew to be the left hand of Thomas Hill, by the letters T. H. being marked on it, they were no longer in suspense about the event.[1]

In his representation of the event, the artist obviously means to capture that moment of perfect conviction, when the members of the search party can no longer doubt that the Maoris are cannibals and that they have eaten British sailors. Confronted by the sign of the most outrageous act of savagery imaginable, these eight white men on the edge of a strange land have been rendered speechless and immobile: their jaws are slack, their gazes are frozen or averted, and their guns are balanced loosely on their shoulders. In their shared sensation of horror, they express a shared "humanity," a moral sentiment that is defined by its abhorrence of all forms of "savagery." But even as the picture invites its European viewers to join in this involuntary expression of an innate morality, it suggests, in the urgency of its invitation, that the humanity of these viewers is peculiarly dependent on the spectacle it abhors. It suggests this in its hyperbolic representation of the hand, not just blown up, but also drawn to our attention by the fixed gazes of the two figures in the foreground and the pointing finger of another man. It suggests it, as well, in its depiction of the meat-tugging dog, which indicates that even the enormous hand requires corroborating evidence. Though these images are intended to point us in the direction of the absent cannibals, they also point us in the direction of the "humane" observers, so anxious to dispel their suspense and so strangely in need of the signs of the cannibal.

Another example may help to make this point more clear. In his 1832 *Narrative of a Residence in New Zealand*, the British artist Augustus Earle reports that during his brief stay on the north island, he got wind of a rumor that the corpse of a female slave was about to be eaten in a nearby village. Because "much [had] been written to prove the non-existence of so hideous a propensity," he and his companion, Captain Duke, immediately "resolved to witness this dreadful scene." As they neared the village, they caught sight of a Maori oven—a hole filled with stones that had been heated in a nearby fire.

> We ran towards the fire, and there stood a man occupied in a way few would wish to see. He was preparing the four quarters of a human body for a feast; the large bones, having been taken out, were thrown aside, and the flesh being compressed, he was in the act of forcing it into the oven. While we stood transfixed by this terrible sight, a large dog, which lay before the fire, rose up, seized the bloody head, and walked off with it into the bushes; no doubt to hide it there for another meal! The man completed his task with the most perfect composure, telling us, at the same time, that the repast would not be ready for some hours!
>
> Here stood Captain Duke and myself, both witnesses of a scene which many travellers have related, and their relations have invariably been treated with contempt; indeed, the veracity of those who had the temerity to relate such incredible events has been every where questioned. In this instance it was no warrior's flesh to be eaten; there was no enemy's blood to drink, in order to infuriate them. They had no revenge to gratify; no plea they could make of their passions having been roused by battle, nor the excuse that they eat their enemies to perfect their triumph. This was an action of unjustifiable cannibalism. Atoi, the chief, who had given orders for this cruel feast, had only the night before sold us four pigs for a few pounds of powder; so he had not even the excuse of want of food. After Captain Duke and myself had consulted with each other, we walked into the village, determined to charge Atoi with his brutality.[2]

Like the picture of the *Adventure*'s search party, Earle's description magnifies the signs of cannibalism in order to legitimate the tableau of humanity frozen in horror by the spectacle of savagery. Even more obviously than in the picture, moreover, Earle's intense desire for these signs overtakes and undermines the nominal subject. Unlike the search party, he has gone looking for these signs for their own sake; it is abundantly clear that he *wants* to see a Maori "occupied in a way few would wish to see." Once he finds the scene he is looking for, he repeatedly reminds us that he and his companion are indeed witnessing it—"Here stood Captain Duke and myself"—and that they are united in horror: "we stood transfixed by this terrible sight." Finally, by dwelling at length on the conclusions he draws while standing there, he indicates both that he understands his own spontaneous reflections on the event to be the preeminent object of interest and that he finds it hard to drag himself away. After being rebuffed by the chief, in fact, he and Captain Duke return to "the spot where this disgusting mess was cooking." They sit "gazing on this melancholy place; it was a lowering gusty day, and the moaning of the wind through the bushes, as it swept round the hill on which we were, seemed in unison with our feelings." In consonance with nature, they too give "full vent to the most passionate exclamations of disgust" and proceed to dig up "the shocking spectacle" of the half-roasted body and rebury it, as the gathered members of two Maori villages look on. It is a purely gratuitous act, as he later admits, for when he goes back the next day the grave is empty. But it is, for that reason, a signal event: a consummate proof of the Englishmen's involuntary humanity and the Maoris' unquestionable savagery.[3]

Earle is not unconscious of the fact that his revisitings of this site, both at the time and in the act of writing about it, might look a little peculiar to his readers. In the midst of an ensuing account of the origin of cannibalism in New Zealand, he suddenly declares, "I will no longer dwell on this humiliating subject. Most white men who have visited the island have been sceptical on this point; I myself was, before I had 'ocular proof.' Consequently, I availed myself of the first opportunity to convince myself of the fact."[4] But neither is he able to keep it from looking peculiar; in protesting that he does not actually take any pleasure in seeing or dwelling on the signs of cannibalism, Earle only calls more attention to the fact that he has been dwelling on the subject for a very long time. And in his allusion to "ocular proof"—a phrase that shows up again and again in early nineteenth-century accounts of cannibalism—he undermines his position still further; whether he intends it or not, he is situating his intense desire for evidence within one of the most damning contexts imaginable.[5] The source of the allusion is the scene in *Othello* in which Othello, his jealousy aroused, says to Iago, "Villain, be sure thou prove my love a whore; / Be sure of it. Give me the ocular proof." The point of the rest of that play, of course, is that if the jealous desire for evidence of infidelity is strong enough, the quality of the evidence is irrelevant; as Emilia says, jealous souls "are not ever jealous for the cause, / But jealous for they're jealous."[6] The object that ultimately satisfies Othello's desire for ocular proof is nothing more than a planted handkerchief, not a "cause" to which his jealousy can be objectively referred, but an indifferent object that Iago's machinations and Othello's mounting jealousy have invested with the aura of a cause. In comparing his visual evidence of cannibalism to Othello's ocular proof, Earle invites a similar critique of his own efforts to discover a "cause" for humane horror in the spectacle of savagery. As Sir John Barrow, a well-known writer and reviewer of travel narratives, would observe a few years later, "though we are not at all disposed to impeach Mr. Earle's veracity, we should much like to have some clear evidence that he was not *hoaxed—in terrorem*."[7] Like the hand, Earle's ocular proof may be said to signify the excessiveness of his desire for it; like the handkerchief, it may also be said to indicate that he does not *discover* his "cause," but that the illusion of that cause was awaiting his arrival.

I want to use these two scenes as a means of evoking an argument that I have made at greater length elsewhere in *The Sign of the Cannibal*: that there is a traumatic absence—what Lacan would call a "missed encounter"—at the heart of the post-Enlightenment discourse on cannibalism.[8] My primary concern in this essay will be to discuss the implications of that fact for critics who analyze the textual figure of the cannibal. For the most part, these critics have begun from the premise that any representation of humanity's encounter with savagery is, by definition, a *mis*representation. They have then moved on to the assertion that we have to abandon the scene of the encounter in order to discover the truth within it. When their mode of analysis has been broadly "anthropological," they have established the structure of a native culture and then placed the acts of the so-called savages in that context. When their mode of analysis has been broadly "literary," they have claimed that the proper referent of "savagery" does not lie in the sphere of native culture but in some other abstract realm: the hearts of colonialists like Earle, for example, or the hearts of all human beings. Historically, these kinds of analyses have been extremely useful weapons in the arsenal of antiracist discourse. But they have come at a significant cost. Whenever someone declares, stepping back from the scene of the encounter, that we are all in fact "cultured," or "humane," or "savage," we lose sight of all the performative and interpretive work that has gone into the production of that encounter. We thereby lose an opportunity to provide antiracist discourse with a fresh point of departure. By holding that point, by staying focused on the scene of the encounter, we can make it increasingly difficult to relocate it within the conceptual spaces of "humanity," "savagery," "discourse," and "culture." If we stop thinking of the encounter as the translucent precipitate of one of these conceptual spaces, we can begin thinking of it instead as the kernel of the Real, the thing that must always be swallowed but can never be digested.

Before applying this argument to some of the recent work on cannibalism in the field of literary criticism, I want to address one of the objections that might emerge at this point. Given my allusion to Lacan's argument that the experiences of all subjects are structured around a missed encounter—"an appointment to which we are always called with a real that eludes us"—why am I bothering to specify the details of these encounters with cannibals? If I believe that it is simply the ordinary practice of all subjects to disavow "this obstacle, this hitch, that we find at every moment" by conjuring up "an Other that is not deceptive, and which shall, into the bargain, guarantee by its very existence the bases of truth," why focus on the figure of the cannibal at the expense of every other image that has, at one time or another, served as the illusory guarantor of the subject's truth?[9]

The answer to this crucial question is, in short, that the figure of the cannibal has been *especially* necessary to the constitution of the humane western subject, and *especially* liable to reveal the traces of the missed encounter that it is structured around. More than any other figure of "savagery," cannibalism has functioned as, in Ernesto Laclau's terms, the "constitutive outside" of the western ideology of humanity—the "ungraspable margin that limits and distorts the 'objective,' and which is, precisely, the real."[10] Nowhere is its constitutive function more clear than in Henry Bolingbroke's 1807 *Voyage to Demerary*, where we learn that the reason westerners consider cannibalism to be unnatural is that "it is a principle of our nature, to be averse to devouring what has been an object of love":

> Man is the object of our strongest affection—the tenderest emotions of the heart are excited by individuals of the human race and these emotions are extended by association in some degree to all mankind. The form, the countenance, the lineaments of man, excite in our minds faint traces of the love which we had felt for individuals of this kind. It is not surprising, therefore, that we should have the most invincible antipathy to eating human flesh; that we should shudder at devouring that which is so peculiarly associated with our strongest affections. . . . Cannibalism is the practice only of the most savage and ferocious nations, of those who have little sensibility of heart to render them capable of loving, and who are devoid of the amiable qualities of the mind, which are the objects of love.[11]

For Bolingbroke, the definition of "humanity" is, in part, "people who love people who love people"; he understands the "amiable qualities of the mind" to be both the agents and the objects of humane love. In order to be able to recognize "humanity" as "a principle of our nature," however, the subject must have some way of stepping outside its tautological structure and thereby establishing it as an object of reflection. For this reason, "humanity" must be additionally defined as "people who do not love people who eat people." In the shudder that passes through his or her body at the very idea of cannibalism, the subject discovers the limit of humanity—"I cannot love a cannibal"—and becomes capable of recognizing himself or herself *as* a humane subject. Cannibalism is constitutive of humanity, then, because it is the limit that humanity requires in order to know itself *as* itself.

What makes it a constitutive *outside*, for post-Enlightenment humanism, is that it is so "ungraspable." As we have seen, the intensity of the "humane" desire for the sign of the cannibal is capable of deforming the nominally objective discourse of humanism, marking it with the trace "of the ever avoided encounter, of the missed opportunity."[12] This desire was particularly intense in the late eighteenth and early nineteenth centuries because, as Earle notes, so many writers had recently attempted "to prove the non-existence of so hideous a propensity." By the mid-eighteenth century, it had been "established as a philosophical truth, capable almost of demonstration, that no such race of people ever did or could exist."[13] Provoked by such doubts, Enlightenment and post-Enlightenment travelers to the Pacific, Asia, and Africa compulsively sought out the kind of evidence that would prevent the cannibal from fading into the ghostly light of fable. These efforts were hindered in several ways. First, the travelers could only communicate with the suspected cannibals through body language and the crudest of pidgins; time after time, they were forced to acknowledge "how far we are liable to be misled by Signs, report, & prejudice" in such encounters.[14] Secondly, as Herman Melville remarks in *Typee*, it was extremely difficult to secure "the testimony of an eye-witness to the revolting practice," since the suspected cannibals were "aware of the detestation in which Europeans hold this custom" and therefore "endeavor[ed] to conceal every trace of it."[15] Finally, as Earle's encounter should suggest, when travelers did succeed in discovering what appeared to be an authentic sign of cannibalism, they had to consider the possibility that they may have been "*hoaxed—in terrorem*." For all of these reasons, it was unusually evident to participants in the post-Enlightenment discourse on cannibalism that the cannibal was yet-to-be-captured, that the image of the cannibal was, as Slavoj Žižek has said of the anti-Semitic image of the Jew, "a scenario filling out the empty space of a fundamental impossibility, a screen masking a void."[16]

I am attending to the figure of the cannibal, then, because: it is constitutive of the discourse of humanity, the master discourse of modernity,
and because its radical "outsideness" helps to reveal the contingency of that
discourse. Over the last 150 years, westerners have learned to take the
objectivity of the cannibal for granted, to forget that that the discursive
visibility of this figure has had to be forcibly established. This is the process
that Laclau, appropriating a term from Husserl, calls "sedimentation"—
"the routinization and forgetting of origins." The work of the historian,
Laclau argues, is "reactivation," by which he means not "returning to the
original situation" but rediscovering the contingency of "stagnant forms
that were simply considered as objectivity."[17] The endpoint of this critical
process is emphatically *not* the recognition that in some putative final
analysis, all experience may be said to be structured around a missed
encounter. As Laclau rightly observes, "[j]ust to say that everything is contingent . . . is an assertion that would only make sense for an inhabitant of
Mars. It is true that in the *final instance* no objectivity can be referred back
to an absolute ground; but no important conclusion can be drawn from
this, since the social agents never act in that final instance."[18] The point of
disrupting the objectivity of the discourse of humanity is not to lend support to a universal theory of the psyche, but to make it possible "to advance
to a *real* humanism; a humanism that acknowledges its radical historicity,
and does not take any of the conditions of its arrival for granted."[19] By
reactivating the sedimented understandings of the figure of the cannibal, I
hope to contribute to the development of that radical democratic project.

It now remains to be said exactly how this mode of analysis impinges
on the work of other critics addressing the figure of the cannibal. As I suggested earlier, these critics have tended to assume that cannibalism is in
fact "cultural" or that it is in fact the projection of a "savagery" located elsewhere. They have assumed, in other words, that the proper object of their
interpretation lies either in a *literal* realm *behind* the representations of
encounters with cannibals or in a *figurative* realm *beyond* such representations. Each of these assumptions is an expression of humanist principles—
one says, "We are all cultured beings," while the other says, "We are all
participants in a struggle between humane and savage principles"—but
neither of them is, to repeat Laclau's formulation, the expression of "a
humanism that acknowledges its radical historicity, and does not take any
of the conditions of its arrival for granted." Each represents a *sedimented*
humanism, based on the exclusion, or forgetting, of the crisis embodied in
the encounter between westerner and cannibal. By reactivating that crisis,
we slow down the interpretive passage into the abstract realms of "culture"

and "savagery," and thereby reconfigure the scene of the encounter as the place where such terms are strategically enacted, rather than the place where their truth is made manifest. In doing so, we reconfigure the two assumptions that have guided most interpretations of the figure of the cannibal. Although these assumptions are unquestionably "humane," they have tended to function as accessories to an especially potent form of colonial discourse, insofar as they have obscured the contingency of its founding event.

Take, for example, the recent controversy between the literary critics Myra Jehlen and Peter Hulme over the proper approach to fifteenth-century European accounts of cannibalism in the Caribbean. In an essay published in *Critical Inquiry* in 1993, Jehlen criticizes Hulme for having treated those accounts in an overly metaphoric way, as signs that tell us a great deal about those who use them and nothing about those whom the signs denote. More specifically, she argues that by moving the discussion of cannibalism "into the realm of the European imaginary," Hulme "erases a particularly sure sign that the Caribbean might constitute a genuinely alternative culture."[20] In his response to Jehlen, Hulme argues that we must maintain a distinction between *cannibalism*, understood as "a term within colonial discourse," and *anthropophagy*, understood "as a much more neutral term for those who want to talk about the consumption of human flesh, in any of the many ways in which such consumption is possible." He goes on to declare that there is nothing wrong with making the term *cannibalism* an object of historical analysis, and that it is "irredeemably romantic" of Jehlen to imagine that a twentieth-century study of colonial discourse could deprive fifteenth-century Caribs of "part of their ability to define themselves as whatever they are."[21] In her counterresponse, Jehlen again insists that it is dangerous to treat "an interpretation independently of its object," arguing that such an approach makes it impossible to illuminate the hidden presence of what she called earlier a "genuinely alternative culture." If we do not "join the undoing of the term *cannibalism* with doing the history of anthropophagy," then "the people whom the myth of "cannibalism" misrepresents, instead of emerging more truly when the myth has been dispersed, disappear altogether. No longer the creatures of colonial fantasy, they do not thereby regain a historical identity."[22]

In her specific criticisms of Hulme, Jehlen is mostly right. By insisting on the real existence of both *cannibalism* and *anthropophagy* and then assigning them to entirely separate realms, Hulme enables himself to treat the discourse on cannibalism as a self-contained sphere with nothing outside of it. In this sense he is not very different from William Arens, who declares near the conclusion of his controversial 1979 book entitled *The Man-Eating Myth* that cannibalism "is a myth in the sense of, first, having an independent existence bearing no relationship to historical reality, and second, containing and transmitting significant cultural messages for those who maintain it."[23] When Hulme asserts that "cannibalism quite simply *is* nothing other than the violence of colonialism incarnate beyond the pale," and that "the early Spanish usage . . . determined the word's subsequent role in European discourse," he reproduces Arens's assumption that "myths" are capable of sustaining themselves without reference to anything outside themselves.[24] As a pure projection that determines subsequent perception, Hulme's "cannibalism" is eternally secure from any deformations that might conceivably result from the colonial encounter. Although Hulme is understandably wary of the "desire for some pure and uncontaminated evidence that can translate itself across the centuries without the elaborate machinery of our interpretive strategies," Jehlen is right to observe that a study of discourse that "focus[es] on coherence" inevitably underplays the effect of the gap between interpretations and their evidence.[25]

The problem with Jehlen's position is that she combines this emphasis on the contingency of the colonial encounter with the entirely noncontingent belief that there is an authentically "cultural" identity beneath the misrepresentations of western discourse. As the most recent generation of anthropologists has convincingly shown, "culture" is no more coherent than "discourse"; it is not the stable truth beneath the lies of colonial representation, but a different representation of the elusive substance that Jehlen calls "material history."[26] In assuming the real presence of a "genuinely alternative culture," and in assuming that the misrepresented people who are the objects of colonial discourse can only emerge as subjects if their words and acts are rearticulated within the terms of this culture, Jehlen subscribes to an idealistic belief in authentic representation that unnecessarily limits our possible responses to the scene of the colonial encounter. This is not to say that "culture" is an illegitimate category of analysis—only that we must not imagine that it is the true and only way of restoring dignity to the objects of a derogatory discourse. We may, for instance, pursue the mode of analysis that Barrow suggests in his response to Earle's narrative, in which the signs of the cannibal are read as simulations, mimicking and mocking the observer's expectations of savagery. Earle himself provides us with a reason to consider this approach, observing later in his narrative that when some visiting Tikopians openly express their dread of the Maori, "whose character for cannibalism had reached even their remote island," the Maori, "with characteristic cunning, perceiving the horror they had created, tormented them still more cruelly, by making grotesque signs, as if they were about to commence devouring them."[27] Without universalizing this style of identification as the essence of "native" subjectivity, we should learn both to recognize it when it appears and to remember its mockery of the dream of real presence when we are piecing together our interpretations of culture.

Among those working in the field of cannibal studies, the critic who has taken the most conspicuous step in the direction of this mode of analysis is the anthropologist Gananath Obeyesekere. In a 1992 essay in *Critical Inquiry* on Enlightenment narratives of Maori cannibalism, he argues that the "discourse on cannibalism tells us more about the British preoccupation with cannibalism than about Maori cannibalism," and that the Maori's ostentatious displays of their cannibal tendencies must be understood within "the context of domination and terror."[28] These are, obviously, important contributions to the project of learning how to think of the colonial encounter as something other than the broadside collision of a totalized discourse and a totalized culture. Their effect is attenuated, however, by their inclusion within the frame of a more general argument that the frequent appearance of the signs of the cannibal in the questions of the British and the answers of the Maori expresses, on both sides, a "latent wish" to consume human flesh.[29] By illuminating the mechanisms of terror, Obeyesekere indicates that the native responses in such encounters may embody what Homi Bhabha has described as "a form of power that is exercised at the very limits of identity and authority, in the mocking spirit of mask and image."[30] But by moving all too quickly to the conclusion that "what gives us all a common humanity is not only our higher nature but also a shared dark side of our being," Obeyesekere effectively replaces the (textual) scene of masking and difference with the (critical) scene of revelation and identity.[31] Just as the contingency of the encounter is swallowed up in Hulme by a reification of discourse and in Jehlen by a reification of culture, it is swallowed up in Obeyesekere by a reification of both humanity and savagery, understood as paired and unbegotten moral presences.[32]

So far, I have considered only those critics who discuss scenes of encounters between westerners and cannibals. It might reasonably be asked, therefore, if my argument has any relevance for those critics who discuss cannibalistic imagery, imagery that may make little or no direct reference to encounters with cannibals. What, for instance, of Maggie

Kilgour's *From Communion to Cannibalism*? In authors ranging from Plato to Melville, Kilgour argues, "cannibalism as an image is related to the breakdown of certain notions of identity and language"—specifically, notions of identity and language that idealize the condition of communion, which she glosses as "benign symbiosis."[33] Kilgour sets herself against all visions of communion that imagine the absolute elimination of antagonism, arguing that while they may seem to escape the taint of cannibalism, they "are essentially cannibalism in its most sterile form" (18), insofar as they bury within themselves the knowledge of the ongoing existence of "bodily appetites and mercenary motives" (118). She aligns herself instead with a vision of communion that simultaneously recognizes the presence of these cannibalistic elements and replaces the sublimation of others by selves with "a more complicated system of relation in which it becomes difficult to say precisely *who* is eating *whom*" (15). Given that her topic is metaphors of incorporation, rather than what she calls "literal cannibalism" (17), does the "outsideness" of cannibalism in the colonial encounter have any bearing here?

I think it does. For one thing, it is impossible to separate the use of cannibalism as a literary figure from the discursive construction of cannibalism as a literal act. When Kilgour describes imperialism as a "form of cannibalism" (186), the derogatory meaning of the metaphor depends on an implied agreement between her and her readers that cannibalism is, as she has said earlier, "obviously the most demonic image for the impulse to incorporate external reality and get everything inside a single body, be it physical, textual, or social" (16). The metaphor makes no sense, in other words, without reference to a discursively constructed agreement that literal acts of cannibalism have definitely occurred and are obviously demonic. To use cannibalism as a derogatory epithet is thus to contribute to the sedimentation of the image of the cannibal, to help close off the modes of analysis that would call its origin into question. Even when we are speaking metaphorically, or analyzing other writers' metaphors, we should be mindful of the colonial provenance of the language we use and attempt to use it otherwise.

The recognition of the missed encounter has implications that go beyond this relatively straightforward reminder, however. If we entertain the possibility that the word *cannibalism* may function as a performative, rather than a substantive—a designation that establishes a presence, rather than a description that confirms a presence—it becomes more difficult to conclude that "cannibalistic" appetites and motives are the obstacles to the realization of a symbiotic ideal. Kilgour tends to speak of these appetites and motives as presences "lurking" (132, 196) beneath the "cloak" (167) of symbiotic ideals, and emerging in a "release of repressed carnivoracity" (17).[34] But what if they are not in fact substantive presences? What if the threat to the symbiotic ideal is not the copresence of "divine and demonic meanings" (222), which makes it hard "to tell where communion stops and cannibalism sets it" (149–50), but the performativity of divine *or* demonic meanings, which makes it possible to reveal each of those meanings, in turn, as fabrications? What if, in other words, the "cannibalistic" functions as a constitutive outside of humanity, in precisely the same way that "cannibalism" does? By asking ourselves these kinds of questions, we make it possible to reframe our analyses of individual texts in ways that are, I think, extremely productive. It may still turn out that just about every author we encounter represents individual and social conflict as a struggle between cannibalistic and benignly symbiotic principles (though I doubt it). But even if it does, we will be capable of reading those representations against their grain, thereby returning them to the uncanny moment of origin that the author, together with other authors, has sedimented with familiarity.

The spirit of inquiry that I am invoking here is neatly captured in an anonymous review of an obscure travel narrative published in 1838. The author of the narrative, Joel Samuel Polack, had written that he had once asked a local Maori chief to show him a piece of cooked human flesh, and that the chief had immediately reached into his cupboard and

> brought down a small flax basket, containing the human viand. At first view I should have taken it for fresh pork in a boiled state, having the same pale, cadaverous colour. My informant stated, it was a piece of the lower part of the thigh, grasping with his hand that part of my body, illustrative of what he advanced. It appeared very much shrunk; and on my observing it must have appertained to a boy, the head of its possessor, when alive, was pointed out to me, apparently a man of forty-five years of age. The sight of this piece of mortality afforded the chief some pleasure, for he stretched out his tongue, pretending to lick the food, and gave other significant signs, indicative of the excessive delight he felt in partaking of human flesh.

The reviewer of the narrative in the London *Athenaeum* reprinted the above passage in full, and then offered the following comments:

In this passage there is nothing to convince those who are disposed to incredulity. The native who showed our author the meat, which was probably pork, was obviously a wag, and well inclined to tickle the white man's prurient sensibility. We do not, indeed, mean to deny that the New Zealanders are cannibals; the concurrent testimony against them, though far from explicit, is yet too strong to be easily thrown away. . . . [Yet w]e cannot but think that Mr. Polack's six years of experience of New Zealand, would have led him to entertain some doubts of the frequency of cannibalism among its inhabitants, if he had not begun with assuming the fact. The disposition most calculated to awaken our mistrust is too conspicuous in his pages, for he absolutely revels in the thoughts of man-eating; he delights to fancy himself quivering in the jaws of some tattooed ogre; he is unable to satiate himself with "supping full of horrors."[35]

Reading in this spirit—reading both cannibalism and the "cannibalistic" in relation to the scenes of their performance—is neither arcane nor arcadian; it is a broadly accessible interpretive practice that has no particular interest in a purer future state. And if the strategy of hitting the "restart key" seems too minimalist or too depressing, consider the alternative: the unending repetition of the "discovery" of cannibalism, and the continuous rejuvenation of all the discourses that the image of cannibalism supports.

NOTES

1. *Journal of the* Resolution's *Voyage* (London, 1775), 94. Burney and his men subsequently drove a group of Maoris away from a fire further down the beach, and there "beheld the most horrible sight that ever was seen by any European; the heads, hearts, liver, and lights of three or four of their people broiling on the fire, and their bowels lying at the distance of about six yards from the fire, with several of their hands and limbs, in a mangled condition, some broiled, and some raw; but no other parts of their bodies, which gave cause to suspect that the cannibals had feasted and eaten all the rest" (95). Even here, we should notice, the evidence is said to give us only a "cause to suspect" that the Maori are cannibals.

2. Earle, *Narrative of a Residence in New Zealand* (London, 1832), 112, 113.

3. Ibid., 114, 115, 116.

4. Ibid., 116–17.

5. The American historian Jared Sparks asserted that while "[i]t was for a long time doubted whether there existed on the globe a race of men, addicted to

the custom of devouring one another," the Cook expeditions furnished "occular proof of the fact" ("New Zealand," *North American Review* [April 1824], 344). Not everyone required such proof; Robert Southey declared that he had not "the least doubt" that the Battas of Sumatra were cannibals, despite the fact that "ocular proof by an European appears to be still wanting" (*"Life and Public Services,"* *Quarterly Review* [March 1830], 435). The British captain John Elphinstone Erskine would later use the currency of the phrase in accounts of cannibalism as the basis of a joke, reporting in 1853 that the sight of a Fijian eating an eye which he had plucked from a skull left members of the Wilkes' expedition "fully satisfied with this ocular proof of cannibalism" (*Journal of a Cruise Among the Islands of the Western Pacific* [London, 1853], 259).

6. *Othello*, 3.3.359–60; 3.4.160–61.

7. Barrow, *"Expeditions on the Amazon,"* *Quarterly Review* (September 1836), 19.

8. Jacques Lacan, *The Four Fundamental Concepts of Psycho-analysis*, ed. Jacques-Alain Miller, trans. Alan Sheridan (New York: Norton, 1981), 55. For the detailed development of this argument, see Geoffrey Sanborn *The Sign of the Cannibal: Melville and the Making of a Postcolonial Reader* (Durham, N.C.: Duke UP, 1998). I have drawn from the introduction to that book in my opening arguments here.

9. Lacan, *Four Fundamental Concepts*, 53, 54, 36.

10. Ernesto Laclau, *New Reflections on the Revolution of Our Time* (London: Verso, 1990), 185.

11. Henry Bolingbroke, *A Voyage to Demerary* (London, 1807), 98–99.

12. Lacan, *Four Fundamental Concepts*, 128.

13. William Marsden, *The History of Sumatra* (London, 1811), 390.

14. Quoted in Ian Barber, "Archaeology, Ethnography, and the Record of Maori Cannibalism before 1815: A Critical Review," *Journal of the Polynesian Society* 101 (1992): 256.

15. Herman Melville, *Typee* (Evanston and Chicago: Northwestern University Press/Newberry Library, 1968), 234.

16. Slavoj Žižek, *The Sublime Object of Ideology* (London: Verso, 1989), 126.

17. Laclau, *New Reflections*, 34, 35.

18. Ibid., 27.

19. Ibid., 245.

20. Myra Jehlen, "History Before the Fact; or, Captain John Smith's Unfinished Symphony," *Critical Inquiry* 19 (1993): 683, 684–85.

21. Peter Hulme, "Making No Bones: A Response to Myra Jehlen," *Critical Inquiry* 20 (1993): 184, 182, 183; Jehlen, "History Before the Fact," 685.

22. Myra Jehlen, "Response to Peter Hulme," *Critical Inquiry* 20 (1993): 188, 189.

23. William Arens, *The Man-Eating Myth: Anthropology and Anthropophagy* (New York: Oxford UP, 1979), 182. I should probably make it clear that I do not agree with Arens's argument that cannibals do not exist. In the case of Burney's discovery, for instance, I think it is highly probable that the bodies of the *Adventure*'s longboat crew were in fact roasted and eaten by the Maori. What I am doing is pointing out the same thing that so many post-Enlightenment reviewers and writers of travel narratives pointed out: that in most reports of cannibalism, the "ocular proof" is remarkably circumstantial. My problem with Arens's argument is that it is only nominally grounded in a study of the circumstantiality of accounts of cannibalism. It is, as he admits at one point, "deductive"; he is "dubious about the actual existence of this act as an accepted practice for any time or place" because "it does not accord with a century of experience accumulated by anthropologists on the human condition" (33, 9, 33). If an anthropological narrative does not square with his sense of what is "human," he rejects it. In dismissing a particularly grotesque account of cannibalism among the Fore in New Guinea, for example, he asks, "could Fore behavior . . . be so far removed from what we and the rest of the world accept as conforming to common standards?" (100). Far from arguing, as Arens does in one of his interviews, that certain acts are "beyond normal human capability" (quoted in David J. Krus, "Russian Cannibals: The Case of the Downed Korean Airliner," *Psychological Reports* 59 [1986]: 4 n.3), I am suggesting that "humanity" has no preexistent rim or bottom, that it is capable of containing any act that we are capable of imagining.

24. Peter Hulme, *Colonial Encounters: Europe and the Native Caribbean, 1492–1797* (London: Methuen, 1986), 67, 308 n.76.

25. Hulme, "Making No Bones," 185; Jehlen, "Response to Peter Hulme," 191. In his introduction to *Cannibalism and the Colonial World* (ed. Francis Barker, Peter Hulme, and Margaret Iverson [Cambridge: Cambridge UP, 1998]), Hulme does acknowledge the contingency of the encounter with suspected cannibals, writing at one point that cannibalism is "an element in cultural contact, an 'entangled object' in the resonant title of Nicholas Thomas's book" ("Introduction: The Cannibal Scene," 21). But he continues to insist that "the discourse on cannibalism" is categorically distinct from "cannibalism itself" and that "the imagery of cannibalism stems in part from denial of the very violence underlying colonising (and other similar) relationships, a violence which is then projected onto its victim" (16, 34). The claim that the discourse on cannibalism has been perpetuating itself for over five hundred years, thanks largely to the ongoing projection of cannibalistic images onto apparently unresisting "victim[s]," sits uneasily alongside the new rhetoric of transformative contact and inextricable entanglement.

26. Jehlen, "Response to Peter Hulme," 189. One of the clearest expressions of the contemporary discomfort with the culture-concept is James Clifford's observation that "Culture, even without a capital c, strains toward aesthetic form and autonomy. . . . [F]or while in principle admitting all learned human behavior,

this culture with a small *c* orders phenomena in ways that privilege the coherent, balance, and 'authentic' aspects of shared life" (*The Predicament of Culture: Twentieth-Century Ethnography, Literature, and Art* [Cambridge: Harvard UP, 1988], 232). While the holisms of culture are clearly preferable to the holisms of race, they nonetheless tend toward the exclusion of Others from the interconnected social spaces that they have always shared with the privileged European observer. Even the best-intentioned evocations of a genuinely alternative culture tend, as Akhil Gupta and James Ferguson argue, to create a subject who "is subtly nativized—placed in a separate frame of analysis and 'spatially incarcerated' in that 'other place' that is proper to an 'other culture'" ("Beyond 'Culture': Space, Identity, and the Politics of Difference," *Cultural Anthropology* 7 [1992]: 14).

27. Earle, *Narrative*, 159.

28. Gananath Obeyesekere, "'British Cannibals': Contemplation of an Event in the Death and Resurrection of James Cook, Explorer," *Critical Inquiry* 18 (1992): 641, 644.

29. Ibid., 635, 642.

30. Homi Bhabha, *The Location of Culture* (New York: Routledge, 1994), 62.

31. Obeyesekere, "'British Cannibals,'" 638.

32. In addition, Obeyesekere shares with Arens and Hulme the conception of the discourse on cannibalism as a self-perpetuating western "myth." In the *Critical Inquiry* essay and in his contribution to *Cannibalism and the Colonial World*, Obeyesekere links the voyagers' obsession with cannibalism to the *topos* of the cannibal in European children's stories and nursery rhymes. He suggests that the voyagers carried to the Pacific an image of cannibalism that had been generated by "infantile bogie fears," and that their subsequent reports of Pacific island cannibalism were received as credible because they "tap[ped]" the same fears in contemporary readers ("Cannibal Feasts in Nineteenth-Century Fiji: Seamen's Yarns and the Ethnographic Imagination," 85).

33. Maggie Kilgour, *From Communion to Cannibalism: An Anatomy of Metaphors of Incorporation* (Princeton, N.J.: Princeton UP, 1990), 194, 122. Subsequent references will be cited parenthetically in the text.

34. She employs the same rhetoric in "The Function of Cannibalism at the Present Time," an essay included in *Cannibalism and the Colonial World*. Here too she expresses a longing for "something higher" than the "material, appetitive [drives] appropriate to our consumer world"; here too, she naturalizes those drives by speaking of them as "our ferocious buried hungers," the "dark truth under our ideals" (259).

35. "Polack, *New Zealand*," *The Athenaeum* (August 18, 1838): 581.

Contributors

Mark Buchan is an assistant professor in Classical Studies at Princeton University. He is currently finishing a book on violence and subjectivity in Homeric epic and has published articles on Latin love elegy and the relationship of exchange to subjectivity in archaic Greece.

Santiago Colás is an associate professor in the Latin American and Comparative Literature department at the University of Michigan. His book, *Postmodernity in Latin America: The Argentine Paradigm*, was published by Duke University Press in 1994. He has also published articles in *PMLA, Social Text*, and *Nuevo Texto Critico*, among others.

Marlene Goldman teaches Canadian Literature at the University of Toronto. Her book, *Paths of Desire: Images of Exploration and Mapping in Canadian Women's Writing*, was published by the University of Toronto Press. She is currently working on a study of apocalyptic and antiapocalyptic discourse in Canadian writing.

Brian Greenspan is an assistant professor at Carleton University where he teaches in the English department and the doctoral program in Cultural

Mediations. He is currently completing a book on American satire and new media.

Kristen Guest is an instructor in the English department at the University of Toronto at Scarborough. Her research interest is in nineteenth-century theater and Victorian culture. She has published articles in *Studies in Romanticism* and *Victorian Literature and Culture*.

Minaz Jooma is an independent scholar in eighteenth-century literature and gender studies. She has published articles in *ELH*; *Literature, Interpretation, Theory*; and *American Transcendental Quarterly*. She is currently writing a book about incest, gender, and consumption in eighteenth-century English literature.

Maggie Kilgour is a professor in the Department of English at McGill University. Her publications include *From Communion to Cannibalism: An Anatomy of Metaphors of Incorporation* (1990) and *The Rise of the Gothic Novel* (1995), as well as numerous articles on cannibalism, gothic literature, and renaissance literature.

Robert Viking O'Brien teaches English at the University of California. A Fulbright scholar, he has published on English Renaissance literature, twentieth-century autobiography, travel writing, and postcolonial literature.

Geoffrey Sanborn is an English professor at Williams College. His book, *The Sign of the Cannibal: Melville and the Making of a Post-Colonial Reader*, was published by Duke University Press in 1998. His essays have appeared in such journals as *Nineteenth-Century Literature*, the *Wordsworth Circle*, and *Arizona Quarterly*.

Julia M. Wright is an associate professor in English at the University of Waterloo. She specializes in nineteenth-century British and Irish literature and has coedited *Romanticism, History and the Possibilities of Genre*, published by Cambridge University Press. Her articles have appeared in such journals as *ELH, Papers on Language and Literature*, and *Mosaic*, as well as various collections of essays.

Index